Luck Egalitarianism

BLOOMSBURY ETHICS

Series Editors

Thom Brooks, Reader in Law, Durham Law School, UK and
Simon Kirchin, Philosophy, University of Kent, UK

Bloomsbury Ethics is a series of books on established and new areas in moral philosophy. Each book is designed both to introduce upper level undergraduates and postgraduates to a key field in ethics, and to develop a particular viewpoint within that field designed to appeal to researchers. All areas of moral philosophy are covered, from the theoretical to the practical. New proposals are always welcome. Please contact the series editors.

Titles available in the series

Intuitionism, David Kaspar
Reasons, Eric Wiland
Autonomy, Andrew Sneddon
Ethics without Intention, Ezio Di Nucci
Moral Motivation, Leonard Kahn
Moral Realism, Kevin DeLapp
Trust, Ethics and Human Reason, Olli Lagerspetz
Virtue Ethics, Nafsika Athanassoulis
Moral Principles, Maike Albertzart

Forthcoming

Moral Skepticism, Basil Smith

Luck Egalitarianism

KASPER LIPPERT-RASMUSSEN

Bloomsbury Academic
An imprint of Bloomsbury Publishing Plc

BLOOMSBURY
LONDON • NEW DELHI • NEW YORK • SYDNEY

Bloomsbury Academic

An imprint of Bloomsbury Publishing Plc

50 Bedford Square
London
WC1B 3DP
UK

1385 Broadway
New York
NY 10018
USA

www.bloomsbury.com

BLOOMSBURY and the Diana logo are trademarks of Bloomsbury Publishing Plc

First published 2016

© Kasper Lippert-Rasmussen, 2016

Kasper Lippert-Rasmussen has asserted his right under the Copyright, Designs and Patents Act, 1988, to be identified as Author of this work.

British Library Cataloguing-in-Publication Data
A catalogue record for this book is available from the British Library.

ISBN: HB: 978-1-47257-043-7
PB: 978-1-47257-042-0
ePDF: 978-1-47257-045-1
ePub: 978-1-47257-044-4

Library of Congress Cataloging-in-Publication Data
A catalog record for this book is available from the Library of Congress.

Typeset by Fakenham Prepress Solutions, Fakenham, Norfolk NR21 8NN
Printed and bound in Great Britain

I dedicate this book to Cæcilie, Hannah, Kira, Samuel and William – in greater love and commitment than might appear in troubled times.

Contents

Acknowledgements x

Preface xi

1 Luck egalitarianism and some close and distant relatives 1

1.1 Introduction 1

1.2 What is luck egalitarianism? 1

1.3 What is attractive about luck egalitarianism? 7

1.4 Three important luck egalitarians: Dworkin 11

1.5 Three important luck egalitarians: Arneson 19

1.6 Three important luck egalitarians: Cohen 22

1.7 Other distributive views 25

1.8 Summary 33

2 Why equality? 35

2.1 Introduction 35

2.2 Formal equality 36

2.3 Equality of human beings 39

2.4 Williams on the idea of equality 40

2.5 Rawls on range properties 42

2.6 Respect and opaqueness 43

2.7 A different proposal 48

2.8 Summary 53

3 Luck 55

3.1 Introduction 55

3.2 Different kinds of luck 56

3.3 Thin luck 57

3.4 Thick luck 59

3.5 Independent notions of luck 62

3.6 How much luck is there? 63

3.7 Constitutive luck 66

3.8 Option luck versus brute luck 67

3.9 Neutralizing luck and equality 72

3.10 Bad luck versus good luck 75

3.11 Summary 76

4 Equality of what? 77

4.1 Introduction 77

4.2 Welfare 78

4.3 The specification objection 82

4.4 The disability objection 84

4.5 The offensive preference objection 87

4.6 The expensive and snobbish tastes objections 93

4.7 The non-instrumental concern objection 98

4.8 Dworkin's resourcist view 101

4.9 Sen's capability metric 108

4.10 Summary 111

5 Telic and deontic luck egalitarianism 113

5.1 Introduction 113

5.2 Some distinctions 115

5.3 Telic versus deontic and the scope of equality 122

5.4 The levelling down objection 129

5.5 Telic egalitarianism and the levelling down objection 135

5.6 Deontic egalitarianism and the levelling down objection 140

5.7 Egalitarian responses 147

5.8 Summary 149

6 The scope of luck egalitarianism 151

6.1 Introduction 151

6.2 Whole lives 152

6.3 Generations 156

6.4 Groups 161

6.5 States 165

6.6 Individuals that are neither persons nor human beings 173

6.7 Summary 178

7 Social relations egalitarianism versus luck egalitarianism 179

7.1 Introduction 179

7.2 Social relations egalitarianism 180

7.3 Anderson's democratic equality 184

7.4 Humiliation and harshness 189

7.5 What is at stake? 194

7.6 The source of the disagreement between social relations and luck egalitarians? 201

7.7 Summary 206

8 Other values 209

8.1 Introduction 209

8.2 Freedom 211

8.3 Demandingness 216

8.4 Community 220

8.5 Publicity and stability 226

8.6 Reflections 231

8.7 Summary 239

Bibliography 241

Index 253

Acknowledgements

A previous version of Chapter 7 was presented at the 3rd Political Theory Workshop, University of Bayreuth, 6 December 2014; a previous version of Chapter 4 at the Department of Philosophy, University of Aarhus, 24 November 2014; and previous versions of Chapters 2 and 8 at the Political Theory Section, Department of Politics, University of Aarhus, 11 November 2014. I thank Søren Flinch Midtgaard, Véronique Munoz Darde, Morten Dige, Lasse Nielsen, Orsolya Reich, Mark Reiff, Raffaele Rodogno, Asbjørn Steglich-Petersen and Jens Damgaard Thaysen for helpful comments. I am extremely grateful to Andreas Albertsen, David Vestergaard Axelsen, Martin Marchman Andersen and Shlomi Segall for written comments on most of a previous draft of the entire book. Finally, I thank the participants at a Chaire Hoover workshop May 26–27 2015 for stimulating discussion and helpful criticisms of the book.

I thank the relevant journals and publishers for permission to reuse material from the following of my publications:

'Review of Kok-Chor Tan: *Justice, Institutions, and Luck: The Site, Ground, and Scope of Equality*', *Mind*, 123 (490) (2014): 653–6.

'Justice and Bad Luck', *Stanford Encyclopedia*. Available online: http://plato.stanford.edu/entries/justicebad-luck/ (accessed 11th April 2014).

'Democratic Egalitarianism vs. Luck Egalitarianism: What Is At Stake?', *Philosophical Topics*, 40 (1) (2012b): 117–34.

'Offensive Preferences, Snobbish Tastes, and Egalitarian Justice', *Journal of Social Philosophy*, 44 (4) (2014): 439–58.

'"Equality of What?" and Intergenerational Justice', *Ethical Perspectives*, 19 (3) (2012): 501–26.

'Telic versus Deontic Egalitarianism', in N. Holtug and K. Lippert-Rasmussen (eds), *Egalitarianism: New Essays on the Nature and Value of Equality*, Oxford: Oxford University Press, 2006, 101–24.

Preface

This book expounds luck egalitarianism in some detail. Roughly, and at a very abstract level, the view holds that it is unjust for some to be worse off than others through bad luck. However, to the extent that they are worse off than others but not through bad luck their disadvantaged position might not be unjust.

These simple thoughts have occupied the centre stage in many discussions in political philosophy/theory generally, and in academic discussions about distributive justice specifically, since the American philosopher and legal theorist Ronald Dworkin's two seminal articles – both entitled 'Equality of What?' – appeared in *Philosophy & Public Affairs* in 1981. On one influential interpretation, Dworkin's main aim there was to argue that, setting aside differences in exercise of responsibility and various special circumstances, people should be equal in terms of resources, not in terms of welfare. Moreover, in these two articles Dworkin showed how egalitarianism could incorporate 'within it the most powerful idea in the arsenal of the anti-egalitarian Right: the idea of choice of responsibility' (Cohen 2011: 32). This has served as inspiration for a large number of theorists since then.

While Dworkin's articles sparked an unprecedented interest in luck egalitarianism itself (e.g. Arneson 1989, 1999; Cohen 2011; Nagel 1991; Rakowski 1991; Roemer 1993, 2000; Temkin 1993; Vallentyne 2002; van Parijs 1991, 1995) as well as in applying it to various practical issues such as health care, climate change and cultural minority rights (e.g. Segall 2009; Norheim and Cappellen 2005; Lippert-Rasmussen 2014b, 2012a, 2009; Kymlicka 1991), the view has important roots in Rawlsian ideas about social and natural lotteries.

In *A Theory of Justice* Rawls contended that which family one happens to be born into – a rich or a poor one – and whether one is born with the natural potential for developing great marketable skills is a matter of luck. These facts are to be seen, metaphorically speaking, as outcomes of the so-called social and natural lotteries, respectively. One is neither responsible for, nor deserves, one's starting point in life. Moreover, Rawls thought that some societies, e.g. ones in which mere formal equality of opportunity prevails in that 'all have at least the same legal rights to all advantaged social positions' (Rawls 1971: 72), but in which no steps are taken to eliminate difference resulting from differential outcomes in the social and natural lotteries, are unjust. They are unjust because they permit 'distributive shares to be improperly influenced by' the outcomes of these lotteries (Rawls 1971: 72). Further back in the history of philosophy, there are affinities between luck egalitarians' insistence that justice is unconditioned by luck and Kant's rejection of the idea that morality is conditioned by luck (Kant 2002).

While luck egalitarianism remains a very influential theory of distributive justice, in recent years an egalitarian contestant has appeared and steadily grown stronger. Presently, many egalitarians reject luck egalitarianism in favour of social relations egalitarianism. Like luck egalitarianism, it sees itself as egalitarian, but, unlike luck egalitarianism, it has no objections to differential luck as such. Rather, it claims that justice requires that citizens be able to relate to one another as equals. One core claim of this book is that not only is the ideal of equality of social relations still to be stated perspicuously, but most of the concerns social relations egalitarians accuse luck egalitarians of being blind to can be accommodated within luck egalitarianism. In any case, one might think that justice is concerned with luck as well as with equal social standing. Indeed, having a lesser social standing through bad luck can be seen as an injustice by luck egalitarians.

This book does not offer a comprehensive treatment of luck egalitarianism, but it covers the main issues raised by the view. It is written as an advanced introduction to its topic, which is accessible to third-year BA students. (That is why, in the interest of accessibility, this book contains no footnotes or endnotes!) However, it also contains a number of novel ideas and claims. For instance, I provide an account of the presumption in favour of equality that connects with a particular and novel answer to the 'Equality of what?' question.

Chapter 1 introduces a core definition of luck egalitarianism. It surveys the views of three influential luck egalitarians – to wit,

Ronald Dworkin, G. A. Cohen and Richard Arneson – and, using this presentation as a springboard, introduces some of the main issues that I return to in later chapters. In the closing section, the chapter contrasts luck egalitarianism with other distributive principles, e.g. utilitarianism, prioritarianism, sufficientarianism and Rawls' difference principle.

Chapter 2 explores the equality component in luck egalitarianism. By this I mean the commitment of luck egalitarians to an equal distribution – as opposed to one that, say, maximizes moral value or leaves everyone with enough – in the absence of non-luck-based justifications of deviations from equality. I argue that this presumption of equality among persons with an equal moral standing is justified by the fact that people have the same capacity to care non-instrumentally about things in a way that is distinctive of persons, e.g. in a way that involves a plan of life or at least planning over extended periods of time.

Chapter 3 clarifies the luck component of luck egalitarianism. Because luck egalitarians ascribe significance to whether inequality results from luck, it is crucial for them to say something about how we distinguish luck from non-luck. The chapter surveys some of the main contenders – e.g. the view that foreseen results of choices do not constitute luck, while other results do. It argues that a desert-based notion of luck is the one that is most relevant from a luck egalitarian point of view.

Chapter 4 turns to the question of in what terms people should be equal. It critically assesses welfare, resource and capability metrics and proposes equality of satisfaction of individuals' reasonable non-instrumental concerns as a new and superior metric. It is superior because it fits well with the so-called anti-fetishist argument, which many participants in the 'Equality of what?' discussion accept, as well as with the justification of the equality component in luck egalitarianism offered in Chapter 2.

Chapter 5 distinguishes between two main forms of luck egalitarianism: telic and deontic. Roughly, the former focuses on the injustice of unequal distributions, whereas the latter focuses on unequal treatment and has no concern for unequal distributions as such. The chapter argues that the distinction is less significant than is often assumed. For instance, while the chapter ultimately defends luck egalitarianism against the levelling down objection – the objection that, as an egalitarian, one has to say, implausibly, that there is something good about levelling down even if no individual is better off in any way as a result – it also argues that telic and deontic egalitarianism are equally vulnerable to the objection.

Chapter 6 addresses various issues in relation to the scope of luck egalitarianism. It defends the view that luck egalitarianism is concerned with inequalities between individuals who have the distinctive kind of non-instrumental concerns described in Chapter 2, wherever and whenever they exist. So, to use a label prevalent in the literature, I defend cosmopolitan luck egalitarianism. I also argue in favour of the view that inequalities between segments of different people's lives are irrelevant from a luck egalitarian point of view, at least if we set aside reductionism about personal identity.

Chapter 7 defends luck egalitarianism against the challenge from social relations egalitarianism. Among other things, it argues that luck egalitarianism can accommodate a concern for equality of equal standing. The chapter also returns to the issue of whether pure natural inequalities, i.e. inequalities that have come into existence without human agency and cannot be eliminated through human agency, can be unjust – a topic that is often thought to separate deontic from telic egalitarians.

Chapter 8 looks at various values, e.g. freedom and community that might, and are often said to, conflict with luck egalitarian justice such that we might have to trade them off against equality. It argues that some, but not all, of these conflicts are real, but that this does not detract from the plausibility of luck egalitarianism. The chapter ends with some meta-reflections on value pluralism and on whether luck egalitarians and their critics simply use the term 'justice' in different ways – a view which I reject.

As might have become apparent at this point, this book is sympathetic to luck egalitarianism and offers responses to some of the main challenges facing it. However, I will not pretend that the theory or, for that matter, the particular brand of luck egalitarianism defended here is uncontroversial or that the way in which I have tried to motivate luck egalitarianism settles the matter in favour of it. Still, in my view luck egalitarianism remains a strong candidate for a plausible theory of distributive justice and this book is an attempt to show why. Inevitably, one must hope for a bit of luck in such an endeavour!

1

Luck egalitarianism and some close and distant relatives

1.1. Introduction

In this chapter, I first offer and explain a preliminary definition of luck egalitarianism (Section 1.2). Then, in Section 1.3, I say something about what makes luck egalitarianism a plausible view of distributive justice. Sections 1.4 to 1.6 present the views of three of the most influential luck egalitarians: Ronald Dworkin, G. A. Cohen and Richard J. Arneson. Section 1.7 contrasts luck egalitarianism with competing distributive principles.

1.2. What is luck egalitarianism?

Since this book is about luck egalitarianism, it is appropriate to start with a preliminary definition of the view – a definition which I will qualify later (e.g. Section 5.5). Initially, however, simplicity is an important virtue. So here is the claim, which I take to be such that to be luck egalitarian one has to affirm it, and if one does, then one is luck egalitarian:

> (1) It is unjust if some people are worse off than others through their bad luck. (cf. Cohen 2008: 300; Elford 2013; Scheffler 2003a: 5; Lippert-Rasmussen 2006)

Call this the *core luck egalitarian claim*. To get a better grasp of it, consider the following two illustrations of the sort of situations that (1) condemns as unjust. In the bad old days of Apartheid most black South Africans were much worse off than most white South Africans. This was so, not because black South Africans were less hard-working than white South Africans or anything of that sort. It was so simply due to the fact that, under Apartheid, South Africans lived in a society in which being born black meant being subjected to all sorts of unjust restrictions and, thus, facing much worse prospects than one's white fellow citizens. While being born black is not in itself an instance of bad luck, under Apartheid it was an instance thereof.

Second, in the bad present days, being born with genes that result in one's suffering from a severe disability renders it likely that one will be worse off than other people who have no such condition. No one has chosen his or her genes. Accordingly, being worse off as a result of a genetically caused disability seems like a paradigm case of being worse off as a result of bad luck and, thus, like racist inequalities in South Africa under Apartheid, a paradigm of injustice according to luck egalitarianism.

The core luck egalitarian claim makes it straightforwardly intelligible why luck egalitarianism is called 'luck egalitarianism'. First, if some people are worse off than others, then inequalities exist. And if inequalities exist, then some people are worse off than others. Hence, it is easy to see that luck egalitarianism is an egalitarian view. Second, it is also clear why the view is a 'luckist' one. Luck egalitarians object to some people being worse off than others through their bad luck. They do not, *qua* luck egalitarians, object to people being worse off than others, when their so being is not the result of their bad luck. Hence, if I freely choose to be worse off than others, say, because I want to spend most of my income on protecting a certain endangered species of flower (cf. Section 4.7), then the core luck egalitarian claim does not condemn the resulting inequality.

Despite the pedagogical advantage just mentioned, the core luck egalitarian claim is not, I hasten to say, one that everyone who is seen as a luck egalitarian accepts. Political philosophers who have been most influential in discussions of luck egalitarianism – whether as proponents or opponents of luck egalitarianism – have offered different formulations and later I will discuss how these formulations relate to the definition I have given. For the moment and before I complicate the picture, I want to expound some important features of the core luck egalitarian claim.

First, luck egalitarianism is a view about justice. It is not a view about moral goodness as such, or a view about moral permissibility, all things considered. On many people's view, justice is one factor among others that determine overall moral goodness and moral permissibility, all things considered, but it is not the only one. For instance, some people think that welfare is another factor, which co-determines moral goodness and moral permissibility. These people might think, say, that a state of affairs where no one is worse off than others through their bad luck is worse than a state of affairs where some people are worse off than others through their bad luck, if people have higher welfare in the latter state of affairs. Similarly, most people think that there is a deontological moral constraint against killing innocent people. Luck egalitarians might consistently think that it would be impermissible to kill all better-off persons, even if that would bring it about that no one is worse off than others through their bad luck. In short: luck egalitarianism is a claim about justice, not a complete theory about moral goodness or moral permissibility.

Second, while luck egalitarianism is a claim about justice, it does not even claim to be a complete theory of justice. Luck egalitarianism simply states a sufficient condition for a distribution to be unjust. Hence, it is open for luck egalitarians to say that something could be unjust for reasons other than that some people are worse off than others through bad luck. So, for instance, as a luck egalitarian you can think that exploitation is inherently unjust and, thus, unjust even if the exploited, worse-off person is not exploited as a matter of bad luck, e.g. if the exploited person freely has chosen to enter into the exploitative relationship. Also, luck egalitarians might think that certain acts are unjust independently of how they affect distributions. G. A. Cohen, to whom I return in Section 1.6 below, subscribes to something very much like the core luck egalitarian claim. Yet he also contends that the kind of anti-Semitic, Montreal racism that he experienced in his childhood was unjust independently of whether it resulted in Montreal Jews being worse off through bad luck – as a matter of fact, it did not harm them much, he thinks (Cohen 2008: 367). In short: while luck egalitarianism is a view about justice, it is not a complete view of justice, where a complete view is one that, for any act or distribution, either implies that it, i.e. the act or the distribution, is or is not just, all things considered.

Third, luck egalitarianism, as I have stated it, is silent on when it is just that people are equally well off. To see that this is not an insignificant point, suppose that Anna and Bruce each live on separate small islands in the South Pacific. Anna is hard-working and Bruce is not. When harvest time comes and, unlike Bruce, Anna stands to enjoy a plentiful harvest, by sheer good fortune (from Bruce's point of view) a big tuna washes ashore on Bruce's island such that, despite Anna's much greater efforts, Bruce ends up as well off as Anna through his good luck. There are reasons why one might think that luck egalitarianism should say something about the injustice of someone's being as well off as others through luck in this way (Cohen 2011: 116–23; cf. Segall 2012; Albertsen and Midtgaard 2014). One such reason is that one's account of why it is unjust for some to be worse off than others through their bad luck commits one to the view that it is unjust for some to be as well off as others through good luck, e.g. because the account is grounded in fairness. However, this is not implied by the core luck egalitarian claim, so in this respect also it is an incomplete view about justice.

Fourth, the core luck egalitarian claim does not say that it is unjust if some are better off than others through their good luck. Some might doubt the significance of this point on the ground that if some are better off than others through good luck, this entails that some are worse off than others through bad luck. However, at least on some accounts of luck this entailment does not hold. Suppose we both have $100. For the price of $100 I am offered a very attractive gamble that gives me 50 per cent chance of $500 and 50 per cent chance of $50. I accept the lottery and win. You are offered $400 for nothing, decline the offer, and donate $50 to a charity devoted to the preservation of endangered species of flowers, ending up with $50. You are now worse off than me, but, arguably, you are not worse off than me as a result of your bad luck. After all, you were offered $400 for nothing and declined the offer, which would have left you as well off as me. However, in part through my good luck I am better off than you are, since there was a significant risk that my gamble would result in my ending up with $50 only. Hence, the putative entailment does not hold (Lippert-Rasmussen 2005; cf. Section 3.10).

Fifth, luck egalitarianism is an essentially comparative view of justice. That is, justice inheres in relations between people and not in how people are situated independently of one another. To see what this comes down to, compare luck egalitarianism with a non-comparative view of justice according to which justice is that everyone gets her due, where one's due is determined by one's level of moral deservingness, and where one's level of moral deservingness is determined solely by one's level of efforts directed at doing the morally right thing. Suppose that on this view you are due more than I am due. Suppose also that while I get exactly what I am due, you get more than what you are due. On the present account, it is unjust that you get more than you are due. But, unlike luck egalitarianism, this non-comparative view implies that there is nothing unjust about your having more than I have relative to what each of us is due. This reflects the fact that this view is non-comparative.

Sixth, the present formulation of luck egalitarianism leaves entirely open what it is to be worse off through one's bad luck. Above I referred to some paradigmatic cases of people being worse or better off through luck – e.g. a person who expectedly enjoys the good fortune of a tuna washing ashore – but these examples leave open what exactly makes these cases of luck. I shall return to this matter in Chapter 3. For present purposes it suffices to distinguish between choice- and control-based conceptions of luck. On the former view, something is a matter of luck for an agent if it is not the result of a choice that the agent made, whereas on the latter view something is a matter of luck for an agent if it is not something over which the agent has or did have any control. Obviously, choice and control often go hand in hand. One has neither chosen one's genes, nor did or does one control them. Yet, analytically we can pry choice and control apart. If, for instance, I end up worse off through indecisiveness – never making up my mind about what to do – this might reflect bad luck on the choice-based conception, but not on the control-based conception, of luck, assuming that I had control over whether I was indecisive.

Finally, while the core luck egalitarian claim says something about *when* a distribution is unjust, it does not say *what makes* it unjust. This difference is often overlooked, because it is natural to assume that to subscribe to luck egalitarianism one has to think that being worse off than others through bad luck is an injustice-making feature, so to speak. However, this assumption might not be true. One might think that what makes it unjust that some are worse off than others through bad luck is that those who are better off cannot justify to these worse-off people that they are worse off. Presumably, the reason why they cannot justify that to the worse-off people is that these people are worse off through their bad luck, but, on the view I imagine, it is not *that* fact, but the fact that the better-off are unable to justify to the worse-off that they are worse off *in virtue of which* the inequality between them is unjust. This distinction between when inequality is unjust and what makes it unjust, when it is, is important because it affects what we can plausibly say about the scope of the core luck egalitarian claim. If luck egalitarianism is a view about that in virtue of which inequalities are unjust or one that is grounded in such a view, then it is difficult not to endorse the widest scope possible for luck egalitarianism, e.g. it would seem impossible not to endorse cosmopolitan luck egalitarianism. I return to this issue in Chapter 6.

To sum up: luck egalitarianism is an incomplete view of justice, which states a sufficient condition for it to be unjust for some to be worse off than others. The view is not opposed to luck as such. For instance, it is silent on the justice of some being equally well off as others through luck and silent on the injustice of some being better off than others through their good luck. Finally, luck egalitarianism as such can be combined with different accounts of what luck amounts to. While there are other aspects of the definition that need to be discussed, I will postpone this to later. The exposition of luck egalitarianism so far should provide a sufficiently clear idea about what the view is for it to make sense in the next section to raise the question of what makes the view attractive in the first place. After all, unless we see that there is something attractive about the view – whether or not we will ultimately want to reject it – it may seem futile to develop it further.

1.3. What is attractive about luck egalitarianism?

There are at least two ways to show that there is something attractive about luck egalitarianism. First, one might demonstrate that the view follows from or justifies other views that one holds and finds attractive. Second, one might establish that the view is one that we are committed to or that it is plausible in itself, e.g. by describing cases of people being worse off than others through bad luck that, once we have eliminated alternative explanations, seem unjust for that reason. In this section, I offer illustrations of both ways of supporting luck egalitarianism.

An illustration of the first way of supporting luck egalitarianism is provided by John Rawls' so-called intuitive argument for the difference principle (Rawls 1971: 65–75; Knight and Stemplowska 2011a: 2–9; Arneson 2001); roughly, the difference principle says that it is unjust if the basic structure of society is such that the worst-off could have been better off. Rawls does not consider the intuitive argument – as opposed to his argument appealing to what hypothetical contractors would choose behind a veil of ignorance – his real argument for the difference principle and in any case, the difference principle is, as we shall see in Section 1.7 below, different from luck egalitarianism, so this might seem strange. However, my treatment of this argument reflects that many have found that, regardless of how Rawls himself uses the argument, it is a compelling argument for something like luck egalitarianism (Kymlicka 2002; Knight and Stemplowska 2011a: 1–23). Others find that it is seriously misleading to see luck egalitarian motifs in Rawls' argument (Scheffler 2003a: 8–12, 24–31; Scheffler 2005; Scheffler 2006; Freeman 2007: 111–42; Mandle 2009: 24–9). For present purposes I set aside such exegetical worries.

The intuitive argument's starting point is equality of opportunity, as laissez-faire libertarians understand it. Equality of opportunity so construed implies, roughly, that there are no legal restrictions that prevent anyone from occupying any job and, thus, that jobs are in this sense 'open to those able and willing to strive for them' (Rawls 1971: 66). Rawls thinks that this conception is untrue to the ideal of equality of opportunity: its 'most obvious injustice ... is that it permits distributive shares to be improperly influenced by [natural and social contingencies] so arbitrary from a moral point of view' (Rawls 1971: 72). By 'natural and social contingencies' Rawls has in mind things such as whether one's genes dispose one to possess marketable talents or whether one is born into a stimulating social environment that would encourage one to develop one's talents. These are contingencies in the sense that they do not in any way reflect any merit or desert on one's part and, in part for that reason, they are morally arbitrary in the sense that the fact that one enjoys good genes or a stimulating upbringing does not render it just that one possesses the superior social position that they enable one to acquire. It is to bring out these points that Rawls uses the metaphors of the social and natural lotteries. Like the outcomes of ordinary lotteries, the outcomes of these lotteries are a matter of good or bad 'fortune' or 'luck' (Rawls 1971: 74, 75). Hence, since one cannot possibly merit, or deserve, an outcome of a lottery, people's starting positions cannot be justified by appeal to merit or desert (Rawls 1971: 7, 104).

Having rejected the laissez-faire conception of equality, Rawls moves on to consider a liberal egalitarian conception of equality of opportunity according to which this ideal enjoins the elimination of social contingencies. On this view: 'assuming that there is a distribution of natural assets, those who are at the same level of talent and ability, and have the same willingness to use them, should have the same prospects of success regardless of their initial place in the social system. In all sectors of society there should be roughly equal prospects of culture and achievement for everyone similarly motivated and endowed' (Rawls 1971: 73). While this passage suggests that Rawls thinks that making an effort negates luck, he also notes that 'the willingness to make an effort, to try, and so to be deserving in the ordinary sense is itself dependent on happy family and social circumstances' (Rawls 1971: 74).

While this ideal of equality of opportunity represents an improvement, it is still deficient according to Rawls. The reason is that the 'natural distribution of abilities' is no less 'arbitrary from a moral perspective' than whether people are born into stimulating or non-stimulating social environments (Rawls 1971: 74). Thus, if one condemns the laissez-faire conception of equality of opportunity as unjust because of moral arbitrariness, on pain of inconsistency, one should also condemn liberal equality of opportunity as unjust.

In its place Rawls proposes what he calls 'democratic equality'. This principle 'is arrived at by combining the principle of fair equality of opportunity with the difference principle' (Rawls 1971: 75). By this Rawls means that out of a set of basic structures that all satisfy the principle of fair equality of opportunitys the one that is just is the one that 'improves the expectations of the least advantaged members of society' (Rawls 1971: 75). In this way, democratic equality mitigates not only social but also natural luck. It does so because under democratic equality those who have had bad luck in the natural lottery could not have been better off under any alternative basic structure.

This interpretation of how Rawls moves from his rejection of laissez-faire libertarianism to democratic equality of opportunity offers some support for luck egalitarianism. It makes us see that perhaps our best reason for condemning laissez-faire equality of opportunity is also a reason for condemning inequalities reflecting inequalities in genetic potential as unjust. It makes us notice that underlying our rejection of this rendering of equality of opportunity is a commitment to luck egalitarianism and it reminds us that this underlying principle commits us to condemn other inequalities as unjust as well. Indeed, one worry is that it makes us condemn all relevant inequalities as unjust. After all, might not differences in motivation, e.g. across men and women, reflect differences in social upbringing, in which case perhaps all inequalities are morally arbitrary? For now, we can set aside this worry to which I will return in Section 3.7.

We have just seen that an important argument by Rawls might manifest an underlying commitment to luck egalitarianism. However, we can also support luck egalitarianism more directly – i.e. in the second way mentioned at the beginning of this section – by considering cases of inequality. Michael Otsuka (2004: 151–2), for instance, points out that people who end up less well off than others as a result of luck often ask 'Why me?'. When no satisfactory answer can be given, they think that life is unfair or unjust. For instance, poor people in Southern Sudan, reflecting how badly off they are relative to rich people in affluent countries, might find it unjust that their prospects are much worse than these people's prospects simply in virtue of their unfortunate birthplace (Caney 2005: 122). Admittedly, some would suspect that what fuels the sense of injustice here is simply the fact that poor people in Southern Sudan's basic needs are unsatisfied. However, since we can see why people living in Greece might ask a similar question when they compare themselves to people living in Germany, and see unfairness even though their basic needs are satisfied, non-fulfilment of basic needs is not of the essence (which is not to say that it is irrelevant). The fact that Greek people's basic needs are satisfied does not defuse their complaint, whether warranted or not, since it concerns the fact that their comparative distributive position reflects bad luck on their part. Unfairness at a high level of well-being might be less of a moral concern than unfairness at a low level of well-being, but a high level of well-being does not eliminate unfairness. Accordingly, a common sense of unfairness seems to involve a commitment to luck egalitarianism (cf. Scheffler 2005: 10).

Some might respond that none of the two considerations above amount to an *argument* for luck egalitarianism. At least, they do not if by 'argument' we mean a derivation of luck egalitarianism from a set of premises containing a more basic principle of justice together with certain additional premises, i.e. the first kind of argument I identified in the first paragraph in this section.

However, it is not clear that to defend a principle of justice one must offer an argument of this kind. Presumably, not all principles of justice are deducible from more basic principles of justice. Some principles are just not derived from others in this sense. Luck egalitarians are not alone in thinking that there are non-derived principles. Nozickean libertarians, say, might think that self-ownership – i.e. that one own oneself and one's labour – is a basic principle in this sense. Thus, they cannot fault luck egalitarians for thinking that there are non-derived principles of justice, though they disagree with luck egalitarians about what these principles are.

This does not mean that this disagreement cannot be settled by argument. For instance, to the extent that a basic principle of justice can account for more of our considered moral judgements than a competing principle of justice, *ceteris paribus*, we might be justified in rejecting the latter principle and endorsing the former. This sort of argument is what is being offered when Nozickean libertarians object that luck egalitarianism implies the following: if one group of people are born with two eyes and an equally sized group are born without any, it would be just to seize one eye from each person in the first group and transplant it onto each person from the second group (cf. Cohen 1995: 70, 243–4). Or when luck egalitarians object that Nozickean libertarianism implies that there is nothing unjust about one person refusing to donate a litre of blood to scientists who could use it to develop a vaccine against Ebola and thereby save thousands of lives. So while no one has tried to deduce luck egalitarianism from a more basic principle of justice, it is unclear that such an argument is needed. Specifically, it seems we can justify luck egalitarianism (or its rejection) by appeal to various intuitions in its favour (that goes against it).

1.4. Three important luck egalitarians: Dworkin

So far I have defined luck egalitarianism and offered two considerations in its support. Newcomers to the field might wonder who are the main *dramatis personae*. Accordingly in this and the next two sections I introduce three main luck egalitarian thinkers (cf. Stemplowska 2013). A selection of this kind is bound to be somewhat arbitrary and, interestingly, one of three theorists below has rejected that label (Dworkin 2003), while another has retracted from luck egalitarianism (Arneson 2000a). Still, many central luck egalitarian themes appear in their writings.

It is probably fair to say that what brought luck egalitarianism into vogue were two articles in *Philosophy and Public Affairs* from 1981 written by Ronald Dworkin and later reprinted in his *Sovereign Virtue* (Dworkin 2000). According to Dworkin, a state is legitimate – i.e. it is such that it has a right to enforce its laws even against citizens that reject them – only if it treats its citizens with equal concern (Dworkin 2000: 1) or, as he put it in previous writing, equal concern and respect. Dworkin thinks different theories of justice interpret the requirement of equal concern differently, but that the best interpretation implies that the state ought to bring about a distribution that is sensitive to differences in ambition, but insensitive to differences in endowment (Dworkin 2000: 89). Assuming that one's ambitions are not a matter of luck and that one's endowment is, this sounds well in line with the core luck egalitarian claim. But, as we shall see, it is neither clear that, despite his many appeals to choice, voluntariness, and the claim that allowing differences in luck to stand is unfair, Dworkin had a luck egalitarian distinction in mind, nor clear that the two distinctions – the distinction between choice and luck and Dworkin's favoured distinction between ambitions and endowment – overlap nicely. I will say more about this later in this section.

Let us start with ambition sensitivity. Dworkin acknowledges that there are many different accounts of welfare. However, he thinks that no ideal of equality of welfare respects ambition sensitivity. Dworkin reasons as follows: suppose a society has set about to realize equality of welfare given a certain chosen conception thereof, e.g. equality of welfare hedonistically construed. Dworkin then imagines the following:

> Suppose that someone (Louis) sets out deliberately to cultivate some taste or ambition he does not now have, but which will be expensive in the sense that once it has been cultivated he will not have as much welfare on the chosen conception as he had before unless he acquires more wealth. These new tastes may be tastes in food and drink: Arrow's well-known example of tastes for plovers' eggs and pre-phylloxera claret. Or they may (more plausibly) be tastes for sports, such as skiing, from which one derives pleasure only after acquiring some skill; or, in the same vein, for opera; or for a life dedicated to creative art or exploring or politics. (Dworkin 2000: 49–50)

Dworkin denies, and many agree with him, that justice requires that resources should now be transferred from others to Louis to reinstate equality of welfare hedonistically construed.

Why does Dworkin think it would be unjust to transfer resources to Louis? In his view, it would be 'quite unfair that [Louis] should be able, at the expense of others, to lead a life that is more expensive than theirs at no sacrifice of enjoyment to himself just because he would, quite naturally, consider that life a more successful life overall' than one without cultivation of expensive preferences or one with, but with no additional resources (Dworkin 2000: 56). Compensating Louis for his expensive tastes trespasses on the fair shares of resources of others. Dworkin concludes that equality of welfare conflicts with the ambition sensitivity desideratum and he then moves on to account for his competing ideal of equality of resources. Before I do so as well, I will highlight two features of Dworkin's discussion of expensive tastes.

The first one is the discrepancy between Dworkin's initial description of Louis and Dworkin's later account of why it would be unjust to compensate Louis. A salient part of the initial description is that Louis 'sets out deliberately' to develop his expensive tastes – a feature that one is bound to find relevant to the case for compensating Louis, if one is a luck egalitarian. However, once we get to Dworkin's account of what makes it unjust to compensate him, this feature plays no role. What makes compensating Louis unjust is that others should not make sacrifices to fund his more expensive life, when the need to do so in order to retain equality of welfare simply reflects his judgement that it is more successful overall. Nothing in this account seems to depend on whether the judgement or the decision to act on it was a matter of choice (assuming that choice negates luck). Indeed, despite his initial description of Louis' case, Dworkin suggests that the distinction between 'expensive tastes that are deliberately cultivated' and 'native desires or socially imposed tastes' might not be so important, because the former are 'cultivated in response to beliefs – beliefs about what sort of life is overall more successful – and such beliefs are not themselves cultivated or chosen' (Dworkin 2000: 52).

Second, it is unclear why Dworkin thinks Louis' case is representative of all expensive tastes. Suppose, for instance, that Louis cultivates an expensive preference, because he thinks that doing so will make everyone equally well off, hedonistically speaking, at a higher level than they would otherwise be, e.g. because others will take much pleasure in his enjoyment of plovers' eggs and pre-phylloxera claret. Suppose this belief is true except for the fact that – bad luck for Louis – he himself will be worse off. It is not clear why Louis should not receive, as a matter of justice, compensation in this case. True, this might not be a matter of Louis seeking what he thinks is a more successful life (for himself only) overall, but there is no reason why it should be, since expensive tastes are not tied to such beliefs in any case.

Turning now to Dworkin's ideal of equality of resources, we should ask when people have equal amounts of resources. One component in Dworkin's complex answer to this question is the envy test:

> Suppose a number of shipwreck survivors are washed up on a desert island which has abundant resources and no native population, and any likely rescue is many years away. These immigrants accept the principle that no one is antecedently entitled to any of these resources, but that they shall instead be divided equally among them ... They also accept (at least provisionally) the following test of an equal division of resources, which I shall call the envy test. No division of resources is an equal division if, once the division is complete, any immigrant would prefer someone else's bundle of resources to his own bundle. (Dworkin 2000: 66–7)

Satisfaction of the envy test is a necessary condition but not, Dworkin thinks, a sufficient one for satisfaction of the requirement that everyone has been treated equally. If all resources are divided into identical resources bundles such that no one envies anyone else's bundle of resources, people who care much about some resources but do not care about others and thus would like to trade have not been treated with the same concern as those individuals who care equally about all resources and thus would not benefit from the option of trading. To refine the envy test, Dworkin proposes that it is combined with a market for resources in the form of an auction (Dworkin 2000: 68). More specifically, he imagines a group of shipwreck survivors who are washed up on a desert island. All are given 'an equal and large number of clamshells' that they can use to bid at an auction where all the resources of the island are sold off. Once the auction is over, the envy test is applied and if it is not satisfied, the auction is repeated and so on and so forth. Through this market mechanism individuals have the opportunity to acquire a bundle of resources that match their preferences within the constraint set by which resources are available at the island and thus avoid the problem of a set of identical bundles of resources.

Satisfaction of the envy test in this setting is a sufficient condition for a distribution of what we can refer to as external resources, e.g. land, minerals and water, to be equal, and respecting it in the initial distribution of external resources among Dworkin's shipwreck survivors secures endowment insensitivity with regard to external resources. But not all resources are external. Our bodies and our labour power are not normally seen in this way.

Suppose that the two of us have identical bundles of external resources, but whereas I have no eyes, you have two transplantable ones. If we apply the envy test to internal resources such as body parts, the test might not be satisfied unless 'your' eyes are redistributed between us. Dworkin wants to avoid this implication, while granting that I have a claim to compensation for my bad luck with regard to internal resources. Similarly, suppose you are more talented than I am such that you produce much more in one hour than I do. Hence, if we apply the envy test to labour power, it might not be satisfied unless I own some of your labour power. Again, Dworkin wants to avoid this kind of 'slavery of the talented', while insisting that I am due compensation on account of my limited endowments. To secure endowment insensitivity in the light of inequalities in terms of internal resources Dworkin proposes an additional device to the envy test: an insurance scheme.

It makes no sense to ask people to insure against being born blind, because once they can answer this question they know whether they were born blind or not. Hence, the insurance scheme Dworkin imagines is counterfactual:

If (contrary to fact) everyone had at the appropriate age the same risk of developing physical or mental handicaps in the future (which assumes that no one has developed these yet) but that the total number of handicaps remained what it is, how much insurance coverage against these handicaps would the average member of the community purchase? We might then say that but for (uninsurable) brute luck that has altered these equal odds, the average person would have purchased insurance at that level, and compensate those who do develop handicaps accordingly, out of some fund collected by taxation or other compulsory process but designed to match the fund that would have been provided through premiums if the odds had been equal. Those who develop handicaps will then have more resources at their command than others, but the extent of their extra resources will be fixed by the market decisions that people would supposedly have made if circumstances had been more equal than they are. Of course, this argument does involve the fictitious assumption that everyone who suffers handicaps would have bought the average amount of insurance, and we may wish to refine the argument and the strategy so that that no longer holds. But it does not seem an unreasonable assumption for this purpose as it stands. (Dworkin 2000: 77–8)

This insurance scheme, and a similar one where one insures against having few marketable talents, reduces sensitivity of distributions to differences in internal endowment. However, as Dworkin realizes, they are unlikely to fully realize the ideal of endowment insensitivity. Some handicaps, whether compensable or non-compensable, may be so expensive to insure against that few would do so. Taking out an insurance for not having the marketable talents of a Bill Gates – a quite common condition, to be sure – would be very expensive and, thus, not one that many would buy and therefore not one that would provide much coverage of the extent to which one falls short of such immensely talented persons. Thus, Dworkin's scheme implies that people with inborn non-compensable handicaps will be worse off than others and people with immense talents will be better off than the rest of us. Does this not conflict with his endowment-insensitivity desideratum?

Dworkin sums up the challenge and responds as follows:

The brute fact remains that some people have much more than others of what both desire, through no reason connected with choice. The envy test we once seemed to respect has been decisively defeated, and no defensible conception of equality can argue that equality recommends that result. This is a powerful complaint, and there is no answer, I think, but to summarize and restate our earlier arguments to see if they can still persuade with that complaint ringing in our ears. (Dworkin 2000: 104)

Dworkin thinks that no other scheme does better than his in meeting the two desiderata and thus that even though it permits inequalities that do 'not reflect any differences in tastes or ambitions or theories of the good, and so does not in itself implicate our first, ambition-sensitive requirement of equality in wage structure', this does not refute his favoured form of resource egalitarianism, since any attempt to address this problem would 'wreak wholesale and dramatic changes in the positions of others, changes which do implicate' the requirement of ambition sensitivity (Dworkin 2000: 105).

It is unclear why Dworkin thinks this provides a satisfying answer to what he admits to be a powerful complaint. After all, he concedes that on his ideal of resources some would be worse off than others because they were less well-endowed than those who were better off, and that is what the complaint says. It also brings out clearly that his reply is not luck egalitarian in the canonical sense of Section 1.1 (but cf. Scheffler 2003b: 200). Finally, it is unclear why, if the resource egalitarian can avail himself or herself of this answer, a welfare egalitarian could not adopt a similar answer to Dworkin's counterexample of expensive tastes – i.e. concede that it is a powerful objection, but insist that it can be answered in no other way but to 'summarize and restate' the arguments that have been offered in favour of welfare luck egalitarianism to see if 'they can still persuade with that complaint ringing in our ears' (Dworkin 2000: 104).

There is also another way in which Dworkin has a less clear-cut commitment to eradicating inequalities due to someone's having bad luck. He makes a very influential distinction between option luck and brute luck (see Section 3.8):

Option luck is a matter of how deliberate and calculated gambles turn out – whether someone gains or loses through accepting an isolated risk he or she should have anticipated and might have declined. Brute luck is a matter of how risks fall out that are not in that sense deliberate gambles. If I buy a stock on the exchange that rises, then my option luck is good. If I am hit by a falling meteorite whose course could not have been predicted, then my bad luck is brute (even though I could have moved just before it struck if I had any reason to know where it would strike). (Dworkin 2000: 73)

Setting aside the 'anomalies' addressed in the paragraph above, Dworkin thinks that inequalities reflecting differential brute luck are unjust. But he also thinks that the inequalities reflecting differential option luck are just. Indeed, he thinks that to eliminate option luck inequality through redistribution from winners to losers would be unjust because it would deprive people who want to take risks of this possibility. This view is clearly luck egalitarian in one respect and not so clearly luck egalitarian in another. It is clearly luck egalitarian in its opposition to inequalities reflecting differential brute luck. Such differences can only exist if some people are worse off than others through bad brute luck.

Dworkin's view is less clearly luck egalitarian in its insistence that inequalities reflecting differential option luck should be allowed to stand. On the one hand such differences are special in the sense that a person who is worse off as a result of bad option luck made a choice to engage in risky behaviour, so, arguably, it is a special kind of luck in that it results from choice. On the other hand, the fact that both the winner and the loser of a gamble chose to engage in the gamble does not change the fact that the resulting inequality between them *is* a matter of luck. True, both of them chose to gamble but the loser neither chose to lose, nor chose to end up worse off than the winner. Hence, assuming that a distribution is unjust when some people are worse off than others through their bad luck, it is hard to see why differential option luck is not unjust. Some luck egalitarians might respond that the relevant injustice-making feature is that some are worse off than others through *avoidable*, or *reasonably avoidable*, bad luck. However, suppose someone declines a gamble and ends up worse off than someone who engages in it and wins and suppose this gamble was one which: i) from the two agents' perspectives was neither unreasonable to decline nor unreasonable to accept; ii) and the former agent would have lost had he or she accepted it. The proposed view would still not explain why the person who declines the gamble is not *unjustly* worse off than the winner.

Dworkin's ambition to defend an ideal of equality of resources that is ambition-sensitive and endowment-insensitive sounds like much of the considerations he adduces in its favour, luck egalitarian. However, his 'Equality of What?' articles' relation to luck egalitarianism, at least as defined in Section 1.1, is not entirely perspicuous. This is so in relation to (a) the reason he gives for withholding compensation for expensive preferences, (b) his rejection of compensation for severe handicaps and for not being very talented, (c) his endorsement of differential option luck, and (d) his acceptance of the role luck plays in relation to which set of external resources is available at his auction – if I hate all the resources available at the auction and you love all of them, you will be better off than me even if I do not envy your bundle of resources – and in how preferences are distributed – something which e.g. determines who enjoys economy of scale (Dworkin 2000: 69). Nevertheless Dworkin's articles set much of the agenda for later contributions to the luck egalitarian literature.

1.5. Three important luck egalitarians: Arneson

In an important article from 1989, Richard Arneson defends equality of opportunity for welfare. He submits that, in his critique of welfarist egalitarianism, Dworkin confuses two distinctions: the distinction between welfare and resources, on the one hand, and the distinction between outcomes and opportunities, on the other. Responding to the case of expensive tastes, Arneson (1989: 84) agrees that, from the point of view of justice, people who deliberately cultivate expensive preferences probably should not receive compensation. However, according to Arneson the reason that, generally, people with expensive tastes are not due compensation is not that justice is not concerned with welfare, but the fact that justice is concerned with equality of *opportunity* of welfare. Since Dworkin stipulates that Louis 'sets out deliberately to cultivate some taste or ambition he does not now have', it is natural to assume that Louis had the opportunity not to develop expensive tastes and accordingly that his opportunities for welfare prior to doing so were equally good as those of others. Arneson (1989: 88) concludes that whereas the example of Louis works as a counterexample to outcome equality of welfare, it has no force against equality of opportunity for welfare. In view of the discrepancy between Dworkin's description of Louis and his claim as to why Louis should be denied compensation, it might be conjectured that Dworkin was not as confused as Arneson thought he was. Perhaps Dworkin's 'confusion' simply reflects the fact that he has a different view from Arneson regarding *why* someone who cultivates expensive tastes should not be compensated – to wit, that one should not be compensated on grounds of one's ambitions – though they agree *that* such people should be denied compensation.

It is one thing to rebut Dworkin's critique of welfarist egalitarianism. It is another thing to present an attractive version of it. In order to do the latter, Arneson states a sufficient condition for there being equality of opportunity for welfare. On his view, equality of opportunity for welfare with respect to two persons obtains when these two persons face effectively equivalent *decision trees*. A decision tree maps the various possible future life-histories of a person from a given moment in time, say, from when he or she becomes morally responsible, falsely supposing there is a sharp cut-off time (Arneson 1990: 179). Or more precisely, it maps all possible future sequences of *choices* among those actions available to the person. Obviously, exactly one of these possible life-histories is realized. The decision tree pertaining to one person is *equivalent* to the decision tree pertaining to another person, if 'the expected value [i.e. welfare] of each person's best (most prudent), second-best ... nth-best choice of options is the same' (Arneson 1989: 85–6). Two equivalent decision trees are *effectively equivalent* decision trees if, among other things, the persons to whom these decision trees pertain do not differ in 'their awareness of these options, their ability to choose reasonably among them, and the strength of character that enables a person to persist in carrying out a chosen decision' (Arneson 1989: 86; cf. Lippert-Rasmussen 1999). Or if they so differ, this is counterbalanced by their options being inequivalent.

This explanation pertains to the opportunity aspect of Arneson's ideal. However, one would also like to know more about the welfare bit. On this matter, Arneson defends a particular preference-based account of welfare:

> I take welfare to be preference satisfaction. The more an individual's preferences are satisfied, as weighted by their importance to that very individual, the higher her welfare ... The preferences that most plausibly serve as the measure of the individual's welfare are hypothetical preferences. (Arneson 1989: 82)

Cases involving preferences based on false beliefs show why Arneson thinks that hypothetical as opposed to actual preferences determine welfare. Suppose I desire to drink the contents of the bottle in front of me. I believe it contains a nice mango smoothie. In fact it contains petroleum. Plausibly, satisfying my actual preference for drinking its contents will not increase my welfare. Moreover, we might say that if I were better informed, e.g. about the contents of the bottle, I would have a preference for not drinking its contents. Plausibly, the satisfaction of this informed preference determines my level of welfare.

There are many different hypothetical preferences. According to Arneson, one's level of welfare is determined by those hypothetical preferences that he calls 'second-best' rational preferences. These are not the preferences one would have if one 'were to engage in thoroughgoing deliberation about [one's] preferences with full pertinent information, in a calm mood, while thinking clearly and making no reasoning errors' (Arneson 1989: 83). These preferences are one's first-best preferences. One gets from one's first-best to one's second-best preference by also taking into account '(a) one's actual resistance to advice regarding the rationality of one's preferences, (b) the costs of an educational program that would break down this resistance, and (c) the likelihood that anything approaching this educational program will actually be implemented in one's lifetime' (Arneson 1989: 83). In short, one's second-best preferences are the preferences one's ideally rational self would want one to have given one's actual irrationality and the cost and prospects of overcoming it. To see what this means, suppose:

> low-life preferences for cheap thrills have a large place in my actual conception of the good, but no place in my first-best rational preferences. But suppose that it is certain that these low-life preferences are firmly fixed in my character. Then my second-best preferences are those I would have if I were to deliberate in ideal fashion about my preferences in the light of full knowledge about my actual preferences and their resistance to change. If you are giving me a birthday present, and your sole goal is to advance my welfare as much as possible, you are probably advised to give me, say, a bottle of jug wine rather than a volume of Shelley's poetry

even though it is the poetry experience that would satisfy my first-best rational preference. (Arneson 1989: 83)

The fact that Arneson's welfarist luck egalitarianism focuses on self-regarding, second-best preferences allows him to dismiss or at least mitigate two objections to welfarist luck egalitarianism, which Dworkin presses. First, Dworkin thinks that external preferences, i.e. preferences that one has regarding others, are irrelevant from the point of view of justice. Yet, on an unrestricted welfarist account such preferences count too. Whether this restriction is plausible or not, Dworkin's objection does not apply to Arneson's welfarism, the scope of which is restricted to self-regarding preference. Second, Dworkin points out that unrestricted welfarism will deem offensive preferences, e.g. racist or sexist preferences, to be relevant from the point of view of justice (cf. Section 4.5). If an individual has less welfare than others, because of the frustration of his racist and sexist preferences, unrestricted welfarists will want to compensate this individual for loss of welfare. Again, whether or not it is plausible to think that justice mandates such compensation, Arneson might say that in most cases people's second-best preferences do not include sexist or racist preferences – say, because such preferences are almost always based on false or incomplete information – and, thus, the frustration of these persons' actual sexist or racist prefer-ences does not detract from their welfare (see Section 4.5). In sum, Arneson's work represents a form of welfarist luck egalitarianism, which avoids many of Dworkin's arguments against it.

1.6. Three important luck egalitarians: Cohen

The last luck egalitarian whose views I will introduce in this chapter is G. A. Cohen. Like Arneson, Cohen does not simply see equality as a condition of legitimacy. Rather, he thinks distributions can be assessed as just or unjust, independently of how they were brought about by the state. Nevertheless, like Arneson, Cohen sets out with an immanent critique of Dworkin's work and then uses it as a springboard for proposing his own competing account of equality. On Cohen's view: 'Dworkin's declared position ... is not congruent with its own underlying motivation' (Cohen 2011: 3). By 'Dworkin's declared position' Cohen has in mind Dworkin's view that 'people are to be compensated for shortfalls in their powers, that is, their material and mental and physical capacities, but not for shortfalls traceable to their tastes and preferences' (Cohen 2011: 19). This distinction is the one we referred to above as the distinction between endowments and ambitions.

Why does Cohen think Dworkin's distinction fails to capture the core of egalitarian justice? One reason is the following. According to Cohen the 'purpose' of egalitarianism 'is to eliminate involuntary disadvantage' by which he means 'disadvantage for which the sufferer cannot be held responsible, since it does not appropriately reflect choices that he has made or is making or would make' (Cohen 2011: 13). This statement is quite in the spirit of my core luck egalitarian claim in Section 1.1 above, because, as Cohen sees it, 'a large part of the fundamental egalitarian aim is to extinguish the influence of brute luck on distribution' where 'genuine choice contrast[s] with brute luck' (Cohen 2011: 29). So for Cohen the crucial distinction is between luck and genuine choice. This distinction, however, cuts across Dworkin's distinction between endowments and ambitions. In principle, deficiencies in 'material and mental and physical capacities' might reflect 'genuine choice', e.g. if I make a genuine choice to donate a kidney of mine to someone else. Also, deficiencies due to expensive preferences might reflect bad luck, e.g. one simply happens to find oneself with expensive tastes that one does not control.

As I said, Cohen is not just making a claim about what is the right reading of egalitarian justice. He is also making a point about what is the impulse underlying Dworkin's own work, i.e. his critique is immanent. He supports this aspect of his claim in various ways. For instance, he points out that whatever attraction Dworkin's hypothetical insurance device has derives from its putative elimination of differential brute luck and not from any alignment with the distinction between ambitions and circumstances. Also, he notes that Dworkin, in 'Why Liberals Should Care About Equality', claims that we should attend to 'which aspects of any person's economic position flow from his choices and which from advantages and disadvantages that were not matters of choice' (Dworkin 1986: 208; quoted in Cohen 2011: 30). This formulation certainly sounds more like Cohen's cut than like Dworkin's official cut in his 1981 articles. Still, as Dworkin's own explanation of why Louis is not entitled, on bar of justice, to compensation for his expensive tastes reminds us, Dworkin's considered position is different from the one suggested by Cohen's cut and different from the one suggested by many of Dworkin's own claims, e.g. in his own answer to why liberals should care about equality.

More positively, Cohen thinks – as Arneson does – that Dworkin's example of Louis with the expensive tastes defeats the ideal of equality of welfare, but that it fails to defeat equality of opportunity of welfare. However, Cohen disagrees with both Arneson and Dworkin about 'what metric egalitarians should use to establish the extent to which their ideal is realized in a given society' (Cohen 2011: 3), where the relevant metric is what matters fundamentally to egalitarians and not just as a proxy for that which matters fundamentally. By way of illustration: egalitarians might regret income inequalities, not because they care about income inequality as such, but because income inequality is a proxy for some other metric which they care about fundamentally, e.g. how well people's lives go. Cohen rejects Dworkin's view on the currency of egalitarian justice, because he thinks welfare matters fundamentally from the point of view of egalitarian justice. He rejects Arneson's view, because he thinks that welfare is not all that so matters. More specifically, he thinks that the involuntary disadvantage that egalitarians want to eliminate includes both welfare as well as resource deficiencies (Cohen 2011: 14).

To show, *pace* Arneson, that welfare is not all that matters, Cohen describes the case of Tiny Tim (to whom I shall return in Section 4.4). Tiny Tim is 'not only actually happy' he 'is also … blessed with abundant *opportunity* for happiness' (Cohen 2011: 15) such that (opportunity for) welfare-wise he is not worse off than others. Yet, 'egalitarians would not on that account strike him off the list of free wheelchair receivers … The essential point is that his abundant happiness is not as such a decisive reason against compensating him for his disability' (Cohen 2011: 15). To show, *pace* Dworkin, that welfare matters, Cohen imagines an individual for whom 'it is not difficult … to move his arms' – indeed he is better at moving them than most – but for whom 'it is very costly ... to do so' (Cohen 2011: 16). The reason it is very costly is that he suffers severe pain whenever he moves his arms. Cohen contends that this person is not worse off resource-wise than others are and yet he is due compensation from an egalitarian point of view: 'there is an irreducible welfare aspect in the case for egalitarian compensation in real-life disability examples' (Cohen 2011: 17).

Let me round off this survey of the views of three important luck egalitarian theorists with the following remarks. First, there are considerable variations across the views of different luck egalitarians. Second, while some luck egalitarians – most clearly G. A. Cohen – endorse the vocabulary of luck, not all of them do. Third, we have seen some of the core issues that I will address in later chapters introduced. Notably, we have seen various ways to flesh out the distinction between luck and non-luck, which I shall return to in Chapter 3, and introduced the disagreement between resourcist and welfarist luck egalitarianism, which will occupy us in Chapter 4. Also, we have seen that whereas Dworkin sees equality as a condition of legitimacy of states, neither Arneson nor Cohen thinks the value of equality simply derives from an obligation of the state to treat its citizens with equal concern. This issue will occupy us on several occasions later, most notably in Chapters 5 and 7.

1.7. Other distributive views

In Section 1.1 I offered a definition of luck egalitarianism and explained various features of it. However, to fully grasp what luck egalitarians believe it is useful to contrast their view with some competing ones. Accordingly, in this section I describe how luck egalitarianism relates to competing or different views. Consider, first, utilitarianism:

(2) An act is morally permissible, if and only if it maximizes the amount of well-being.

Utilitarians have different conceptions of well-being. Some think it consists in pleasant mental states, while others think it consists in preference satisfaction.

Utilitarianism is often said to have some tendency to justify equality of resources. The reason for this is the decreasing marginal well-being from additional units of resources. By way of illustration: the first $1,000 I get makes a huge difference to my well-being, since it means a difference between starving to death and being able to survive at a very modest level. However, as I get more and more money I will get less and less additional well-being out of an additional $1,000. Presumably, at some point additional money will make no difference to my level of well-being.

In response to this observation, we can note two things. First, at best the relevant tendency is just that – a tendency. There are bound to be cases where utilitarianism will not favour equality. For instance, grumpy people are bad converters of resources into welfare. All else being equal, utilitarianism favours their being worse off than others.

Second, to the extent that utilitarianism has a tendency to justify equality, it favours equality in a way which is very different from the way in which egalitarianism does so. To the extent that utilitarianism favours equality, it does so in its capacity to function as an instrument of maximizing the sum of welfare. Luck egalitarians, of course, might value equality instrumentally as well, but they also think that equality is valuable independently of whether it promotes other values such as welfare.

There are other ways in which utilitarianism and luck egalitarianism differ. Most importantly, utilitarianism is a view about moral permissibility, while luck egalitarianism is a view about justice. This means that, in one way, the two theories are not competing – that is, if one rejects utilitarianism it is still an open question which alternative theory of moral permissibility one should adopt and luck egalitarianism cannot be an answer to this question. In another way they are competing. Unlike utilitarians, luck egalitarians think that justice is one consideration among others – perhaps one of the most important considerations – that determine what is morally permissible. Accordingly, if one is a luck egalitarian one cannot be a utilitarian, since presumably there will be cases where weighty luck egalitarian justice concerns favour a distribution that does not maximize the sum of welfare. In these cases luck egalitarians, who think that justice is more important than a tie-breaker that determines which among several acts that are permissible on the utilitarian criterion is to be preferred, will favour a distribution that does not maximize the sum of welfare on grounds of distributive justice.

Second, while utilitarians are only concerned with welfare, luck egalitarians may be concerned about other things as well, e.g. they might care about the distribution of resources. Indeed, like Dworkin, as far as justice goes luck egalitarians may only be concerned with something *other than* welfare.

Third, there is no 'luckist' element, as it were, to utilitarianism. That is, utilitarians ascribe no fundamental significance to whether someone's level of welfare is a matter of luck or non-luck. Like with some of the other views introduced below, in principle, it is possible to construct a luckist version of utilitarianism. Suppose one adopts a desert-based conception of luck (see Section 3.3) according to which one has good luck if one has more than one deserves and bad luck if one has less. On this view of luck, one could argue that some have been attracted to a luckist version of utilitarianism. Fred Feldman, for instance, defends a version of consequentialism that adjusts utility for desert on the basis that a pleasure is more valuable if it is deserved and less valuable, or perhaps even disvaluable, if it is undeserved (Feldman 1997). Given an appropriate account of desert, this position might be looked upon as luck-utilitarianism (or luck-consequentialism). On one version of this kind of view (one differing from Feldman's), the moral value of an outcome always increases with increasing welfare for individuals. But the moral value of an extra unit of welfare to a person is greater, the larger the degree to which the person deserves this gain (loss avoidance).

Fourth, utilitarianism is indifferent between whether a certain gain in well-being falls on non-human animals or on human beings, all other things being equal. As it is normally understood (but see Section 6.6), luck egalitarianism is concerned with inequalities between human beings, but not with inequalities between different non-human animals or between human beings and non-human animals.

I now move on to consider a second view, which is different from, but related to, luck egalitarianism, i.e. sufficientarianism. At least in the relatively straightforward version that I introduce here, it holds that:

(3) It is unjust if some people do not have enough.

In some ways, this view is considerably closer to luck egalitarianism than utilitarianism. Like the former, it leaves open what the relevant currency of justice is. Moreover, while, as usually stated, sufficientarianism has no luckist component, it is easy to see how we can revise it such that it does:

(3*) It is unjust if some people do not have enough through their bad luck.

On this view, it need not be unjust if some people have less than enough as a result of their knowingly being imprudent, just as, according to luck egalitarianism, it need not be unjust if some people are worse off than others as a result of knowingly being imprudent (cf. Fabre 2012: 16).

What does it mean to have enough (cf. Casal 2007)? There are two ways to answer this question. One might answer it through a comparison with others, e.g. one might say that one has less than enough resources if one has less than 50 per cent of the resources people have on average (cf. Axelsen and Nielsen 2014; Huseby 2010). An extreme version of comparative sufficientarianism, which is difficult to distinguish from egalitarianism, holds that one has less than enough when one is worse off than others.

Alternatively, one might answer it independently of any comparison with others, e.g. one might think that there are certain basic capabilities such as being able to have good health and to be attached to others that are necessary for living well, independently of how well off others are, and that anyone who does not have these capabilities does not have enough (Nussbaum 2000: 76–8). Obviously, any view as to where the relevant threshold of sufficiency is located is bound to be controversial and difficult to defend adequately.

For present purposes, we can set these difficulties aside and note that just as sufficientarianism normally is endorsed in a non-luckist form, sufficientarians tend to have a non-comparative view of sufficiency. This means that one crucial difference between luck egalitarianism and sufficientarianism is that the former is essentially comparative across individuals in a way that the latter is not. That is, in order to know whether a distribution is just, we need to know how people's distributive positions compare to one another. This is something we do not need to know according to sufficientarianism. One way to see this is to imagine a situation where everyone enjoys blissful lives far above the level of sufficiency but some are slightly worse off than others through bad luck (cf. Benbaji 2005; Frankfurt 1987). Sufficientarians see no injustice in this situation because no one has less than enough. However, luck egalitarians do.

Some are initially attracted to sufficientarianism because they think morality is more concerned about worse-off people than about better-off people and yet feel some unease with the fact that sufficientarianism completely ignores inequalities above the level of sufficiency. Some such people find prioritarianism, which is the third non-luck egalitarian view to be introduced in this section, attractive (e.g. Holtug 2010; Parfit 1995):

> (4) The moral goodness of an outcome is determined by the sum of individual well-being weighted by how well off the relevant individuals are.

Prioritarianism has two core ideas: (i) whenever some individual is benefited, the outcome becomes better, all other things being equal, and (ii) a unit of well-being has greater moral value if it accrues to someone who is at a lower rather than a higher level of well-being. (i) entails that prioritarianism always implies that it is valuable if an individual receives an additional unit of welfare. This is so even if this person is already much better off than others. If we formulate luck egalitarianism as a view about moral value:

> (1*) It has negative moral value if some people are worse off than others through their bad luck.

This view clashes with prioritarianism in that it implies that there is some value to eliminating inequality by making everyone worse off.

(ii) implies that prioritarianism, absent other morally relevant concerns, favours a more equal to a less equal distribution. It does so for a reason which would apply even if there were no decreasing marginal well-being from additional resources – namely, that additional benefits at lower levels of well-being have greater, non-instrumental value than benefits at higher levels. In this way, prioritarianism has a more robust tendency to favour equality than utilitarianism does. This is why many are inclined to think of prioritarianism as an egalitarian view in a broader sense but have no such inclination in the case of utilitarianism.

If we combine prioritarianism with the view that:

(5) An act is morally permissible, if and only if it maximizes the amount of moral value (understood in purely prioritarian terms).

we get a view – weighted beneficence – which differs from utilitarianism only in that it weighs units of welfare according to how well off its bearers are. Weighted beneficence clashes with luck egalitarianism for the same reason that utilitarianism does. There could be cases where one maximizes the sum of moral value by making some worse off than others through no fault of their own. In these cases prioritarians will unequivocally favour the more unequal distribution, whereas luck egalitarians will think that the more unequal distribution is more unjust even if, all things considered, it is morally best. I shall return to the issue such situations give rise to in Chapter 5.

Before leaving prioritarianism, I should mention that Richard Arneson has proposed a luckist version of prioritarianism that accommodates the 'generic egalitarian intuition' that 'fortunate individuals should give up resources to improve the life prospects of those whose initial conditions are unpropitious [i.e. the upshot of bad luck]' (Arneson 1999a: 227). According to this view, 'the moral value of achieving a gain (avoiding a loss) for a person' is 'greater, the lower the person's lifetime expectation of well-being prior to receipt of the benefit (avoidance of the loss)' and 'greater, the larger the degree to which the person deserves this gain (loss avoidance)' (Arneson 1999a: 239–40).

Having introduced prioritarianism, it makes sense to briefly discuss Rawls' celebrated difference principle – the fourth non-luck principle to be discussed in this section:

(6) The basic structure of a society is just only if the worst-off group, primary goods-wise, is as well off as possible.

The difference principle is different from prioritarianism in that it gives absolute weight to the position of the worse-off. This may

seem problematic. Suppose we can benefit everyone else tremendously by modifying the basic structure of society such that we make
the worst-off group slightly worse off. According to the difference
principle the relevant modified basic structure would be unjust.
Prioritarians find this implausible.

While the difference principle is often seen as an egalitarian
principle, it is clear that it differs from luck egalitarianism in a number
of respects. First, the site of justice – i.e. that to which principles
of justice apply – is the basic structure of society and not distributions as such. Second, it has no luckist element. Third, it implies
that an unequal distribution might be just even in the absence of
responsibility-related factors justifying this inequality. This is so if an
unequal distribution would imply that the group of worse-off people
under that distribution would be better off than under the equal distribution. Fourth, the difference principle is concerned with groups,
not individuals. Normally, luck egalitarianism is seen as a view that
pertains to inequalities between individuals (see Section 6.4). This
means that it avoids an important objection to the difference principle
– namely, that it ignores inequalities *within* groups. However, the
luck egalitarian principle, as I have stated it, can be interpreted both
ways and, in any case, it is easy to see how it might apply not to
individuals, but to the same groups as the difference principle.

To complete this comparison of luck egalitarianism with alternative principles, I want to end this survey by considering a fifth
principle – the principle of Rawlsian fair equality of opportunity –
which I briefly touched upon in Section 1.2 on the first part of Rawls'
intuitive argument for the difference principle. This principle says:

(7) It is unjust if any individual, who has the same native talent
and the same ambition as another individual, does not have
the same prospects of success in competitions that determine
who gets positions that generate superior benefits for their
occupants. (Rawls 1971: 73)

In one way this principle is a more restricted one than luck egalitarianism. By 'positions' Rawls has in mind first and foremost things like
jobs and by 'benefits' he has in mind the sort of benefits typically
associated with jobs such as income. However, many benefits derive

from features not attached to positions in this sense. For instance, whether one is cheerful by temperament or whether one has attractive looks makes a big difference to the quality of one's life. Yet, Rawls' principle of fair equality of opportunity does not apply to such benefits. Thus, one's favoured version of luck egalitarianism – say, welfarist luck egalitarianism – might not be satisfied even though Rawls' principle of fair equality of opportunity is, i.e. because some people have suffered differential bad brute luck in spheres of life not covered by Rawls' principle. For a similar reason, a distribution might satisfy one's favoured luck egalitarian principle even though Rawlsian equality of opportunity is not satisfied, i.e. because an unfair inequality of opportunity is counterbalanced by luck favouring those having worse opportunities in relation to the sort of position to which Rawlsian equality of opportunity applies.

To bracket the previous two points, let us assume that the only relevant sort of goods that exist are those to which Rawlsian fair equality of opportunity applies. Under this assumption, would Rawlsian fair equality of opportunity imply that no one is worse off than others through bad luck? There are at least two reasons why not. First, differences in natural talents are presumably a matter of brute luck. But Rawls' principles allow that two persons who are equally ambitious and thus put equal amount of efforts into reaching a position that generates superior benefits do not have the same prospects of success when one has a greater natural talent than the other. Yet this would be ruled out by luck egalitarianism.

Second, to the extent that one can suffer bad luck in terms of one's ambitions, there is a second reason why the satisfaction of Rawlsian fair equality of opportunity does not satisfy luck egalitarians. To see that, plausibly, there could be such a thing as bad luck in terms of ambition, consider the following not so hypothetical example offered by Richard Arneson:

Suppose that [equality of fair opportunity] obtains in a society but overwhelmingly boys develop the ambition to pursue challenging and lucrative careers and girls overwhelmingly do not. The explanation is that boys and girls alike are subjected to a rigid form of socialization which instills ambition in boys and quashes it in girls. (Arneson 2008)

In this society it would seem plausible to say that girls suffer from bad ambition luck – due to circumstances beyond their control they are led to develop fewer ambitions than boys in a way, let us suppose, that is bad for them. Many luck egalitarians contrast ambitions and efforts with luck, and Arneson's example suggests compellingly that at least some differences in ambitions and efforts might be due to luck and, thus, might have no power to justify inequality. If so, this is a second way in which Rawlsian fair equality of opportunity is not enough for luck egalitarians. Moreover, it indicates a way in which the satisfaction of luck egalitarianism might not suffice for there being Rawlsian fair equality of opportunity. Consider two people who have the same high level of natural talents and ambition. They differ in that one's high level is due to good luck, e.g. having been fortunate to be raised in a sexist society favouring members of his sex, the other person's high ambitions are not due to good luck. On luck egalitarianism, this would seem to call for equalization such that the person whose high ambitions are not due to luck has better prospects than the person whose high ambitions are due to luck. If such equalization is implemented, we might have a situation where luck egalitarianism is satisfied, but Rawlsian fair equality of opportunity is not. On the basis thereof, I conclude that luck egalitarianism and Rawlsian fair equality of opportunity are distinct views. This is not to say that one cannot explore versions of the ideal of equality of opportunity that have impeccable luck egalitarians credentials, as indeed some luck egalitarians have done (Roemer 2000; Segall 2013).

1.8. Summary

In this chapter I first introduced a core luck egalitarian claim, i.e. that it is unjust if some people are worse off than others through their bad luck. Having explained this claim, I proceeded to explain its attraction. Specifically, I rejected the view that the principle needed to be derived from a more basic moral principle. I then introduced the views of three influential luck egalitarians – Dworkin, Arneson and Cohen – pointing out various differences between them, e.g. whether equality is a moral requirement independently of conditions of legitimacy or whether equality concerns resources or welfare.

Finally, in order to locate luck egalitarianism on the map of normative views about or pertaining to distributions, I contrasted it with a number of competing views which have some affinity with luck egalitarianism in that they have some tendency to favour more egalitarian distributions and, thus, are harder to distinguish from views, e.g. Nozick's right-libertarianism, that have no such tendency. Lessons so far include that standard luck egalitarianism is a view (at least also) about distributions across individuals; that it leaves open what the relevant currency of justice is; that it is essentially comparative across individuals; that it is a justice view, not a moral permissibility view; that it has an equality element which can be detached from its luckist element. In the next chapter I take a closer look at the justification for the former element, while in Chapter 3 I unfold the luckist element.

2

Why equality?

2.1. Introduction

In effect, luck egalitarianism holds that justice requires that people be equally well off unless those who are worse off are worse off through their luck-negating choice or exercise of responsibility. One might challenge luck egalitarians to justify this presumption in favour of equality. Why is the baseline distribution from which deviations can be justified by differential exercise of choice or responsibility not one where the total sum of welfare is maximized or, as prioritarians have it, one where the total sum of weighted welfare is maximized? This question arises once we bear in mind the luckist versions of utilitarianism and prioritarianism that I briefly described in Section 1.7. As Susan Hurley has argued at length, the aim to neutralize luck cannot in itself justify this presumption, since even equal distributions might come about through luck (Hurley 2003: 147; cf. Cohen 2011: 116–23; cf. Christiano 2006: 46).

To justify the basis of equality it seems that one has to identify 'the features of human beings in virtue of which they are to be treated in accordance with the principles of [egalitarian] justice' (Rawls 1971: 441). Unfortunately, many luck egalitarian writers have addressed an all-egalitarians audience, who accept the relevant presumption and simply want to know how it is most plausibly fleshed out. This chapter speaks to those who want the presumption of equality justified in the first place. In doing so I shall bracket the luckist element of luck egalitarianism, which I will return to in Chapter 3. Section 2.2 explores whether the presumption in favour of equality can be derived from a formal principle of justice. Section 3.3 investigates how the presumption of equality relates to the idea that all human beings have an equal, basic moral status. Sections 3.4–6 assess three attempts to ground equality in features that, unlike, say, sympathy or intelligence, (most) human beings have to an equal degree: Bernard Williams' (having awareness of oneself and one's place in the world), Rawls' (moral personhood) and Ian Carter's (being entitled to opacity respect). Section 3.7 distinguishes the problem of justifying the presumption of equal standing from another question with which it is often confused, and which is not a problem for egalitarians in particular – the question of in virtue of what, if anything, persons or human beings have a higher moral status than non-persons or non-humans. On this basis it proposes that equality of moral standing of persons is grounded in their capacity to be non-instrumentally concerned with things in a distinctive way.

2.2. Formal equality

One argument in favour of the presumption of equality that immediately springs to mind is one that appeals to the principle of formal equality, i.e. the principle that cases that are relevantly alike should be treated alike, while cases that are relevantly different should be treated relevantly differently. On the assumption that people who have not exercised their responsibility or chosen to act differently are relevantly alike, they should be treated alike, according to the principle of formal equality, and this in turn requires some kind of equal distribution. If the presumption in favour of equality could be established in this way it would be very good from the point of luck egalitarianism, since if any principle of justice is undeniable the principle of formal equality is surely one.

Unfortunately, this argument will not do. For suppose that by making one individual better off than others we can maximize the sum of welfare. In that case, there is a relevant difference between the two individuals, according to utilitarians – namely, that by making the former better off than the latter we can maximize the sum of welfare. In itself the principle of formal equality is compatible with any view about what constitutes relevant differences and, thus, does not in itself rule out utilitarianism. Hence, it cannot in itself justify distributive equality.

Thomas Christiano concedes that the formal principle of treating the alike alike and unalike unalike does not in itself establish equality. However, he thinks it does so together with a few other plausible principles. Here is his own short summary of his long, complex argument appealing to formal equality ('the generic principle of justice' in his terminology):

> If there are two people and we believe that one person ought to be better off than the other, it follows that we think that there is a reason for the better-off person to be better off than the other and justice requires that this reason be a relevant difference between them. But, by hypothesis, there are no relevant differences and the persons have equal status, so it follows that the same reason holds for the other person to be that well off. So, if the other person is not as well off, then that person is being treated in violation of the generic principle of justice or of his equal status. Hence, either the better-off person does not have reason to be treated that way or there is a relevant difference or the generic principle is false. By hypothesis there is no relevant difference between these persons of equal status, and the generic principle of justice is true. Therefore, the better-off person does not have reason to be treated better than the worse-off person. There is only one level of well-being that can satisfy the generic principle of justice, the fundamental value of well-being, and the fact of no relevant differences among equals, and that is the level at which there is equality of well-being. (Christiano 2006: 63)

The hypothesis to which Christiano refers in the second sentence of the above passage derives from a stipulation to the effect that his argument applies only to people before they reach the age of adulthood and his assumption that at such an age there are no differences in desert or productivity or any other factor that constitutes relevant differences between them (Christiano 2006: 35).

There are several problems with this argument. However, I want to focus on the assumption that comes out in the second sentence of the passage quoted above. Suppose that the better-off person, whom Christiano refers to, is better off because this is required by the priority principle – moral value would not be maximized if the two persons were exactly equally well off. Christiano wants to claim that if this difference is the only difference between then, assuming that they have the same moral standing, there is just as much reason why the worse-off person should be as well off as the better-off person. Accordingly, the inequality violates the principle of generic justice.

But why cannot the prioritarian say that there is a morally relevant difference between the two – namely, that benefiting the better-off person results in more moral value than benefiting the worse-off person, say, because the former person is a better converter of resources into moral value? In what appears to be a response to this suggestion Christiano contends that the:

> requirement to maximize a person's well-being cannot be conjoined with the generic principle of justice if one thinks that each person's well-being is important. To treat everyone alike in the way specified by the principle of maximization is impossible. (Christiano 2006: 59)

However, prioritarians are not concerned with persons' well-being as such, so for this observation to have any bite, the relevant requirement, which Christiano mentions, must be a requirement to maximize the moral value of a person's well-being. His point would then seem to be that maximizing the moral value of one person's well-being (presumably by maximizing her level of well-being) would mean that, having spent so many resources on the first person, we could not maximize the moral value of other people's well-being and that would violate the generic principle of justice. However, prioritarians do not accept any requirement to maximize the moral value of *each person*'s well-being. Unlike the moral requirement to maximize *overall* moral value, it is not a moral requirement that follows from the definition of prioritarianism and, indeed, for the reason indicated by Christiano, a moral requirement that clashes with the moral requirement to maximize overall moral value.

A further point is that in affirming the permissibility of inequalities, prioritarians could deny that this involves any violation of generic justice. In a sense it is true that, according to prioritarianism, 'the well-being of a person who is better off is worth less than the well-being of that same person or some other person who is worse off' (Christiano 2006: 59). But this is true in a sense that is compatible with the principle of generic justice and the equality of moral status of persons. To those who are better off and to whom extra benefits have less moral weight, we can say: 'It is not as if you have a lesser moral status than those who are worse off. If you were as badly off as those who are worse off or if they were as well off as you are, extra benefits to you and them would count for exactly the same, morally speaking. The reason why benefits to you have less moral weight is that it is more urgent to benefit people who are worse off'. Prioritarianism might be a false view, but there are no plausible notions of equal status and formal justice that together imply its falsity. Formal equality, on its own or together with the relevant additional premises, will not justify the presumption of equality.

2.3. Equality of human beings

Even if we cannot appeal to the formal principle of equality, there is another principle that we can appeal to which seems very attractive as well – namely a principle to the effect that all human beings have an equal basic moral status – which might justify the equality baseline. To see what this principle involves, consider the following plausible implication of the principle – that the interests of some individuals do not count for more, morally speaking, than the interests of others just because they have a favoured gender or race. After all, these people are all human beings.

Unfortunately, it seems doubtful that this appeal can justify the presumption of equality either. First, even if the principle is true, it is not clear that inequality will necessarily clash with equal basic moral status. Peter Singer, for instance, holds that giving equal weight to the equally important interests of individuals is a plausible way of understanding equal moral standing (Singer 1993: 21–2). On that view, if a certain redistribution will harm me just a little, but benefit others much more, the interests of others in this redistribution taking place are more weighty than my interest in its not taking place.

Accordingly, a redistribution of this sort would not, on Singer's view, clash with equal basic moral status even if it would result in inequality.

Second, there is a more basic reason why this appeal is problematic – namely, that, on reflection, it is hard to see why all human beings should be thought to have the same basic moral status. Mere species membership seems just as odd a reason for moral status as membership of a particular race. As Richard Arneson puts it: 'If we were to encounter alien beings from another planet' and the aliens 'showed a capacity for rational, autonomous agency, we would be required to include them within the scope of our moral principles' (Arneson 1999c: 103). This suggestion might seem innocuous in itself. But now we may ask the following question: if it is the capacity for rational agency, not species membership, that entitles aliens to be included within the scope of our moral principles, what about those human beings who have no capacity for rational agency? Clearly, there are some such human beings, e.g. newly born infants or severely demented elderly people. Moreover, the distinction between those who have and those who do not have a capacity for rational agency is a very simplifying and ultimately arbitrary-looking distinction. Different human beings have different capacities for rational agency. This fact makes the following questions very relevant: if moral status derives from the capacity for moral agency, why not say that the greater one's capacity for rational agency the higher one's moral status is? And why say about human beings who have no capacity for moral agency that they are to be treated as equals with human beings who have such a capacity? Since neither of the two candidate justifications for the presumption of equality reviewed so far seems convincing, and since we would like to have a justification for the presumption in favour of equality, we need to face the following question: in virtue of which characteristics do human beings enjoy moral equality and, presumably, a superior moral status to non-human beings?

2.4. Williams on the idea of equality

In some of his early work, Bernard Williams notes that human beings are unequal in physical as well as mental abilities. Specifically, this is true of our moral agency. Some people have a great capacity for sympathetic understanding, while others do not. Indeed, it seems that whichever natural property we have in mind, people have that property in varying degrees, thereby rendering it an unsuitable basis for equality. Of course one could deny that there is any natural property of ours that forms the relevant basis and appeal to a non-natural basis instead. One such basis is that we are all children of God. Another is the Kantian suggestion that our capacity for rational agency is rooted not in our empirical, but in our noumenal self. On the assumption that this is true of all human beings, and not any non-human beings, such a noumenal self might form a suitable basis for equality. The drawback is that the Kantian idea of a noumenal self is 'a kind of secular analogue of the Christian conception of the respect owed to all men as equally children of God. Though secular, it is equally metaphysical: in neither case is it anything empirical about men that constitutes the ground of equal respect' (Williams 1973a: 116). Hence, Williams presents us with a dilemma. Equality is grounded, if grounded at all, in either natural or non-natural properties. If it is the former, there is no basis for equality, since, for any natural property, it is something that human beings possess in varying degrees. If it is the latter, it is doubtful that we have this property. On either horn of the dilemma, a suitable basis of equality eludes us.

Williams, however, proposes a way out of the dilemma. Instead of grounding equality in agency, he suggests that the basis of equality consists in a kind of self-awareness possessed by all human agents (Williams 1973a: 117). Simplistically, we all have a particular perspective on the world and it is this feature of us that entitles us to being treated as equals. As Williams puts it: 'men are beings who are necessarily to some extent conscious of themselves and of the world they live in' (Williams 1973a: 237). In short, people are entitled to some sort of equal treatment – in Williams' view 'each man is owed the effort of understanding' (Williams 1973a: 237) – in virtue of having consciousness of themselves and of their place in the world.

Does Williams' proposal meet the challenge? There are at least two reasons why not. First, Williams immediately adds that mad people and mentally defective people are special exceptions to 'what is in general true of men' (Williams 1973a: 238). It might be added that foetuses, infants and small children, while not 'mentally defective' in the normal sense, do not have the sort of perspective that people in general have. Hence, to the extent that these people are thought to fall under the scope of equality, Williams' attempt to ground equality is inadequate.

Second, as pointed out by Ian Carter, even the sort of consciousness mentioned by Williams reflects empirical capacities and 'like other empirical capacities' they are 'possessed in different degrees by different individuals. People are more or less conscious, and more or less able to be conscious, of their own activities, of their own future, of their own life plan, of the world around them and the options it makes available to them' (Carter 2011: 547). While Williams may not disagree with this claim – viz. his use of the phrase 'to some extent' in the quote cited two paragraphs above and his remark about mentally defective persons – arguably, it implies that he does not succeed in avoiding the dilemma he describes.

2.5. Rawls on range properties

While Williams' suggestion might be defective as it stands, we could more charitably note that perhaps he means to suggest that what really grounds equality is not the possession of reflective consciousness as such, but the possession of at least a certain level of consciousness. The idea here is that the latter suggestion is immune to the challenge. To explore this, we can take a look at Rawls' distinction between scalar and range properties. A scalar property is one that one can have in many different degrees. Intelligence is a scalar property in this sense. Having a level of intelligence at least as high as the average level of intelligence is a range property. Either you have it or you do not. Moreover, if two persons have this property they might still vary in their levels of intelligence and yet not vary in terms of their possessing the range property of having a level of intelligence that is at least as high as the normal level of intelligence.

Rawls suggests that equality is grounded in the range property of being a moral person. A moral person is one who has a certain minimum capacity for having a conception of the good and a capacity for a sense of justice. While Rawls concedes that the two capacities involved are scalar properties, having a minimum capacity is a range property, which either you have or you do not have.

While this proposal avoids the second objection to Williams' proposal, it still faces two objections. First, some human beings are not moral persons. We might think that they fall outside the scope of egalitarian justice and if so, Rawls' proposal is fine at least as far as this point goes. However, if not, it cannot ground equality rightly construed.

Second, while grounding equality in having the range property of being a moral person avoids the problem that many of those persons whom we would want to say fall under the scope of equality differ in terms of their capacity for having a conception of the good and a sense of justice, the proposal faces a different problem. Consider an individual who falls just below the relevant minimum level of capacities for having a conception of the good and for having a conception of justice and compare this individual to one who is barely above this minimum level. On the Rawlsian view, the difference in terms of the range property – being a moral person or not – is very important, even though the difference in terms of the underlying scalar property out of which the range property is constructed is very small. Indeed, this difference might be much smaller than the one that exists between the latter person and a third person whose capacities for having a conception of the good and for having a conception of justice are extraordinarily rich. This much greater difference does not, according to Rawls, make any difference from the point of view of equality. Carter expresses the disquiet about the Rawlsian view on this matter as follows: 'If the basis of a range property is more fundamental than the range property itself, why not concentrate directly on the more fundamental scalar property (or set of properties)?' (Carter 2011: 549). While there is no logical inconsistency involved in basing the presumption of equality on a range property such as being a moral person, it is unsatisfactory to do so for the reason indicated.

2.6. Respect and opaqueness

Carter is not just critical of other proposals in the literature regarding the grounding of equality. He offers an ingenious proposal himself which, as he sees it, avoids the shortcomings of the previous proposals. He proposes that the basis of equality is a requirement to respect agents by treating them as opaque, paying attention to their outward features as agents only. This, Carter argues, shows that the answer to the 'Why equality?' question determines which is the right answer to the 'Equality of what?' question (see Chapter 4). Before I address this implication, I need to present Carter's account of the basis of equality.

Carter starts out from what he claims is a duty of opacity respect – a duty which is plausible independently of any prior commitment to egalitarianism. This duty is a duty to refuse to 'evaluate persons' varying capacities' (Carter 2011: 550). The duty requires us to adopt a 'perspective that is external to the person, and in this sense holding back from evaluating any of the variable capacities on which her moral personality supervenes, be they capacities for rational thought or capacities for evaluative judgement or capacities for awareness and understanding of one's place in the world' (Carter 2011: 551; cf. Wolff 1998). This duty has a restricted scope, however – it is a duty to treat people as opaque only once it has been established that their relevant capacities are at least as great as required for them to have moral personhood (Carter 2011: 552). Once that has been established, the opacity duty kicks in and agents have a duty not to treat them on the basis of such assessments, or indeed to form such assessments, of how much their capacities on which moral personhood supervenes exceeds the minimum threshold required for moral personhood.

Why assume that we have a duty to treat persons as opaque? Carter offers three reasons. First, the duty 'has at least as good a claim as that of Williams' to qualify as an intuitively plausible interpretation of the idea of treating persons as ends in themselves' (Carter 2011: 552). Second, Kant thought respect involves maintaining a proper 'distance' and even between friends 'we must be blind to the other's faults' (Carter 2011: 552). Finally, states have a duty to treat citizens independently of their agential capacities, e.g. the state has a duty 'to view the citizens simply as an agent' and, thus, not to compensate people whom it considers deficient in terms of rationality (Carter 2011: 557).

How does the duty of opacity ground equality, setting aside those who, compatibly with this duty, are deemed not to possess moral personhood? Carter's idea is that once 'the absolute minimum is recognized, opacity kicks in. And once opacity kicks in, there can be no grounds for locating individuals along the scale of variable agential capacities (above the threshold)' (Carter 2011: 553). Hence, we ought to treat people whose agential capacities reach or surpass the relevant minimum as equals, because we are required by the duty of opacity to ignore those differences between them that might ground unequal treatment.

Carter makes an additional claim – that this basis for equality constrains the range of possible answers to the 'Equality of what?' question which will occupy us in Chapter 4. More specifically, he contends that any practice of equalization must pass what he calls the 'opacity test': 'a practice passes the opacity test if and only if the carrying out of that practice neither constitutes nor presupposes any violation of the requirement of opacity respect' (Carter 2011: 561). The reason for this test is that the basis for equality is the opacity duty and, so Carter contends, it would seem to involve a certain kind of conceptual incoherence to violate the opacity duty in the interest of equality. More specifically, Carter thinks that agential properties, e.g. one's level of intelligence, cannot be part of the egalitarian *equalisandum*, since to assess such properties one will have to look beyond the exterior of an agent.

Having presented Carter's argument, I shall now critically assess it starting with his claim that the right answer to the 'What is the basis of equality?' question constrains the range of possibly right answers to the 'Equality of what? question. I want to make two points in this connection. First, under some circumstances, equalization of agential capacities might pass the opacity test. Suppose that, as an unintended by-product of another engineering development project, medical engineers develop a device that detects inequalities in agential capacities and boosts agential powers, e.g. through non-invasive electrical stimulation of the brain, in those with fewer capacities. The good thing about this device is that it can be operated without the operator, or for that matter anyone else, ever looking beyond the 'exterior' of those on whom the device is used, i.e. no one will ever know who had lesser capacities. Using this device seems compatible with opacity respect.

Second, Carter thinks the opacity duty constrains which *equalisanda* are plausible. However, one might turn this argument on its head and say that the right answer to the 'Equality of what?' question constrains which duties we can plausibly be said to have. So, for instance, if you think that it is very plausible that from an egalitarian point of view one should seek to equalize agential capacities, e.g. by spending more resources on pupils with lesser such capacities than on pupils with greater, then you might infer that this constrains the set of duties that can plausibly be attributed to us. More specifically, assuming that such equalization would require not treating people as opaque, attributing such a duty to us is not plausible.

In my view, the 'Basis of equality?' and the 'Equality of what?' questions are interdependent. There could be reasons why the answer to one question constrains the other, but not the other way round. However, the reasons Carter offers in favour of the opacity duty – i.e. appeal to moral intuitions and Kant exegesis – are not of a kind that would warrant any such asymmetry. As far as moral intuitions are concerned, the very same kind of reasons are offered in favour of agential capacities being one respect in which people ought to be equal.

Turning now to those reasons, I find it striking that while there is something attractive about such a duty in some contexts, Carter does not provide convincing support for it. First, to appeal to the fact that it coheres well with what Kant wrote seems like an argument by appeal to authority and not a very successful one at that. Kant thinks that respect requires that friends ignore each other's faults, but, of course, noticing each other's merits would seem to do no such thing even though this involves looking beyond each other's interior.

Second, fulfilling one's opacity duty towards another seems neither sufficient nor necessary for treating them as ends in themselves. A concentration camp guard who kills people with a yellow star on their clothes, meticulously avoiding looking beyond their exterior, does not treat those whom he kills as ends in themselves. Conversely, someone who assesses everyone's agential capacities in order to boost these further – suppose he needs to know their level to boost them – might treat everyone as ends in themselves even though he violates the opacity duty.

Finally, while there might be special contexts where some agents have opacity duties towards others, there seem to be no such general duties and, in any case, in those special contexts where such duties obtain, right-holders might waive those rights. For instance, people who have close personal relations do not have a duty not to assess each other's agential capacities. Indeed, in some cases they may have duties – including duties of justice, e.g. between family members, to assess them in order to help their loved ones. Moreover, presumably citizens might waive their right to the state treating them as being opaque. Suppose all citizens do so and suppose the state can equalize agential capacities. On Carter's view, there is no egalitarian basis for doing so in this case, since the basis for equality is absent, given that citizens have waived their right to be treated as opaque. Yet, plausibly egalitarians think that equality applies even in such a case.

As is probably obvious by now, I do not think that Carter's proposal succeeds. So let me end this section by adding one more reason. Even setting aside the previous points, it is not really clear that Carter's proposal has the right form. Compare two persons, one whose agential capacities (have been established to be/) are just below the minimum required for moral personhood and one whose capacities (have been established to be/) are located just at that threshold. There is a tiny difference between them in terms of the underlying scalar properties that determine whether one has the relevant range property, i.e. a minimum of (established) agential capacities, and yet, according to Carter, they differ significantly in terms of the duties owed to them – the latter person is owed a duty of opacity, but the former is not. Here we might ask the very same question Carter puts to Rawls: 'If the basis of a range property is more fundamental than the range property itself, why not concentrate directly on the more fundamental scalar property (or set of properties)? … Why not say that moral personality varies in degree in accordance with variations in the scalar property (or properties)?' (Carter 2011: 549–50). When we ask these questions in the context of Carter's theory, the suggestion could be that people below the relevant threshold are not owed full opaqueness but something very close to it (reflecting that in terms of the more fundamental property underlying the range property they are almost indistinguishable from those who are owed a duty of full opacity). In that case, we are in effect back to a scalar degree of moral status.

Carter, of course, is likely to retort that the whole point is that this is not so, once we are above the threshold, and that the duty of opacity respect enjoins that we disregard differences in agential capacities above the threshold. However, even if we grant Carter the latter claim, this makes no difference to what egalitarian justice requires, unless facts that one is under a duty to disregard cannot affect one's duties. And I think they can. Suppose that I have promised Cid to disregard information acquired through Facebook. Suppose also that for some reason I know that Aisha and Bassam have informed me about their needs via Facebook and that one of them is in urgent and much greater need than the other. Suppose I have no other way of knowing who is in greater need than through taking into account information acquirable through Facebook and that I can only help one of them. In this case, arguably I have a duty to help the person in greater need even if it is also true that, in effect, I have a duty to disregard information about who that is.

2.7. A different proposal

I now offer my own take on the question about the basis of equality. Initially, I will distinguish between two different questions, which are often run together in the literature. Moreover, I shall argue that once we distinguish between these two questions, we see that the first question, while intriguing, is not one that poses problems for egalitarianism in particular. The second question is one to which the answer is the unfairness of a state of affairs where individuals whose moral standing is the same are unequally well off for reasons not related to the exercise of their agency.

The first question is one that pertains to the moral status of persons:

(1) In virtue of which properties do all persons have (i) equal moral standing and (ii) a moral standing which is different from that of non-persons?

Call this question the question of moral standing. This question is different from the question of equal treatment:

(2) Why is it desirable that persons with equal moral standing are treated equally or are equally well off in the absence of

considerations about differential responsibility that motivate unequal treatment or inequality?

These two questions are different in that the equal treatment question pertains most naturally to a group of persons who are assumed to have equal moral standing, while the moral standing question pertains most naturally to a group of individuals where we ask why some of them, i.e. those who are persons, have an equal moral standing to one another, and a moral standing which is higher than those of non-persons, e.g. mice. In principle egalitarians and non-egalitarians could agree about the answer to the first question even though, by definition, they disagree about the answer to the second question, since non-egalitarians do not think that persons with equal moral standing should be treated equally or be equally well off. For instance, take Robert Nozick. Nozick thinks that persons have a different moral status from non-persons in virtue of our being rational, having moral agency and free will and in virtue of the 'ability to regulate and guide [our lives] in accordance with some overall conception [we choose to accept]' (Nozick 1974: 49). However, while Nozick thinks that persons have equal moral standing in that they have the same rights, he does not think that persons are entitled to equal treatment in a more extensive sense required for the notion of equal treatment in the egalitarian sense. Admittedly, this conjunction of views might be inconsistent, but it might also simply be that our answer to the question of moral standing does not in itself entail any particular answer to the equal treatment question. It entails neither the Nozickean nor the egalitarian answer.

On the assumption that what I have just suggested is true, I want to make the further suggestion that while it is indeed a hard question what makes persons equal in terms of moral standing and, setting aside God etc., higher in moral standing than non-persons, it is a question that is not a problem for egalitarians in particular. Thus, whatever difficulties egalitarians may have in answering it are not reasons to reject egalitarianism in favour of one of those competing theories whose proponents face a similar challenge. I have already mentioned Nozick as an example of a libertarian who faces this problem. However, sufficientarians and prioritarians, who think sufficiency and priority apply, and apply equally so, to persons, but not to non-persons, face a similar problem. This is not to say that all distributive principles must answer the question of equal moral standing. Utilitarians, for instance, might reject the question as embodying a false assumption, namely, that persons have a moral standing different from non-persons (see Section 1.7). However, even they will face a similar question, to wit, the question of why all sentient beings have the same moral standing and one that is higher than non-sentient beings and mere things.

Before turning to the question of equal treatment, I want to make a few additional remarks about the equal moral standing question. First, I claimed that the equal moral standing and the equal treatment questions are often run together in the literature. By way of illustration of this, let us return to Carter's account. At various points in his article he says that egalitarians had better supply an account of what makes all human beings equal that does not simply appeal to the 'Aristotelian principle that equals are appropriately treated equally whereas unequals are appropriately treated unequally' (Carter 2011: 541). In his view, they need to do so because otherwise they are unable to explain why we do not 'accord equal entitlements indiscriminately to humans and cats and oysters' (Carter 2011: 541). At this point the question which he thinks egalitarians must face is what I called the question of equal moral standing. However, as I have argued, this is not a question for egalitarians specifically, but one that a broad range of moral and distributive theories must answer, and yet Carter takes himself to be responding to a challenge to egalitarians – people who 'favor according people equal (or less unequal) degrees or amounts of something' – specifically, though he mentions the possibility that non-egalitarians might also face a similar challenge (Carter 2011: 540).

Second, as I have noted, the question of equal moral standing is a challenging question and one where we cannot simply appeal to the intuition that all human beings are equal. After all, this equality in moral standing must be grounded in some property of all human beings and, in the light of non-human persons and human non-persons, mere species membership seems not to be what underlies such equality. However, whatever other property one proposes apparently one runs into a dilemma: either we select a property for equal moral standing such that all human beings possess it, e.g. being a living organism, in which case the group of beings with equal moral standing is implausibly large, e.g. it includes bacteria, or we select a property, e.g. rationality, such that we can exclude implausible candidates for equal moral standing, in which case many human beings do not possess equal moral standing and, possibly, some non-human animals, e.g. chimpanzees, do so as well. At this point we seem to have uncovered a set of conflicting moral intuitions, some of which will have to be rejected (cf. McMahan 2002: 228–32). This is a significant problem, but as I have argued, it is not one that constitutes a reason to reject egalitarianism, since other distributive theories involve similar problems.

Third, while I find Carter's suggestion regarding the basis of equality implausible, I do think there is something to his contention that – putting his point in my terms – our answer to the question of equal standing constrains our answer to the 'Equality of what'? question. So, for instance, if we think the basis of equal moral standing is the capacity to experience pain and pleasure, it would be odd to think that causing pain or pleasure are irrelevant to wrong- or right-making features. Similarly, because I shall propose in Chapter 4 a certain answer to the 'Equality of what?' question – namely, that individuals should be equal in terms of what they are non-instrumentally concerned about in a certain way – this, I think, has repercussions for what answer I can give to the question of equal moral standing. Specifically, it seems natural to combine this view with the view that the equality of moral standing of persons is grounded in their capacity to be non-instrumentally concerned with things in a distinctive way, say, one that involves long-term planning.

As it happens, I am happy to do that. The resulting view is not very different from some of the other plausible answers that have been offered in the literature in response to this question, e.g. Williams' or Nozick's. I would add, however, that on some views about justice, justice is a very special moral concern, e.g. one that is constrained, for instance, by considerations of publicity. If one holds such a view (to be critically assessed in Section 8.5) there is much less reason to think that the answer to the question of equal moral standing constrains the answer to the 'Equality of what?' question, since in that case, presumably, justice is so specialized a value that it is insensitive to some or many of the properties that bear on our overall moral status.

With these remarks in the background, we can now turn to the equal treatment question and ask it in a way that clarifies it. For questions such as this one always have an explicit or, as in this case, implicit contrast class. So, for instance, 'Why did he marry Emily?' has a different import depending on whether the relevant contrast class is '... rather than Sue' or '... rather than simply continuing living together with her'. Similarly, the equal treatment question involves a certain implicit contrast, which seems to be the italicized bit in what follows:

(3) Why is it desirable that persons with equal moral standing are treated equally, *and not unequally*, or are equally well off *and not unequally well off* (absent considerations about differential responsibility motivating unequal treatment or inequality)?

Once the question is posed this way, it becomes quite manageable. For treating people with equal moral standing unequally when there is no difference between them that can justify the relevant differential treatment is plainly unfair. Similarly, it just is plainly unfair that some people with equal moral standing are worse off than others when there is no difference between them that could justify the inequality between them (cf. Segall 2013: 15–33). This conception of fairness coheres well with considerations about luck, because most luck egalitarians accept that differential exercise of responsibility might justify deviations from equal treatment or equal outcome. However, they do not accept that anything else renders inequality fair, because whatever else these justifiers would be, they would not be suitably related to responsibility and, thus, the relevant inequality would be a matter of luck.

Suppose that this answer to the equal treatment question is accepted. Those who posed it in the first place might respond by noting that it rests on an appeal to fairness and that the answer does nothing to ground fairness. So, while the answer succeeds in grounding equality, it does so by grounding it in another ungrounded value and that doing so is just as arbitrary as simply postulating equality without seeking to ground it in another value.

In response, luck egalitarians should reject what seems to be the underlying assumption of this challenge – namely, that values are arbitrary unless grounded in other values. This assumption is problematic because if grounding of one value in another takes place by deriving the former from the latter, then any chain of grounding will end at some ungrounded value. As noted in Section 1.3, if this results in arbitrariness, any value claim must ultimately be ungrounded. Assuming that it is not in principle impossible to justify values, we might appeal to the notion of reflective equilibrium. On this view, fairness is a value that is fundamental in the sense that it is not derived from other values. However, this does not render it arbitrary. For it explains and, thus, is justified in part because it explains other moral judgements that we make, such as the judgement that it is unfair to treat two persons unequally, when there is no consideration about differential exercise of responsibility that justifies differential treatment. Obviously, this reply raises some difficult and general questions about moral justification. However, it is also clear that insofar as we find the present grounding of luck egalitarianism in fairness problematic for the reason indicated, this does not reflect any problem with luck egalitarianism in particular, but a more general problem with grounding of moral values, be they luck egalitarian or non-luck egalitarian.

2.8. Summary

To conclude this chapter, we can note that the basis of equality question really splits into to two different questions: the equality of moral standing question and the equal treatment question. Both questions are about equality, of course, but in different senses. The first is a question about equality of moral standing of persons. This is a tough one and whichever answer we give to it, it seems that some intuitively plausible claims, e.g. that all human beings are equals, will have to go. However, it is not a problem specifically for luck egalitarians, because many distributive theories other than luck egalitarianism similarly impute equal moral status to persons. Admittedly, not all do – e.g. utilitarians might say that, according to them, there is nothing fundamentally special about persons as opposed to sentient beings – but even in this case we could imagine relevantly matching non-standard versions of luck egalitarianism that range over sentient beings and, thus, like utilitarianism avoid the equality of moral standing question. I have also suggested a particular answer to this question – that the moral equality of persons is grounded in their capacity for caring non-instrumentally about things in a distinctive way. Admittedly, this proposal needs to be developed in various ways, but it is one that coheres well with the answer to the 'Equality of what?' question that I offer in Chapter 4.

The second question – the equal treatment question – is one that pertains specifically to luck egalitarians. However, once we distinguish it clearly from the former question, equality seems grounded in fairness. What makes it just that two persons are treated equally or are equally well off, when there are no considerations about differential exercise of responsibility that motivates inequality, is that anything else would be unfair. There is a sense in which fairness is ungrounded – it is not derived from some more basic value. But this, I argued, is unproblematic unless you think that any value must be grounded in a way that implies that no value ever can be other than ultimately ungrounded. If so, this would be a problem. But it would be one which would be a problem for everyone, not just luck egalitarians. On this optimistic note – 'optimistic' from the point of view of luck egalitarians at least – I turn to the notion of luck.

3

Luck

3.1. Introduction

Luck egalitarianism, as formulated in Section 1.2, is distinctive in finding it unjust that some people are worse off than others when this is simply their bad luck. This makes it imperative for them to account for what luck amounts to. For that purpose we can largely set aside – the exception being Section 3.9 where I explore the connection between equality and the aim to neutralize luck – the aspect of luck egalitarianism that occupied us in the previous chapter, i.e. that it is committed to equality, at least in the absence of non-luck considerations justifying differences in people's relative positions. This commitment is not essential to the luckist aspect of luck egalitarianism and as we saw in Section 1.7, it is possible for other distributive views, e.g. sufficientarianism, to be luckist in the same way as luck egalitarianism. This is so even if, as a matter of fact, only prioritarianism has been defended in a luckist version.

Sections 3.2 to 3.5 survey some of the main accounts of luck that are on offer in the literature and show that there are significant differences between different accounts of luck. On some of them, luck nullifies responsibility. On others, the ones I myself am inclined to favour, it nullifies desert, or, more precisely, differential luck rules out proportional differential desert. Sections 3.6 and 3.7 raise the question of whether everything, including one's own constitution, is a matter of luck. Section 3.8 discusses the influential distinction between brute and option luck in relation to the aim to neutralize differential luck and argues that the distinction is quite complex.

Section 3.9 casts some light on the idea that the aim of luck egalitarianism is to neutralize luck. Section 3.10 distinguishes between good and bad luck and argues that while luck egalitarians are opposed to some being worse off than others through bad luck, they are not opposed to some being better off than others through their good luck per se (see Section 3.9). Section 3.11 sums up.

3.2. Different kinds of luck

Luck is a pervasive feature of human life (Williams 1981: 21; Nagel 1979; Statman 1993: 11). First, the outcomes of our actions are affected by luck (resultant luck). In the mid-1990s it may have seemed prudent to take a degree in computer science. Someone who did so and completed a course just before the IT bubble burst unforeseeably in 2000 may rightly see his ensuing unemployment as bad resultant luck.

Second, the circumstances in which one acts introduce luck (circumstantial luck). A person who is offered proper incentives and plenty of time to deliberate may make a wiser decision than he would under less favourable conditions; it may be by accident that he finds himself in the favourable conditions and hence makes the wiser decision (but see Pritchard 2005: 254–61).

Third, luck affects the kind of person you are (constitutive luck). Genetically, some people are at greater risk of cancer through smoking than others, and because of this it makes sense to say that some smokers are lucky to avoid cancer.

Finally, there is luck in the way one's actions are determined by antecedent circumstances (antecedent causal luck). As Rawls' notion of the social lottery reminds us, children who grow up in a stimulating environment perhaps become more motivated than they would in a duller setting; yet children do not determine the time and place in which they are raised.

When we add up resultant, circumstantial, constitutive, and antecedent causal luck, the area of life that is free of luck seems to shrink 'to an extensionless point' (Nagel 1979: 35; cf. Parfit 1995: 10–12). To many this seems a very radical implication. One hope might be that once we clarify the notion of luck and non-luck, we will see that luck occupies a more restricted place in our lives.

3.3. Thin luck

In the endeavour to elucidate the notion of luck, it is helpful to start with distinguishing thin from thick luck (Hurley 2003: 107–9). To say that something is a matter of *thin* luck for someone is to say merely that this person does not stand in a certain moral relationship to a certain object, where such moral relationship essentially involves this individual in his or her capacity as a rational agent. To say that something is a matter of thick luck is to say this *and* to commit oneself to a certain account of the non-moral properties in virtue of which this moral relationship obtains. Accordingly, a thick concept of luck is a more specific version of the corresponding thin concept of luck. In either case, to say that something is a matter of luck for someone, in the sense of 'luck' that is relevant to justice, is to imply that it affects this person's interests for good or bad.

There are several varieties of thin notion of luck. One is the following kind of responsibility luck:

(1) Y is a matter of luck for X if, and only if, X is not morally responsible for Y.

In this definition, like those set out below, 'X' ranges over individuals and 'Y' ranges over items that can be a matter of luck for an individual, e.g. events, states of affairs, personality traits, actions, omissions, and much else.

A number of views about what makes an agent responsible for something have been taken (for an overview, see Matravers 2007: 14–64). On responsibility for actions (and omissions), (a) some emphasize the role of the ability to act otherwise (Ayer 1982; Moore 1912), (b) others focus on whether an act is appropriately related to the agent's real self (Frankfurt 1988; Watson 1982), and (c) yet others think that what matters is whether the agent acted from a suitable reasons-sensitive mechanism (Fischer and Ravizza 1998; Fischer 2006). A fourth account (d), which has been proposed specifically in relation to luck egalitarian justice, is that agents are responsible for outcomes unless it would have been unreasonable for society to expect them to avoid it (Segall 2010: 20; cf. Andersen and Nielsen forthcoming). To say that an outcome conforms to (1) is to remain neutral on which of these accounts, if any, is correct.

Thin notions of luck need not be notions of responsibility luck. Thus the following notion of desert luck is thin:

(2) Y is a matter of thin luck for X if, and only if, it is not the case that X deserves Y.

As with responsibility, a number of views about what makes an agent deserving have been taken (Kagan 2012: 6–7; Sher 1987: 7). Some accounts hold the basis of desert to be the value of one's contribution, while others hold the desert basis to be one's level of effort. People who think that justice should neutralize the luck specified by (2) can disagree over these accounts.

It is worth emphasizing that thin responsibility luck and thin desert luck are independent of one another. First, X may be responsible for Y and yet not deserve Y. Thus a man who heroically throws himself onto a grenade to save his comrades, thereby losing his life, is responsible for his own death – indeed this is what makes his act praiseworthy – even if he did not deserve to die. Second, X may deserve Y without being responsible for Y. Thus a poor saint who stumbles, entirely fortuitously, upon a gold nugget might deserve (in the wider scheme of things) to be enriched by his discovery even though he is not responsible for making it.

While my main aim in this section is taxonomical, I should note, just for the record, that to my mind these two examples also suggest why luck egalitarianism based on the desert notion of luck is more plausible than luck egalitarianism based on the responsibility notion of luck. It is unjust that the heroic soldier who is morally more deserving than most lives a shorter life than most. Similarly, it is just that the poor and deserving saint is made as well off as others by his stumbling on the gold nugget. More generally, because of what I called resultant luck above, one's moral deservingness can vary independently of the degree to which one is responsible for one's level of the relevant *equalisandum*. In cases where the two diverge, desert luck seems to be a notion of luck that is more pertinent from the point of view of justice than responsibility luck.

Suppose we adopt a desert-based notion of luck such that we think that it is unjust if some are worse off than others through their bad desert luck. If so, one might sensibly ask how luck egalitarianism differs from the ideal of comparative desert, i.e. that it is unjust if people's relative positions do not only reflect their respective comparative desert, that is, how deserving they are relative to one another. The answer is that they differ in that, unlike comparative desert, the luck egalitarian desert-based position does not imply that it is unjust if unequally deserving persons are equally well off (Segall 2014: 37–40). Certainly, this difference implies that the two positions are distinct. However, it also raises the question of whether comparative desert is not a more plausible view than desert-based luck egalitarianism (Cohen 2011: 116–23). After all, the following seems arbitrary: If X is much more deserving than Z, it is unjust for Z to be better off than X and it is unjust that X is somewhat better off than Z, but not to a degree which appropriately reflects that X is much more deserving than Z. Yet, it is not unjust for X to be exactly as well off as Z.

Other thin notions of luck can be described, but thin desert luck and (especially) thin responsibility luck have received the lion's share of attention in the literature on distributive justice. While clearly different, they are occasionally conflated (as pointed out in Hurley 2003: 191–5).

3.4. Thick luck

The claim that something is a matter of thin responsibility luck can be combined with various accounts of responsibility and thus various accounts of luck. It is these latter accounts – *thick* accounts of responsibility luck – that tell us what makes a person responsible for something. On the thick, control-based account of responsibility luck:

(3) Y is a matter of luck for X if, and only if, (i) X is not responsible for Y; and (ii) X is not responsible for Y if, and only if,

X does not and did not control Y. (Otsuka 2002: 40; Zimmerman
1993: 219)

A competing thick, choice-based account of responsibility luck says:

(4) Y is a matter of luck for X if, and only if, (i) X is not
responsible for Y; and (ii) X is not responsible for Y if, and only if,
Y is not, in an appropriate way, the result of a choice made by
X. (Cohen 2011: 13)

One who has adopted a choice-based version of luck is G. A. Cohen:
In his view, 'the fundamental distinction for an egalitarian is between
choice and luck in the shaping of people's fates' (Cohen 2011: 4).

To see how these control-based and choice-based notions diverge,
consider a Frankfurtian scenario in which Y comes about as a result
of X's choice, but X did not control whether Y came about because
had X not chosen to bring about Y, then Y would have been realized
through some alternative causal means (Frankfurt 1988). Conversely,
in a case in which X fails to make up his mind whether to prevent Y
coming about and then finds he can no longer control the outcome,
it might be said that Y does not come about as a result of X's choice
even if X controlled Y.

Often it makes a crucial difference for whether something counts
as luck which items Y ranges over (see Cohen 2011: 24–5; Price
1999). Suppose, for instance, that a person deliberately, and in full
control, cultivates a preference for spending leisure hours driving
about in her car reasonably foreseeing that the prices of fuel will
stay low (Arneson 1990: 186). Unfortunately, and unpredictably, the
price of fuel skyrockets and her preference becomes very costly.
In this case, the fact that this person prefers to spend her leisure
hours driving her car is neither bad control luck nor bad choice luck.
However, the fact that she is worse off as a result of her preference
may be both, since she neither chose to act in such a way to make
this fact obtain nor controlled whether it did.

It has been argued that both the control-based and choice-based
thick notions of luck are too broad. First, against the choice-based
account one could describe what seems like a decisive counterexample to the view, i.e. one where two persons facing very different
choice situations – e.g. one has much better options than the other and

better choice-making capacities – make different choices and, thus, the better-placed chooser ends up better off than the worse-placed one. In such situations it is implausible to say that the former person's greater gain is not his good luck. To accommodate objections of this sort, friends of the choice-based conception tend to emphasize that only 'genuine choice' justifies inequality. Or that only if the persons between whom the inequality obtains made their choices under equally (un)favourable choice-making circumstances can it justify inequality.

Second, most people neither control nor choose their religion, yet it seems odd to ask for compensation for feelings of guilt engendered by religious belief on the grounds that it is a matter of bad luck that one holds those beliefs (Scanlon 1975; Cohen 2011: 33–7). To accommodate this intuition Cohen introduces the notion of *counterfactual* choice (cf. Elford 2012). One can explain this notion with the following claim:

> (5) Y is a matter of luck for X if, and only if, (i) X is not responsible for Y; and (ii) X is not responsible for Y if, and only if, Y is not the result of a choice made by X and X would not choose Y if X could.

Given the opportunity to do so, the theist would not choose to be free of the feelings of guilt engendered by his religious convictions. Therefore, it is not a matter of luck that he has such feelings and so justice does not require him to be compensated for the feelings. As Cohen says, the costs of the unchosen and uncontrolled commitments of the religious believer 'are so intrinsically connected with his commitments that they' are not bad luck (Cohen 2011: 36; compare Cohen 2011, 88). Hence, if by 'responsible for' we simply mean 'should bear the costs of' (cf. Ripstein 1994: 19n), the theist is responsible for his religiously mandated feelings of guilt.

Just as there are different accounts of thick responsibility luck, there are different accounts of thick desert luck. These correspond to competing accounts of the basis of desert. One notion is that of thick, non-comparative desert luck, which can be elaborated as follows:

> (6) Y is a matter of luck for X if, and only if, (i) it is not the case that X deserves Y; and (ii) X deserves Y if, and only if, it is fitting that X has Y given the moral or prudential merits of X.

The notion fleshed out here contrasts with that of thick, comparative desert luck:

> (7) Y is a matter of luck for X if, and only if, (i) it is not the case that X deserves Y; and (ii) X deserves Y if, and only if, it is fitting that X has Y given the relative moral or prudential merits of X and Z and given what Z has.

It may be a matter of bad thick, non-comparative desert luck that the crops of a talented, hard-working farmer are destroyed by cold weather. If, however, the crops of a farmer who is equally talented but even more hard-working are also destroyed, it will not be a matter of bad thick, comparative desert luck that the first farmer's crops are destroyed.

The list of thick notions of luck mentioned so far is not intended to be exhaustive, and each notion may of course be developed in several directions. Clearly, thick luck is quite complex.

3.5. Independent notions of luck

Some accounts of luck are neither thin accounts of luck nor aim at capturing a general moral notion such as responsibility or desert. Instead they appeal to an independent conception of luck. Lottery luck is arguably one example:

> (8) Y is a matter of luck for X if Y, from the perspective of X, is the outcome of a lottery.

The underlying idea here is that there is a sense in which the outcome of a (fair) lottery is a matter of luck for the person who participates in it whether or not he is responsible for it – as some accounts of responsibility imply and others do not. It can be maintained that justice is concerned with this notion of luck independently of how it relates to responsibility and desert. Thus an egalitarian may think that it is bad if people are unequally well off as a result of differential lottery luck even if he has not made up his mind whether people are responsible for differential lottery luck. He might add that it would be illegitimate for the state to enforce equality in face of inequality resulting from a fair lottery to which all parties consented. Also, lotteries might be excellent means of making outcomes independent of the unjust biases of distributors (compare Stone 2007: 286–7), even if the outcome might be unjust despite the fact that such biases played no role in their genesis.

In principle, one could also care about choice and control luck independently of how these relate to thin luck, e.g. responsibility and desert. However, philosophers who think that justice is a matter of eliminating differential luck have studied choice and control mainly because they assume that the absence of choice and control nullifies responsibility or desert.

3.6. How much luck is there?

Above I mentioned the worry that once we take fully into account how much luck there is, the area of non-luck shrinks to an 'extensionless point'. However, accounts of responsibility or desert differ with regard to their implications on this matter. For instance, if a hard deterministic account of responsibility is true, everything is a matter of responsibility luck. A hard deterministic account of responsibility says that responsibility and determinism are incompatible, that determinism is true, and, hence, that no one is ever responsible for anything. If, on the other hand, one accepts a compatibilist, reason-responsiveness account of responsibility, many outcomes will not be a matter of responsibility luck, at least for some agents. A compatibilist, reason-responsiveness account of responsibility for outcomes says that an agent is responsible for outcomes that he or she brings about in the right sort of way through the agent's action (or omissions) where these issue from an action-generating process that is sufficiently sensitive to practical reasons, e.g. normal human deliberation, and that actions may issue from such mechanisms whether or not determinism obtains (Fischer and Ravizza 1998). Still, agents who act from reason-responsive mechanisms may face choice situations that differ much in terms of how favourable they are, in which case inequalities reflecting such differences may not be just, even if they obtain between agents who are responsible for the choices they made. For this reason (among others), it is open for compatibilist luck egalitarians to think that little inequality can be justified by differential exercises of choice (Barry 2005).

One issue, which has received quite a lot of attention in the debate about justice and luck is the regression principle governing luck:

(9) If the causes of Y are a matter of luck for X, so is Y.

Assuming that everything is caused by prior causes, if this principle is coupled with control or choice accounts of luck (setting aside the counterfactual choice-based account of luck, i.e. (5)), everything turns into luck. For if we couple (9) with, say, the thick, choice-based account of responsibility luck, it follows that for my present reckless driving not to be a matter of (bad) luck, it will have to be the case that I am responsible for, and hence have chosen, the causes of my present reckless driving. In turn, for me to be responsible for these causes I will in turn have to be responsible for, and hence have chosen, the causes of these causes of my reckless driving; and so on. Obviously, at some point, moving back through the causal chain (e.g. prior to my coming into existence, if not long before that), choice, and thus responsibility, will peter out. So it will follow that I am not responsible for my present reckless driving: it is my bad luck that I drive my car in a totally irresponsible way. Generalizing this sort of reasoning, it seems no one would ever be responsible for anything – that everything would be a matter of responsibility luck. As Thomas Nagel writes: 'Everything seems to result from the combined influence of factors, antecedent and posterior to action, that are not within the agent's control. Since he cannot be responsible for them, he cannot be responsible for their results' (Nagel 1979: 35; compare Strawson 1994; Watson 2006: 428).

Suppose that it turns out that everything is a matter of luck, say, determinism and incompatibilism are true and the appropriate conception of luck is moral responsibility luck. In that case, luck egalitarianism will collapse extensionally speaking into outcome egalitarianism, i.e. there will be no cases where someone is justly worse off than others through something other than bad luck. But this means, it seems, that only equality of outcome is just according to luck egalitarianism. Some might think that this implies that luck egalitarianism is then no longer a distinct view. However, this is not so. It still differs from outcome egalitarianism in that, unlike the latter, it implies that if some people were worse off than others through something other than their bad luck this need not be unjust (Cohen 2011, 116–23; Stemplowska 2008). Indeed, even given the truth of determinism, luck egalitarianism is more plausible than outcome egalitarianism because it has more plausible implications if not all inequalities turn out to be a matter of luck.

The view that everything is a matter of responsibility (and desert) luck obviously flies in the face of our everyday ascriptions of responsibility. Accordingly, this implication of the regression principle is often deployed in a corresponding *reductio ad absurdum* (Hurley 1993: 183; Hurley 2003; Nozick 1974: 225; Sher 1997: 67–9; Zaitchik 1977: 371–3). However, this *reductio* is perhaps too hasty. It has been argued that the principle (applied to control) is not simply a matter of 'generalization from certain clear cases'. Rather, it is a condition that we 'are actually being persuaded' is correct when we apply it to cases 'beyond the original set', where, on reflection, we find that 'control is absent' (Nagel 1979: 26–7). If this is right, we need an alternative explanation of why moral responsibility is absent in those cases where control of causes is absent. So, for instance, if we agree that a person who offends, as an adult, as a result of childhood deprivation is not responsible for his action, we need to explain what, here, nullifies responsibility if not lack of control over causes of the agent's actions. That is, we need to explain why certain kinds of causal background to action threaten control while others do not, even if we are dealing with cases with the shared feature that the agent does not control the early parts of those causal backgrounds.

Addressing this problem, Fischer and Ravizza suggest that a 'process of taking responsibility is necessary for moral responsibility' (Fischer and Ravizza 1998: 200). They add that, since processes are necessarily historical, it follows that their account of responsibility attends to an action's genesis or origins. With the same problem in mind, Susan Hurley suggests that responsibility requires that the process 'by which reason-responsive mechanisms and self-percep- tions in relation to these mechanisms are acquired' (Hurley 2003: 51) is one in which the agent is equipped with mechanisms that are sufficiently responsive to objective reasons (Hurley 2003: 51–2). That is, the reasons for which the agent acts must match the reasons for action that there in fact are sufficiently well, although this match need not be perfect. Whether either of these suggestions accommodates cases where initially responsibility is undermined by lack of control of causes remains to be seen.

3.7. Constitutive luck

One of the four forms of luck mentioned in Section 3.2 is constitutive luck – luck in being the kind of person one is (Nagel 1979: 28). Personal constitution may include contingent as well as necessary features of a person, such as inclinations, capacities and temperament. On the other hand, it may consist of necessary features only. For example, on common, origin-focused views about the essence of a human being, the fact that one developed from a particular sperm and ovum is a non-contingent fact about one (cf. Section 7.3). On the first view here, one could have existed with a different constitution, while on the latter one could not. On the latter account, a world in which no one exists with the constitution I have is a world in which I do not exist.

This may be thought to show that Rawls' idea of a natural lottery is seriously misleading. For, normally, lottery luck is identity-dependent. That is, we say that someone has good luck in buying the winning ticket because we compare two outcomes in both of which this person exists. One of these outcomes – the one which was *ex ante* very unlikely to be realized – is much better for this person than the other. That is why this person had lottery luck. However, when we talk about the natural lottery luck in connection with one's essential properties, the very idea of lottery luck seems to involve an incoherent conception of bare selves that exist before they acquire their essential properties, or for that matter any properties at all (Hurley 2003: 120–3; Rescher 1993: 155).

This observation seems sound, but it hardly follows that the idea of natural lottery must be rejected altogether. Suppose a person's constitution involves the fact that he developed from the particular sperm and ovum from which he in fact developed. The question then is whether this limits the range of benefits metaphysically available to this person. If it does, there are necessary limits to how lucky or unlucky this person could be. However, it is not clear that this view about the essence of a person does anything at all to limit a person's good or bad luck. Genetically determined, benefit-influencing properties may vary independently of origin, e.g. as a result of genetic changes occurring before or after conception; and obviously the social environment in which the relevant person grows up, and in which his properties constitute talents or non-talents, may vary widely. Accordingly, it is doubtful that anyone is ever in a position in which he can point to another individual with a level of benefits different from his own and correctly deny that it is metaphysically possible for him to have had that level of benefits. So while constitutive luck, understood in one way, may be incoherent, this has no tendency to show that Rawls' idea of a natural lottery is incoherent.

3.8. Option luck versus brute luck

Many luck egalitarians think that not all instances of differential luck are unjust. For example, they often distinguish between option luck and brute luck and deny that bad instances of the latter are unjust. Recall Dworkin's notions of option and brute luck introduced in Section 1.4: 'Option luck is a matter of how deliberate and calculated gambles turn out – whether someone gains or loses through accepting an isolated risk he or she should have anticipated and might have declined' (Dworkin 2000: 73). Brute luck is 'a matter of how risks fall out that are not in that sense deliberate gambles' (Dworkin 2000: 73).

In Dworkin's view, insurance provides a link between brute and option luck. For 'the decision to buy or reject … insurance is a calculated gamble' (Dworkin 2000: 74). This means that a person may suffer bad brute luck, and for that reason end up worse off than others, and yet the resulting inequality might reflect differential option luck. Roughly, this will be so if the person who ends up worse off could have insured against the sort of bad brute luck that she later suffered but declined to do so (Dworkin 2000: 74, 77). So although it may be bad brute luck that I suddenly go blind as a result of a genetic condition, the fact that I end up worse off as a result of going blind (if this occurs) will reflect bad option luck provided suitable insurance was available to me.

Dworkin's distinction needs to be clarified and amended in certain ways (Lippert-Rasmussen 2001; Vallentyne 2002; Vallentyne 2008; Sandby 2004: 294–9; Otuska 2002: 45; Steiner 2002: 349; see also Dworkin 2002: 122–5). First, consider a case where an individual can choose between two alternatives. One involves a 75 per cent chance of having one's crops destroyed by cold weather. The other one involves a 70 per cent chance of having one's crops destroyed by flooding. In one sense, either risk is avoidable. Yet, if one were to go for the first alternative, and if one's crops were destroyed by cold weather, it would seem odd to say that the full extent to which one becomes worse off as a result of that choice is a matter of bad option luck. After all, the chances of becoming just as badly off via a different causal route, had the agent chosen the other alternative, were almost as great. So it seems we should often think of a given piece of luck as a mixture of brute luck and option luck where the exact mixture depends on the extent to which one could influence the expected value of the outcome of one's choice. In the present case, I could only marginally influence the expected value of the outcome. Hence the disadvantages resulting from my choice should be seen as mostly a matter of bad brute luck.

Second, suppose I am morally required to perform a certain action, say, to save someone from a burning house, thereby risking some moderate burns in the process. Let us also suppose that I am worse off than the person I save and that my doing so happens to make me even worse off than this person, since I do get burned in a way that requires expensive medical attention. While the extra inequality that results from my doing what I am morally required to do, on Dworkin's definition, reflects bad option luck on my part, the view that the resulting extra inequality is in no way unjust is implausible. In fact, the same conclusion would seem to apply to cases where the risk of severe burns is so high that one's intervention is supererogatory and one ends up worse off as a result of one's choosing to engage in a supererogatory rescue mission (Eyal 2007: 4; but see Lazenby 2010; Temkin 2003(b): 144; cf. Temkin 2011: 68).

Third, suppose you and I face a prisoners' dilemma. I know that there is some chance that you may defect, in which case I will end up worse off. However, because I do not want to exploit you by defecting myself in case you do not, I cooperate. As it happens, you defect and I end up worse off. Again, since I am now worse off as a result of a calculated gamble, I am worse off through bad option luck. Yet, it seems plausible to hold that the inequality that results from your exploiting my resistance to exploiting you is unjust (Lippert-Rasmussen 2011a, 2011b; for a different, but related problem, see Seligman 2007).

Setting aside refinements to it, in what way does Dworkin's distinction matter from the point of view of justice? We can split this question into two, one concerning brute luck and one concerning option luck. Most egalitarians believe that justice requires the nullification of all differential effects of brute luck (Cohen 2011: 5, 29; Dworkin 2000; Rakowski 1991; for a recent critique see Elford 2013; Lazenby 2014), feeling that it cannot be just that some people are worse off than others simply because they have been unfortunate, say, to have been born with bad genes. Not all egalitarians, however, take this position. Peter Vallentyne believes that while it is true that justice requires compensation for congenital dispositions to develop serious diseases, this is because justice requires not the neutralization of bad brute luck but equality of initial prospects (Vallentyne 2002: 543). This equality obtains between two people when at some early stage in their development – say, the time at which they become sentient – their prospects are equally good. A genetic defect, at this point in time, would limit one's opportunities, and so such defects will often provide grounds for compensation. However, if two people face the same initial risk of developing malaria and have equally good initial opportunities, justice does not require us to compensate the one who gets malaria as a result of bad brute luck.

It is an advantage of Vallentyne's approach (over brute luck-neutralizing egalitarianism) that it avoids the costs incurred in neutralizing the effects of differential brute luck. Of course, such costs may lower everyone's *ex ante* prospects. Hence, brute luck egalitarians are committed implausibly, in such cases, to worsening everybody's prospects – or, at least, to saying that it would be better to do so from the point of view of equality even if it may not be better *tout court* (cf. Section 5.4). However, as Vallentyne concedes, initial equality of opportunity also raises problems. Suppose we live in a caste society but make sure that babies are assigned starting positions in that society by a fair lottery. This society may well realize initial equality of opportunity, yet it does not seem just (Barry 1989: 224n). Indeed, it is far from clear that the lottery reduces the injustice of this society at all.

Turning now to option luck, three positions should be noted. First, some believe that justice requires the differential effects of option luck not to be nullified. Dworkin takes this view (Dworkin 2000; see also Rakowski 1991: 74; Williams 2013). He thinks it would be unjust if the state were to compensate people who suffer bad option luck by taxing people who enjoy good option luck: '... people should pay the price of the life they have decided to lead, measured in what others give up in order that they can do so ... But the price of a safer life, measured in this way, is precisely foregoing any chance of the gains whose prospect induces others to gamble' (Dworkin 2000: 74).

Others believe that justice permits, but does not require, the nullification of the effects of differential option luck. Peter Vallentyne defends this position. According to him, justice requires initial equality of opportunity, and this can be achieved through a scheme that provides equality of initial opportunities for advantage and no compensation for bad option outcome luck. However, initial equality of opportunity can also be achieved if the state, say, taxes all good option outcome luck (and all good brute luck) and compensates all bad option outcome luck (as well as all bad brute luck). This, in effect, will deprive people of the opportunity to gamble and hence ensure that everyone ends up equally well off. In Vallentyne's view, the latter is required by justice when, and only when, this increases the value of people's initial opportunities, and when the scheme is introduced publicly and proactively so that people know the rules of the game before it starts (Vallentyne 2002: 549, 555). The first of these conditions may be met where people are very risk-averse and the transaction costs involved in the tax scheme are not very great.

In a third position, justice requires the nullification of some or all effects of differential option luck (e.g. Barry 2008). This view comes in several versions. In one, justice requires compensation in some but not all cases of bad option luck. For instance, Marc Fleurbaey argues that justice has a sufficientarian component such that it requires differential option luck outcomes, where some people end up very badly off, to be eliminated. Suppose, for instance, that someone decides to use his motorcycle without wearing a helmet, knowing the risks involved, and ends up in a traffic accident in which he is seriously hurt as a result. According to Fleurbaey, justice requires us to help this person (Fleurbaey 1995: 40–1; Fleurbaey 2001: 511; Fleurbaey 2008: 153–98; see also Segall 2007; Stemplowska 2009: 251–4; Voigt 2007; cf. Section 7.4). Those attracted by Dworkin's position on bad option luck might reply that we confuse an obligation of justice with an obligation of charity. It would be unfair for the motorcycle driver to impose costs on us simply because he prefers to take the gamble of driving without helmet without insurance. He, not others, should pay the price of his decisions (which is not to say that he deserves his bad fate). By contrast, friends of Vallentyne's view might urge that there is nothing unjust about a system that publicly and proactively declares that bad outcome option luck will be compensated by means of taxing away good option luck. Hence, while a refusal to assist the unlucky motorcyclist need not be unjust, the imposition of assistance costs on others, under the circumstances mentioned, would not be unjust either.

A more extreme egalitarianism – 'all-luck egalitarianism' to use an apt phrase coined by Shlomi Segall (2010: 46) – has it that 'differential option luck should be considered as unjust as differential brute luck' (Segall 2010: 47). For if what really drives egalitarians is the conviction that one group of people should not be worse off than others as a result of causes for which they are not responsible, then, arguably, it follows that differential option luck is bad. After all, a gambler is not responsible for the outcome of her gamble being what it is rather than something else it could have been. One promising way of fleshing out this view has been proposed by Carl Knight. According to Knight (2013: 1061; cf. Andersen 2014), 'individuals should receive the warranted expected results of their gambles, except insofar as individuals blamelessly lacked the ability to ascertain which expectations were warranted'. On this view, a beneficiary of good option luck who received more than what she was warranted in believing that her gamble would yield should compensate a victim of bad option luck who received less than the warranted expected outcome of her gamble. This view leaves open that, in a limited range of cases, inequalities due to differential option luck are just, e.g. in cases where two individuals had access to the same gambles, one chose a more favourable gamble and the other a less favourable one, and both received the outcome which it was warranted to expect.

All-luck egalitarianism does not commit its advocates to the position that the state (or, for that matter, anyone else) should prevent conduct that might lead to inequalities reflecting differential option luck: advocates of the view may care about welfare too and rightly think that welfare is promoted when the outcomes of gambles are allowed to stand, or they might distinguish between legitimacy – 'the property something has when ... no one has a just grievance against it' (Cohen 2011: 125) – and justice and think that state intervention to eliminate differential option luck would be illegitimate even if it would thereby bring about a less unjust distribution. Again, the claim that differential option luck is bad is consistent with the view that, given that people do choose to gamble, it is better if differential option luck is not eliminated, even if it would be better if people had chosen not to gamble in the first place (Lippert-Rasmussen 2001: 576; compare Cohen 2011: 124–42; Persson 2006).

3.9. Neutralizing luck and equality

Many passages in the luck egalitarian literature suggest that justice is luck-neutralization, not luck-amplification, not luck-mitigation (Mason 2006), and not luck-equalization. Consider, for instance, Rawls' remark that 'Intuitively, the most obvious injustice of the system of natural liberty is that it permits distributive shares to be improperly influenced by these factors [i.e. social circumstances and such chance contingencies as accident and good fortune] so arbitrary from a moral point of view' (Rawls 1971: 71). On the admittedly disputable assumption that Rawls thinks that factors that are 'arbitrary from a moral point of view' and affect people's interests are a matter of luck, one might read this passage as saying that under a just distribution, luck does not influence distributive shares (Rawls 1971: 72). A similar passage can be found in Cohen's work: 'anyone who thinks that initial advantage and inherent capacity are unjust distributors thinks so because he believes that they make a person's fate depend too much on sheer luck' (Cohen 2011: 30). This passage can be read as suggesting that the aim of neutralizing luck justifies equality and that realizing equality will eliminate luck.

Such passages can, however, be read in other ways. Thus Rawls might simply mean to say that, while luck influences distributive shares under a just distribution, it does not do so improperly. Likewise, Cohen might be saying that, while people's fates depend on luck under a just distribution, they do not depend on sheer luck. And the fact that there is room for these different readings encourages us to ask exactly what role luck-neutralization can play in relation to a theory of distributive justice.

Addressing this question, Hurley distinguishes between a specificatory and a justificatory role for the aim of luck-neutralization. In the first role, the aim specifies what egalitarianism 'is and what it demands' (Hurley 2003: 147). In the second, it provides a justification for favouring egalitarian over non-egalitarian theories of distributive justice. Hurley believes that the luck-neutralizing aim fails in both roles (cf. Lang 2006). If the aim were to play either role, it would have to be the case that the favoured distribution – e.g. equality, utility maximization, or maximizing the position of the worst-off – limits the influence of luck on outcomes. However, there is no clear sense in which this is the case (cf. Parfit 1995: 12). For the sake of simplicity, suppose the favoured distribution is an equal one. Suppose also that the inequality that we are concerned with exists between two people who have each been stranded on a small island. Through sheer good luck, the first person's island is lush and fertile, and through sheer bad luck the other person's island is arid. It does not follow from the fact that this unequal outcome is the result of luck that, if we eliminate the inequality, the resulting equal outcome will not be the result of luck to the same degree, i.e. will not be one in which factors for which people are not responsible play no (or a smaller) causal role in bringing about the outcome. To see this, assume we are dealing with thick, control-based responsibility luck and imagine that a powerful egalitarian intervener dumps a shipload of fertilizer on the second island so that equality in the Robinson Crusoe-like setting is realized. Since neither of the two people controlled what happened, the resulting equality here is just as much a matter of luck for them as the prior inequality was. Since we can implement equality without eliminating luck, this shows that we can neither justify equality as a means of neutralizing luck, nor specify what equality requires as neutralizing luck. The same applies to other end-result principles, e.g. sufficiency (Hurley 2003: 146–80).

In response to this important point, it might be argued that when luck egalitarians write about 'neutralizing luck', this is really shorthand for something like 'eliminating the differential effects on people's interests of factors which from their perspective are a matter of luck'. This is no different from saying that affirmative action in favour of women is a way of neutralizing the effects of sexist discrimination. In saying this, we do not imagine that affirmative action programmes remove sexist discrimination and all its effects; we mean merely that the affirmative action programme eliminates the differential effects on men and women of sexist discrimination, e.g. in university admissions. On this reading, considerations about luck serve not to justify equality, but to select the appropriate egalitarian view from among the large family of views that ascribe intrinsic significance to equality. As Arneson puts it: 'The argument for equal opportunity rather than straight equality is simply that it is morally fitting to hold individuals responsible for the foreseeable consequences of their voluntary choices' (Arneson 1989: 88). Equality is the default position, morally speaking. It is not justified by appeal to luck. Such an appeal, however, explains why some deviations from this default position need not be bad from an egalitarian point of view, for in the relevant deviations it is not a matter of luck that some people are worse off than others. In response to Hurley's point, Cohen offers a related reply: 'That it extinguishes the influence of luck is no more of an argument for egalitarianism than that it promotes utility is an argument for utilitarianism and in each case for the same reason, to wit, that the cited feature is too definitive of the position in question to justify the position in question' (Cohen 2011: 118–19; see also Vallentyne 2006a: 434; Hurley 2006: 459–65). In fact, he goes on to offer something that is more radical than the shorthand description of the luck egalitarian aim offered in the opening sentence of this paragraph. Since luck egalitarians are opposed to luck 'in the name of fairness' (compare Temkin 2003(a): 767) and since, no less than inequality, equality is unfair when 'in disaccord with choice', equality might be unjust for exactly the same reason as inequality might (Cohen 2011: 121; cf. Segall 2012). Pragmatic, not principled, reasons explain why unjust equalities tend to not to be mentioned by luck egalitarians.

3.10. Bad luck versus good luck

Many discussions of justice and bad luck assume that bad (brute) luck somehow calls for compensation (cf. Section 1.2). This raises the question whether justice is not concerned with good luck. Does good luck call for reverse compensation such as taxation? Interestingly, this way of approaching justice's preoccupation with luck makes the ideal of justice seem less attractive: it may suggest that envy lies behind that ideal (Nozick 1974: 240). Yet egalitarian justice is not best formulated this way.

Assume again, for the sake of simplicity, that a just distribution is an equal one; and assume that we are dealing with thick control luck. We can then distinguish between the following two views:

(10) It is in itself bad if X is worse off than Z through bad luck on X's part.
(11) It is in itself bad if Z is better off than X through good luck on Y's part.

It might be thought that the difference between these views is merely nominal. For if X is worse off than Z through bad luck on X's part, how can it fail to be the case that Z is better off than X through good luck on Z's part, and vice versa? However, this is a mistake.

Suppose that X and Z are equally well off. X is unable to alter his level of benefits, while Z is offered a benefit that he accepts. X is now worse off through bad luck, i.e. through circumstances over which he exercised no control. Z, on the other hand, might not be better off than X through his own good luck: he may not have controlled whether he would be offered the benefit, but he controlled, we can assume, his acceptance of it. Thus, if we subscribe to (10), we should be concerned with the resulting inequality in this scenario, but we need not be if we subscribe to (11).

Suppose again that X and Z are equally well off. X, but not Z, is then offered an avoidable gamble, which he decides to take, and as a result he ends up worse off than Z. Although it is a matter of luck for Z that he is now better off, it is not a matter of bad luck for X that he is worse off. X controlled whether he ended up worse off than Z, because he controlled his decision to gamble, and if he had not gambled, he would not have ended up worse off than Z. If we subscribe to (10), we might be indifferent to the resulting inequality in this scenario, but we may not be if we subscribe to (11).

These cases show that egalitarians can resist the envy-attributing formulation of their view. They need not be hostile to some people being better off than others through good luck. Consistently with this, they can disapprove when some are worse off than others through bad luck. This is not to deny that, as a matter of fact, one person's being worse off than another through bad luck tends to go hand in hand with the latter being better off through good luck (compare Temkin 1993, 127; Lippert-Rasmussen 2005).

3.11. Summary

This chapter has zoomed in on the luckist component of luck egalitarianism. We have seen that the notion of luck can be fleshed out differently. In particular, I have drawn a distinction between thin and thick luck and between various conceptions of thick luck, e.g. choice- and control-based conceptions. I have also taken a closer look at the distinction between option and brute luck. Not only is this distinction more complex than is often thought, its relation to the luck egalitarian opposition to some people's being worse off than others through bad luck is complicated due to the fact that many luck egalitarians accept that differential option luck is just. Finally, we have seen that equality cannot be justified by appeal to the aim to neutralize luck and that luck egalitarians are not opposed as such to some people being better off than others through good luck. It seems fair to say that the core notion of luck is complex and raises a number of challenging issues, which luck egalitarians still need to struggle with.

4

Equality of what?

4.1. Introduction

According to the core luck egalitarian claim (Section 1.2) it is unjust if some people are worse off than others through their bad luck. But what are the kinds of good or goods it is bad, if some are worse off than others are though their bad luck? Many inequalities between people are irrelevant from the point of view of justice. For instance, you may have more hair or a bigger collection of stamps than I have, but in itself these inequalities are of no concern from the point of view of egalitarian justice. Hence, to know what luck egalitarianism implies more concretely, one must provide an answer to this question – the question of currency of egalitarian justice, as it has come be called due to an influential contribution by G. A. Cohen (2011).

While it is indeed true that luck egalitarians must provide an answer to this question, a similar question faces friends of other distributive principles. For instance, sufficientarians must say what the currency of sufficiency is. In short, there is a more general question about the currency of distributive justice. This is important because some of the difficulties that egalitarians face in providing a plausible answer to the question of the currency of egalitarian justice might reflect difficulties that pertain to the more general question about the currency of *distributive* justice and not to the more specific question of the currency of *egalitarian* justice. If so, these difficulties are not an indication of any weakness of luck egalitarianism as such.

The chapter will take a look at three main contenders: welfare accounts, resource accounts, and capabilities accounts. Section 4.2

starts with sketching a forceful argument – the anti-fetishist argument – for why the currency of egalitarian justice is welfare. Even if it is successful – in Section 4.7 I argue that ultimately it is not – this argument, however, does not provide a complete answer to the question of the currency of egalitarian justice, since there are different accounts of what welfare amounts to. The section proceeds to present the three most common answers without adjudicating between them. Sections 4.3 to 4.7 discuss six objections to welfarist egalitarianism. I shall dismiss the first five challenges – the specification, the disability, the offensive preferences, the snobbish tastes, and the expensive tastes objections – but concede that it is unclear why egalitarians should not take into account non-self-regarding concerns – the non-instrumental concern objection – and, thus, suggest what we might coin *concern luck egalitarianism*. Section 4.8 critically assesses Dworkin's resourcist metric, while Section 4.9 explores Sen's capabilities-based approach. Section 4.10 concludes.

4.2. Welfare

Suppose we make everyone equal in terms of the amount of money they have over their lifetime. Suppose also that no differences in efforts etc. justify inequalities in income. Would that satisfy luck egalitarians? It seems not. Consider a person suffering from a serious medical condition. This person has to use almost all of her money on purchasing medical services just to survive. Others, who do not have similar medical problems, can spend most of their money on trekking in the Himalayas or living pleasurable lives in nice, warm houses. This strongly suggests that money is not the relevant currency of egalitarian justice. Moreover, there is an obvious explanation of the inadequacy of money as the answer to the currency question – namely, that we care about money, but only as an instrument to achieving something that we care about non-instrumentally. To care non-instrumentally about the amount of money one disposes of is to treat money as some kind of fetish. Dworkin articulates a closely related worry as follows: 'If we decide on equality, but then define equality in terms of resources unconnected with the welfare they bring, then we seem to be mistaking means for ends and indulging in a fetishistic fascination for what we ought to treat only as instrumental' (Dworkin 2000: 14). These considerations suggest that the currency of egalitarian justice must be something that we care about non-instrumentally. Moreover, since each of us cares non-instrumentally about his or her own welfare, this might lead some to endorse the following (simple and fallacious) line of argument:

(1) The currency of egalitarian justice is something that each of us cares about non-instrumentally.

(2) Each individual cares about her own welfare non-instrumentally.

(3) Thus, the currency of egalitarian justice is welfare.

As I will argue in Chapter 7, this argument, which models a line of argument suggested, but not endorsed, by Dworkin (2000: 20–1, 31), is not sound. Until then it will, however, serve to structure my discussion.

The anti-fetishist argument concludes that the currency of egalitarian justice is welfare. However, because there are different competing accounts of what welfare is, this in itself does not fix what welfare luck egalitarians are committed to. The three main contenders are: mental-state-based, preference-based, objective list-based accounts of welfare. Let us briefly consider them in this order.

First, it seems like a truism that, *ceteris paribus*, a life with many pleasurable sensations is better than a life with many painful experiences. In support of this view, we might point to the fact that many people are willing to undergo an operation to relieve themselves of chronic pains even if the operation might shorten their lives. On a simple hedonistic version of mental-state-based theories of welfare, only pains – such as those mental states caused by physical torture – and pleasures – such as those mental states involved in having an orgasm – count. However, mental-state-based theories of welfare might take a broader, non-hedonist view and say that pleasant mental states are those we prefer to be in, while unpleasant ones are those we prefer not to be in. It is often said that at the end of his life Freud declined morphine to dull constant pains resulting from cancer, because he preferred to remain clear-minded. On the broader mental-state-based account he lived a better life by declining morphine, because, as a result, his mental states were to a higher degree those that he preferred to be in.

Second, once we move from hedonist mental-state-based theories to broader mental-state-based theories, there is a certain argumentative pressure in the direction of saying that welfare consists in the satisfaction of one's preferences *tout court* and not just the satisfaction of a narrow subset of them, i.e. one's preferences regarding one's mental states. Some resist this pressure, arguing that the satisfaction of preferences regarding something other than one's mental state are not sufficiently closely related to what happens to oneself to bear on one's welfare (Kagan 1992). Others reject this worry and endorse a preference-based account of welfare. However, almost all who do pay some lip service to the reservation mentioned by Kagan, by conceding that only a subset of a person's preferences – those that are in some sense, which is hard to capture, self-regarding – count from the point of view of welfare. Suppose, for instance, that I have a preference for getting a job as a philosopher and a preference for there being glaciers in the Alps in 2300. It seems clear that the former preference is self-regarding and that its frustration makes my life worse, *ceteris paribus*. It also seems plausible that the latter preference is non-self-regarding and that its frustration will not make my life have gone any worse. Not only are most preference-based accounts refined in the sense that their scope is restricted to self-regarding preferences. As indicated by my discussion of Arneson in Section 1.4, most preference-based accounts stress that it is preferences that a person would have under certain ideal circumstances, where the person is better informed than she is as a matter of fact, that count from the point of view of welfare. As we saw, one motivation for this claim is that there are cases where the satisfaction of a preference that is based on false empirical beliefs – e.g. I devote my life to become rich in the belief that this will make me happy, only to discover once my desire is satisfied that it makes me no more happy – will not make the preference-holder's life better (Griffin 1986: 12).

Third, once we make the move from actual to idealized preferences there is argumentative pressure to go beyond preference-based accounts altogether. For if an individual is well informed, is not one of the things that she is well informed about the desirability of possible objects of preferences? If we answer this question affirmatively, it seems that we have deserted preference-based accounts of welfare and instead endorse the view that an individual's life is better the more objectively desirable goods that it contains – 'objectively' because the desirability of something depends on characteristics of the object and not on whether the subject is related to it in a particular way, e.g. by desiring it. In support of such an objective list account, it might be said that, intuitively at least, in many cases we desire things because they are valuable, we think, and it is not the case that we think they are valuable because we desire them. For instance, we think that deep personal relationships make our lives better and if presented with a person who has no desire, actual or idealized, for such relations and, thus, no such relations, we are likely to think that his life is worse for that reason. Conversely, if a person has a desire, actual or idealized, for something trivial – say, counting grass blades – we are likely to think that the satisfaction of this desire in itself does not make his life go better. True, we might think it does so indirectly, because if it is not satisfied this might cause frustration. However, this is further support for objective list accounts, because plausibly frustration is an objectively undesirable state to be in.

Objective list accounts form a large family of views. Typical items on the list other than deep personal relations include 'moral goodness, rational activity, the development of one's abilities, having children and being a good parent, knowledge, and the awareness of true beauty' (Parfit 1984: 499). Indeed, hedonism might be seen as a deviant objective list theory according to which only pleasure is objectively valuable.

Which of these three accounts one should endorse is a large question in itself and, possibly, not one that we need resolve for present purposes. The reason we need not is the following. Suppose I defend hedonist luck egalitarianism and you reject it, because you accept objective list luck egalitarianism. If you reject hedonist luck egalitarianism because you think hedonism is a false theory of well-being, you might still agree with me that well-being is the currency of egalitarian justice and that luck egalitarianism is the correct theory of justice. Hence, our disagreement regarding the true theory of well-being has no implications regarding the latter two questions and, indeed, it is a disagreement that is mirrored in our disagreements about all competing non-luck egalitarian distributive principles – e.g. you will reject hedonist sufficientarianism for a reason I will not. Accordingly, in what follows I want to focus on five objections to welfarist luck egalitarianism that do not focus on the falsity of any of the three main theories of well-being presented in this section, keeping in mind the diversity of theories of well-being as well as the general appeal of welfarist luck egalitarianism as brought out by the anti-fetishist argument.

4.3. The specification objection

This section critically assesses the so-called specification objection. According to Dworkin, for reasons brought out in the anti-fetishist argument, welfare metrics are indeed appealing in the abstract (Dworkin 2000: 14). However, we need to specify what welfare consists in. As we saw in the previous section, there are three main ways to go and – so Dworkin, and with him Cohen, claims – whichever of them we take, it is implausible to say that justice requires equality of welfare relevantly specified. Hence, the specification objection does not presuppose the falsity of any particular theory of welfare. It simply says that whichever of them is true equality of welfare is implausible. Hence, an acceptable form of the ideal of equality must be equality of something other than welfare. This undermines whatever appeal the unspecified welfare metric might have.

Why do Cohen and Dworkin think that any specification of equality of welfare renders the pertinent ideal implausible? The main underlying reason is one that we will elaborate in the sections below: because some theories of welfare imply that frustration of offensive preference and snobbish tastes reduces one's welfare. In this way the specification objection presupposes the soundness of the objections based on expensive and offensive preferences and snobbish tastes addressed below. Hence, despite its initial attractiveness, the abstract view that the metric of justice should be what really matters for people – the quality of their lives and not just the resources they have – should be rejected (Cohen 2011: 85; Dworkin 2000: 31).

Despite its ingenuity the specification objection is flawed. First, it is an exaggeration to say that the ideal of equality of welfare loses all of its attractions once specified. For instance, it still seems that it is unjust if, hedonically speaking, one person's life is much worse than another person's through the former person's bad luck. At any rate, Cohen cannot deny that there is some plausibility to this view given that he thinks hedonic welfare is one component in a plausible metric of egalitarian justice (cf. Section 1.5).

Second, if the specification objection is to show that resource egalitarianism is superior to welfare egalitarianism and not just that welfare egalitarianism is problematic, it must also be shown that not all resource, or mixed (welfare-resource), metrics have comparable, counterintuitive results. But neither Dworkin nor Cohen offer any argument to show that this desideratum is satisfied. Offhand it seems that they could not have done so. Welfare measures are attractive in general, as both Dworkin and Cohen agree, because they are non-fetishistic: that is, they focus solely on things people care about non-instrumentally. This gives us a reason to reject any specification of a resource measure, which by definition must focus on something other than what people care about non-instrumentally. At the very least, friends of the specification objection must explain why it provides a reason for rejecting welfare metrics that is stronger than the reason the anti-fetishist argument gives us to reject resource metrics. It is an exaggeration to say that the welfare metric is plausible only in its unspecified form: e.g. the claim that it is unjust if some people are worse off than others in terms of their hedonic welfare seems plausible in itself. At least, Cohen seems to think so, given his use of the example of a very mobile person who nevertheless experiences pain whenever he moves his body to defeat a pure resource-based metric (Cohen 2011: 16).

There is a further point here. One might suspect that something like the specification objection applies to resource-based views as well. That is, it is plausible to say in the abstract that people should have equal resources, but that when we try to specify resource metrics we might find that each has counterintuitive implications of its own (cf. Dworkin's own complaint against it discussed in Section

1.3). Because Cohen thinks that the relevant *equalisandum* has an irreducible welfare element, he seems to accept that any specification of the resource view has counterintuitive implications; and this makes it pertinent to ask why, on his view, something like the specification objection does not apply to resource-based views as well. This might not defeat the specification objection, but it shows that, unlike Dworkin, Cohen is not in a position to endorse it.

A final problem with the specification objection is that it requires the claim that any specification of the welfare measure will have strongly counterintuitive results. Dworkin acknowledges that he does not do this, as he does not discuss all possible elaborations of the welfare metric (Dworkin 2000: 16). It might be unreasonable to demand exhaustive coverage here; the most Dworkin can reasonably be expected to do is to support his generalization by attending to welfare metrics that are commonly deployed and/or plausible. However, he does not even do this. As we saw in Section 1.4, Arneson has defended the sophisticated and robust-looking view that welfare consists in satisfaction of preferences my ideally informed self would have for my actual self – a view Dworkin does not address (Arneson 1990: 161–4). For the specification objection to carry any weight, it should at least address those specifications that the main contender of welfarist luck egalitarianism endorses rather than the welfarist specification that resourcist luck egalitarians deem most interesting to defeat.

4.4. The disability objection

A second objection to a welfarist metric of egalitarian justice, which is due to Cohen, involves an adaptation of Dickens' Tiny Tim (cf. Section 1.5). Tiny Tim is unable to walk and thus worse off resource-wise than others. However, he has an unusually sunny temperament and is thus better off welfare-wise than most others. According to Cohen, justice requires Tiny Tim to be supplied with a wheelchair even if he is better off welfare-wise than most others; thus the metric of justice needs a resource component. In Cohen's view this does not show that welfare is not one component among others in a defensible metric of egalitarian justice, but it shows that it is not the only one. On his view, resources are part of a plausible metric too.

I am sceptical about this example's dialectical significance. First, if I think carefully about the case, I do not think justice is promoted when people who are able to walk are forced to give up resources to provide Tiny Tim with a wheelchair and as a result end up even worse off than him in terms of how well their lives go welfare-wise. Some theorists, of course, will agree that Tiny Tim should be compensated, but this might simply reflect a prior theoretical commitment – e.g. to liberal state neutrality, where state neutrality is (mistakenly, according to Cohen) taken to require that the state disregards welfare concerns (Arneson 1990). However, people's intuitions may simply differ at this point, so I do not want to put any argumentative weight on this other than by noting that, for me, the case is not a reason to reject welfare egalitarianism.

Second, Cohen suggests that part of the problem with denying Tiny Tim compensation and, more generally, part of the reason why '(u)tility is an unsuitable guide to policy' is that 'a person may adjust his expectations to his condition' (Cohen 2011: 46). In the light of Cohen's later and, in my view, very fruitful distinction between applied and fundamental principles of justice (see Section 8.5), this objection is misarticulated in that our present enquiry concerns not the proper 'guide to policy', but the *equalisandum* of the fundamental principle of egalitarian justice (Cohen 2008: 279). In this context the objection from adaptive preference formation seems to be grounds not for including a resource component in the *equalisandum*, as Cohen suggests, but for revising equality of opportunity for welfare so that it applies to preferences that individuals would have had in the absence of objectionable processes of adaptive preference formation. Interestingly, Cohen makes an analogous point in relation to the offensive taste objection to welfare outcome egalitarianism (Cohen 2011: 10).

Third, even if it is agreed that most, or many, of us have the intuition that justice requires us to compensate Tiny Tim for his resource deficit, the argument would be far from over. The ability to move around is such an important prerequisite of whatever constitutes welfare – or even an objective component of welfare – that there is a real danger that we will fail to take fully on board, when we react to the Tiny Tim case, the fact that Tim has a life that goes better than other people's. In support of this suggestion, consider the following example. Normal Tim has the ability to move around that people in our society normally enjoy. However, he lives among people whose ability to move around has been boosted and is super-human – people who can move around much faster and for much longer than he can. Accordingly, Normal Tim has a resource deficiency relative to his fellows. However, like Tiny Tim, Normal Tim is blessed with a sunny temperament and cares very little about his inability to move around faster or for longer periods. He likes reading, and writing novels, and even if his legs were enhanced, he would rarely use this enhancement. Few will say that the justice-based reason for enhancing Normal Tim is as strong as the justice-based reason for supplying Tiny Tim with a wheelchair in Cohen's example. Indeed, few will think there is *any* reason to compensate Normal Tim. But since Normal Tim's resource deficit relative to his fellow human beings is equivalent to Tiny Tim's deficit relative to unenhanced human beings, we can infer that it is not that deficit alone that motivates the response in the case of Tiny Tim. More generally, the Cohenian response to the case of Tiny Tim may reflect a normality bias. To test this we can stipulate that not only does Tiny Tim possess normal mobility, and others super-normal mobility, but he also has a normal temperament. It is just that, through no fault of their own, others have a gloomy, sub-normal temperament. I suspect this stipulation further weakens the Cohenian intuition. Some might respond that the Cohenian response to the case of Tiny Tim reflects sufficientarian intuitions. However, this suggestion is compatible with the present account, since intuitions regarding sufficiency might also reflect normality bias.

Let us briefly take this a little bit further. Suppose Tiny Tim has a gloomy temperament, but no disabilities. Suppose you can give him a pill that will enhance his temperament, but paralyse his legs, and, unlike in the case that I imagined in the previous section, suppose that your only concern is acting for Tiny Tim's own sake – no reasons of justice bear on the case. Assume, say, that Tiny Tim has consented to your doing whatever you think is best for him. Also, assume that you and Tiny Tim are the only two persons who exist such that any inclination you may have not to enhance his temperament while paralysing his legs does not derive from the fact that you subscribe to resource egalitarianism. (If the person who is worse off resource-wise is so because he freely transferred part of his resources to the better-off person, there is no resource-egalitarian objection to the relevant inequality. I need the pertinent assumption to rule out a resource-egalitarian *explanans* of my conjecture.) I conjecture that, pretty much irrespective of how much we emphasize what Tiny Tim would gain welfare-wise from consuming the pill, many of those who share Cohen's view of what justice requires in the case of Tiny Tim would not be in favour of giving Tiny Tim this pill for his own sake. If this conjecture is correct, it suggests that these people do not think that Tiny Tim has as much welfare as others, despite his sunny temperament; and the fact they think he should be offered a wheelchair fails to show that they are committed to something other than equality of welfare. I conclude that the disability objection fails.

4.5. The offensive preferences objection

Some people have preferences, e.g. sexual preferences, which others find offensive, e.g. because they find them vulgar. This, however, it not the distinctive sense of offensiveness that is at stake in the offensive preferences objection to welfarism. Rather, what is at stake here are preferences that are offensive because they are preferences for outcomes that clash with the ideal of equality to which egalitarians are committed, e.g. a preference for discriminating against other people or a preference for 'subjecting others to a lesser liberty' as a means of enhancing their own self-respect (Cohen 2011: 9; cf. Rawls 1971: 30–1; Dworkin 2000: 22–4). In short, preferences are offensive in the sense relevant to the present point when they are anti-egalitarian preferences. A number of theorists, e.g. Rawls, Dworkin and Cohen, have argued in the light of offensive preferences that welfare cannot be the currency of egalitarian justice. Here I focus on Cohen's articulation of the offensive tastes objection.

Before zooming in on offensive preferences, I need to surface a brief methodological point about what, in the present context, counts as a relevant objection to welfare egalitarianism. Cohen distinguishes between objections to welfare-based conceptions of

the *equalisandum* 'which are (i) plainly not egalitarian, (ii) arguably
... egalitarian, and (iii) problematic with regard to how they should
be classified' (Cohen 2011: 6). To object to the ideal that people
should be equal in terms of welfare on the grounds that its
implementation would violate people's privacy is an objection of
type (i). The objection focuses on a conflict between equality and
a different value, privacy. On the pluralist assumption that it is
possible for values such as these to clash, it casts no doubt on the
welfare-based construal of the ideal of equality. However, to object
to welfare egalitarianism on the grounds that, due to their own
recklessness, some people are bad converters of resources into
welfare is in Cohen's view an objection of type (ii). It shows that
welfare egalitarians have misconstrued equality: in Cohen's view,
we should infer that equality demands not equal welfare outcomes,
but equal *access* to welfare.

It is not clear whether an underlying criterion is being applied here
to classify the objections, or whether the classification is intuitive.
In his handling of various objections, Cohen appeals to two ideas:
(a) that objections of type (ii) rest on the thought that people do not
'get an equal amount of something that they should have an equal
amount of'; and (b) that the relevant objectionable feature involves
'an exploitative distribution of burden' (Cohen 2011: 7–8). Cohen
connects (b) with his view that the 'primary egalitarian impulse is to
extinguish the influence on distribution of both exploitation and brute
luck' (Cohen 2011: 5).

With this methodological point having been raised, let us return
to offensive preferences. Applying neither (a) nor (b) shows that an
offensive preference-based objection is properly categorized as type
(ii). First, including offensive (and, for that matter, snobbish) preferences in one's comparison of welfare involves the idea that there is
something – i.e. preference-satisfaction or hedonic welfare – that
everyone should 'have an equal amount of'. Second, the inclusion of
such preferences need not involve any exploitation where X exploits
Y when X takes 'unfair advantage' of Y, because there seems to be
no sense in which people who are compensated for welfare deficits
deriving from frustrated offensive (or snobbish preferences), with
which they are stuck, *take* advantage of others (Cohen 2011: 5).
Despite these two observations, Cohen treats the objection that

welfare egalitarianism is committed to compensation for frustrated offensive preferences as an objection of type (ii). He writes:

> From the point of view of justice, such pleasures deserve condemnation, and the corresponding preferences have no claim to be satisfied, even if they would have to be satisfied for welfare of equality to prevail. I believe that this objection defeats welfarism, and, hence, equality of welfare. But the natural course for a welfare egalitarian to take in response to the offensive tastes criticism is to shift his favour to something like equality of *inoffensive* tastes. (Cohen 2011: 10)

In suggesting this move he makes no distinction between offensive preferences that have been deliberately cultivated and those that have not been cultivated in that way. Thus he seems to think that even welfare deficits deriving from involuntarily acquired offensive preferences are irrelevant from the point of view of justice. Certainly, the reason he gives for disregarding them – that they clash with the ideal of equality – applies whether the offensive preferences have been deliberately developed or not.

Is Cohen right to classify the offensive tastes objection as type (ii)? I think not. Consider, first, the way Cohen himself formulates the requirement of egalitarian justice: it implies that everyone enjoys 'equal access to advantage' (Cohen 2011: 14). Assuming this requirement demarcates justice, and that something deserves condemnation only if it is incompatible with the requirement, a taste for discrimination should not be condemned as unjust. Consider a case where a woman's desire to discriminate against men – say, by refusing to hire male applicants as such – is frustrated. As a result she enjoys less welfare than others. Suppose, moreover, that had she satisfied her preference, this would have reduced the inequality of access to advantage between men and women within the relevant domain. In this case, at least, egalitarian justice, when construed as indicated, does not appear to require us to condemn the preference. It might be suggested that the offensive tastes objection just *is* of type (ii), and that if Cohen's account of egalitarian justice implies otherwise, this shows his account to be flawed. This response strikes me as forceful. Note, however, that my aim in the present paragraph is the limited one of exploring how this objection should be classified *given* Cohen's account of egalitarian justice.

Several things can be said here in defence of Cohen's position, or something like it. First, when Cohen refers to the standpoint of justice, perhaps he does not have in mind the requirement that everyone has equal access to advantage. Perhaps his concern is with the 'primary egalitarian impulse', which, so he claims elsewhere, 'is to extinguish the influence on distribution of both exploitation and brute luck' (Cohen 2011: 5). Presumably the primary impulse is satisfied if, and only if, everyone has equal access to advantage. Even if Cohen's description of the primary egalitarian impulse is correct, this would not offer Cohen a robust response to the present line of criticism. The female employer we considered may prefer to discrim-inate against men, even though she does not prefer that men are exploited (clearly, if she simply abstains from hiring male applicants she does not take 'unfair advantage' of them, even if she may treat them unfairly in other ways) and does not prefer that men are worse off than women as a result of bad brute luck.

Second, in support of Cohen it might be proposed that while his examples are unfortunate, his main point stands. Specifically, a preference that some have less access to advantage than others clashes with the requirements of egalitarian justice as he describes it: if the preference is satisfied, Cohenian luck egalitarian justice does not obtain. In some sense, such a preference *does* 'deserve condemnation' from the point of view of egalitarian justice. Focusing on this preference is therefore helpful, because it enables us to set aside the more peripheral issue of exactly *what* content a preference must have if it is to merit condemnation from the point of view of egalitarian justice and instead highlights the question whether egali-tarian justice actually condemns any preferences at all.

In response to this suggestion, note first that offensive prefer-ences might be instrumentally valuable from the point of egalitarian justice. For example, it may be that the fact that some people have offensive tastes makes it the case that there is less inequality in access to advantage (whether or not advantage includes welfare arising from the satisfaction of one's offensive preferences).

Second, it is not clear that the fact someone has offensive prefer-ences (i.e. preferences for unjust states of affairs) is intrinsically bad follows from the view that the state of affairs which it is a preference for is intrinsically bad. There is no inconsistency involved in thinking that it is bad if p, but not bad if someone prefers p. The issue is not, as Cohen suggests, whether, say, offensive preferences 'have [a] claim to be satisfied' – no preferences have such a luck egalitarian claim – but whether the bearer, who involuntarily harbours the preference, has a claim to be compensated, e.g. in terms of the greater satisfaction of her non-offensive preferences, for the welfare deficit its frustration involves.

It might be bad if there are Martians and Venusians, since Venusians would be worse off through no choice or fault of their own, even if it would make the present distribution no more unjust if someone were to harbour an offensive preference for Martians over Venusians in hypothetical cases where they both exist. Even more clearly, individuals who have offensive preferences regarding existing individuals could be unjust. But presumably this is not in itself regrettable from the point of view of luck egalitarian justice, since this ideal can, conceptually speaking, be satisfied in a world in which everyone is unjust; it is not an ideal about the character of just persons (see however Section 8.4).

Third, even if it did follow from the fact that p is unjust that justice is less well realized if someone prefers that p, it would not follow from offensive preferences being condemned as unjust that their satisfaction, or frustration, is irrelevant from the point of view of justice. The consequent of this conditional is implausible anyway. Imagine a society with two ethnic groups, Danes and Finns. Danes have an offensive preference for discriminating against Finns, who in turn have a similar preference vis-à-vis Danes. Suppose the offensive preferences of Danes are satisfied, but that the offensive preferences of Finns are not. In terms of the satisfaction of all other preferences, members of the two groups are identically situated. In my view, this situation is worse, *ceteris paribus*, than one in which members of both groups have their offensive preferences satisfied or frustrated to an equal degree (cf. Lippert-Rasmussen 2013b: 110). If this is right, offensive preferences do count from the point of view of equality. I conjecture that failure to see this rather simple point reflects a tendency to think of offensive preferences as preferences concerning members of minorities who are already unjustly disadvantaged. However, offensive preferences can be held in situations where there is no disadvantaged minority. This concludes my treatment of the first reason for thinking that Cohen misclassifies the offensive preferences objection.

Turning now to the second reason, consider a case in which someone leads a life that is worse than that of others, welfare-wise, because, through no choice or fault of his own, he was kidnapped by a brain surgeon who tampered with his brain so as to make him harbour strong offensive preferences – which, as it happens, are frustrated. Compare this with an otherwise comparable case where the victim non-voluntarily acquires strong expensive tastes, again not satisfied. On Cohen's account, there is no injustice in the first person being worse off, but there is injustice in the second person being so. However, the contention that there is a luck egalitarian distinction to be made between these two cases seems incredible. The two people do not differ in their exercise of responsibility and, thus, the impulse guiding luck egalitarianism suggests that they could not justly be unequally well off given that such an inequality cannot be justified by a differential exercise of responsibility (Cohen 2011: 121). Their preferences differ simply as the result of the neurosurgeon tampering with the brain of the former person and direct brain manipulation undermines moral responsibility (Fischer 1994: 151; Fischer and Ravizza 1998: 230–6; Pereboom 2001: 112–17). Indeed, intuitively the luck egalitarian case for compensating the person with offensive preferences is very strong, and this makes it noteworthy that the person in question here is not responsible for his or her offensive preferences. Perhaps it is tacitly assumed that people with offensive preferences have some degree of indirect control over them. This, at any rate, would lend (in the context, illicit) support to view that the frustration of (involuntary) offensive preferences is irrelevant from a luck egalitarian point of view. In sum, the case of offensive tastes does not motivate a rejection of welfare egalitarianism and for the view that Cohen misclassifies an objection appealing to such preferences as a type (ii) objection, i.e. as an objection to unrestricted welfare luck egalitarianism.

4.6. The expensive and snobbish tastes objections

I now turn to the other anti-egalitarian preference that Cohen and, in effect, Dworkin discuss, i.e. expensive and, in particular, snobbish preferences. In Section 1.3, I described how, to defeat welfare egalitarianism, Dworkin imagines the case of Louis, who has deliberately cultivated expensive tastes for plovers' eggs and pre-phylloxera wine (Dworkin 2000: 48–59). People who favour equality of welfare would approve of Louis getting extra resources to compensate him for the fact that in order to reach the same level of welfare he now requires more resources than others do. Dworkin thinks it would be unjust to compensate Louis for his expensive tastes and that this fact defeats the welfare metric.

Cohen thinks Dworkin misdiagnoses the case. He makes two points in this connection. First, like Arneson (see Section 1.4), Cohen points out that in his description of the case, Dworkin foregrounds Louis' *deliberate* cultivation of his expensive tastes. This distorts matters: the case involves a loss of focus on expensive tastes per se, so it does not show that people with expensive tastes per se do not deserve compensation (cf. Arneson 1989: 77–93). This has become the standard, and to my mind convincing, welfarist response to the objection from expensive tastes. However, Cohen proposes a variant of Louis' case which suggests an interestingly different objection to the welfarist metric – one which Cohen is much more sympathetic to.

Second, Cohen distinguishes between deliberately cultivating a preference that just happens to be expensive and deliberately cultivating a preference because it is expensive, where 'because' means *for the reason that* (Cohen 2011: 99). In the latter case alone an expensive taste is, or might be, snobbish. A preference for expensive goods is not snobbish if the reason underlying the preference is a belief that high price is a reliable sign of good quality. Cohen speaks of 'Louis-like snobbish reasons that justify less sympathy' (Cohen 2011: 95). He acknowledges that people who simply desire things that happen to be expensive may well deserve compensation. This helps us clarify Cohen's position. Essentially, Cohen believes that, like the expensive tastes objection, the snobbish tastes complaint is a type (ii) objection – see the methodological point in the previous section – to the ideal of equality of welfare. In his view, the objection to compensating people for a welfare deficit deriving from frustrated snobbish tastes does not derive from values other than equality, e.g. from the value of overall welfare.

Before facing the normative question whether Cohen is right to deny that people are due compensation when their welfare deficit is due to expensive, snobbish tastes, I need to sort out a couple of conceptual issues. First, how do offensive preferences and snobbish preferences relate? A natural view here is that snobbish preferences are a sub-species of offensive preferences. Snobbish preferences clash with the value of equality because they reflect a desire to see oneself as superior to others (see Chapter 7). On reflection, however, it is unclear that snobbish tastes must take this form. It is possible for someone to have a snobbish taste without being motivated by a desire for superiority. You might have a preference for expensive sports gear in part because of its being expensive and you conceive of yourself as someone who only uses expensive sports gear, while in all other areas you have inexpensive preferences. You might not mind the fact that your tastes in these other areas are inexpensive, nor that others have satisfied their expensive, snobbish preferences. In this kind of case, your snobbish taste is not offensive, surely, whether a welfare deficit resulting from it should be compensated for or not.

By way of further support for the claim canvassed in the previous sentence, consider the fact that someone with an expensive, snobbish preference in some category of goods need not require more resources in total than another person if both are to reach the same level of welfare. Imagine you have expensive tastes in beer. To reach the same level of welfare as others reach by buying Heineken, you need access to some fancy microbrewery equipment. However, *unlike* your friends you have inexpensive tastes in cars, so the bundle of resources that will leave them with the same level of welfare as you is more expensive than the bundle of resources you require to reach this level, despite your expensive preference for beer. Against this background your preference does not seem to be expensive. The key thing here is that an individual preference might be expensive even if the overall set of preferences of which it is a member is not.

It might be objected that the concept of expensive tastes does not apply to preferences for goods within a particular sub-category, such as alcoholic drinks or means of transportation. It only applies to individuals' complete set of preferences. If so, my example of a person who has snobbish, expensive preferences regarding the sub-category of alcoholic drinks but cheap preferences overall is misconceived. However, my main claim – that a person may have snobbish and yet inexpensive preferences – survives the objection.

Cohen discusses a case in which a person has snobbish *and* expensive preferences, but this overlap is contingent. Cheap, snobbish preferences are possible, as are expensive, humble ones (see next paragraph). This can be seen most clearly if we imagine someone who falsely believes beer to be expensive and cultivates a preference for beer on the basis of this belief. To ensure that this badly informed snob reaches the same level of welfare as others, we may need fewer resources than we require to ensure that a better informed person without snobbish preferences reaches the same level of welfare as others. So the objection to snobbish preferences per se cannot appeal to the consideration that it is unjust to demand a greater share of resources than others on account of one's expensive preferences. This raises the question of what one should say about snobs with cheap preferences. If welfare deficits arising from frustrated snobbish preferences should be disregarded, such snobs should be denied the resources needed to bring them up to the same level of welfare as non-snobs even if they already command fewer resources than others. With his multidimensional metric, Cohen might think snobs with cheap preferences are due some compensation for being under-resourced, but given his refusal to accommodate snobbish preferences, he would presumably be committed to denying compensation on welfare deficit grounds.

Snobbish preferences, as defined above, are a species of desire whose object is the price of the good desired. Accordingly, there are two other species of desire belonging to this genus. First, there is what I shall call humble preferences, where a humble preference is a preference for something on the grounds that it is cheaper than the relevant goods others prefer. So if someone prefers beer not because he likes its taste, but because it is cheaper than the drinks others prefer, he has a humble preference. Second, there is what

I shall call neutral tastes. These are tastes for something on the grounds that it is neither cheap nor expensive. Humble preferences are interesting, because they clash with the ideal of equality in some of the ways snobbish preferences do. Accordingly, some of the egalitarian objections to snobbish preferences will apply to humble preferences as well. To date, no one has addressed the issues raised by humble preferences.

Turning now to the normative issue mentioned above – i.e. whether Cohen is right to deny that people are due compensation when their welfare deficit is due to expensive, snobbish tastes – let me note first that, analogously with the case of offensive tastes, it is not plausible to hold that snobbish preferences are simply irrelevant from the point of view of justice. This can be seen if we imagine a case where everyone holds snobbish preferences through no choice or fault of their own, and where they are unequally well off as a result of the fact that some people's snobbish preferences are satisfied and others' are not. This case seems worse, from the point of view of equality, than one in which everyone's snobbish preferences are satisfied or frustrated to an equal degree.

Second, if snobbish preferences clash with egalitarian justice, so do humble preferences – an implication which seems implausible. While people with humble preferences have a better character than people with snobbish preferences, *ceteris paribus*, humble preferences are, like snobbish preferences, a preference for inequality, i.e. put in third-person terms it is – like snobbish preferences – a preference for some people being worse off in some respect than others.

Third, Cohen puts a lot of emphasis on the fact that bearers of non-snobbish, expensive preferences typically identify with the preference as such while regretting that the preference is expensive (Cohen 2011: 92–6). This distinguishes them from people with snobbish, expensive preferences, and it is why the latter are less deserving, or not deserving at all, of compensation. However, I doubt that snobbish preferences, in the ordinary sense, typically involve the bearer's identification with the expensiveness in the relevant sense. For instance, a snob who prefers Chateau Margaux to ordinary red wine might think that he obtains superior satisfaction relative to others as a consequence of his discriminating taste. The situation is not that he gets (and identifies with his getting) less satisfaction out of ordinary red wine and thus needs more resources than others do to reach a given level of satisfaction. It is that that he obtains superior satisfaction relative to that achieved by people with less discriminating tastes out of superior red wine. Let us, however, set aside the issue of how rare such preferences are and instead focus on expensive, snobbish tastes, where the bearer really *does* not regret, or even identifies with, their being expensive in the relevant sense.

Even in this case a distinction similar to the one Cohen rightly presses – the distinction between regretting the preference and regretting that it happens to be expensive to satisfy it – may apply to snobbish, expensive preferences. The distinction I have in mind is the distinction between regretting that it happens to be expensive to satisfy one's preference and regretting that one is in a social context in which it is valuable for one to satisfy snobbish preferences. Just as a bearer of a judgemental preference that happens to be expensive can 'regard it [the expensiveness of satisfying their preference: KLR] as a piece of bad luck for which they should be compensated, on pain of incoherently repudiating their own personality, on pain of confessing to a most bizarre alienation from themselves', so bearers of expensive, snobbish preferences can 'regard it as a piece of bad luck for which they should be compensated' that they find themselves in a context where the satisfaction of such preferences has value for them (Cohen 2011: 93). *If* the former shows, as Cohen believes, that the case for compensating expensive preferences is not defeated, so does the latter. In neither case do the claimants repudiate their personality. The snobs who claim compensation on the grounds indicated do not repudiate their personality. They think that, given the circumstances under which they regrettably live and over which they have no control, the satisfaction of snobbish preferences is good for them. They would not want their personality to be any different from what it is. In a sense, of course, this situation involves alienation from one's personality. After all, snobs prefer a situation in which their circumstances as well as their preferences are different from those in the present situation. However, this is not the sort of bizarre alienation that Cohen has in mind, i.e. the alienation involved in seeing the expensiveness of satisfying one's preferences as one's bad luck and at the same time deeming such preferences to be one's good luck in that one thinks that it would involve a loss were one to have non-snobbish preferences despite changes in one's circumstances. By way of contrast, the snobs I have in mind have no thought to the effect that, given their circumstances, their personality is not as it should be.

Finally, much of the reasoning presented above in connection with offensive tastes seems to apply here as well. The satisfaction of snobbish preferences is compatible with everyone having equal access to advantage; and even if the content of these preferences is specified in such a way that their satisfaction really does prevent everyone from having equal access to advantage, it is unclear why this should be taken to imply that they should be disregarded. Accordingly, like offensive tastes, snobbish tastes do not motivate a rejection of welfare luck egalitarianism.

4.7. The non-instrumental concern objections

In the last four sections I have surveyed objections to the welfarist account of the currency of egalitarian justice and dismissed them as inconclusive. Given the force of the anti-fetishist objection – something which critics of welfarist metrics like Dworkin and Cohen concede – this makes the welfarist metric a strong contender. As Dworkin puts it: 'The basic, immediate appeal of equality of welfare … lies in the idea that welfare is what really matters to people … Equality of welfare proposes, that is, to make people equal in what is really and fundamentally important to them all' (Dworkin 2000: 31; cf. Sen 1980: 218). Of course, this cannot be entirely right, because, as Dworkin acknowledges, things other than people's own welfare matter non-instrumentally to them, though Dworkin offers independent reasons for why these concerns should not be included in the metric of equality – reasons countered in the sections above. In this section I want to suggest that the anti-fetishist argument actually motivates a position somewhat different from a welfarist metric.

Recall the anti-fetishist argument presented in Section 4.2. I mentioned that the argument is flawed. There are two reasons why.

First, at best it is contingently true that people care non-instrumentally about their welfare. Fanatics or, more positively, idealists, for instance, might care about their own welfare only as a means of bringing about some end unrelated to their own welfare. Hence, the most someone who presses the fetishistic-objection can claim is that, as it happens, equality requires equality of welfare, whereas it is non-contingently true that individuals should be equal in terms of the satisfaction of what they care about non-instrumentally. This includes, but, significantly, is not exhausted by, their own welfare.

One line of response to this complication would be to say that the relevant fetishism derives from the resource metric's failure to focus on what people *have reason* to care about non-instrumentally (whether or not they care about it). It could be added that, necessarily, we all have reason to care non-instrumentally about our own welfare. No such line of argument is available to advocates of resource metrics of equality.

Second, we care non-instrumentally about things other than our own welfare. For instance, parents care non-instrumentally about the welfare of their children. Altruistic people care non-instrumentally about the welfare of everyone. Idealists care non-instrumentally about things other than welfare, e.g. that certain species do not become extinct. While we might be able to say to people who do not care about their own well-being that they ought, as a matter of reason, to do so, it is implausible that people who care about things other than their own well-being care about things they ought not care about, as a matter of reason.

In the light of these concerns we might say that what is really salvageable from the anti-fetishist argument is a revised version of its major premise:

(1*) The currency of egalitarian justice is something that each of us cares about non-instrumentally provided we do not have reason not to care about it.

Call this metric non-instrumental concern. *Non-instrumental concern luck egalitarianism* (or for short: concern luck egalitarianism) holds that:

(4) It is unjust if some people are worse off than others in terms

of the degree to which that which they care non-instrumentally about, non-unreasonably, is realized through their bad luck.

The qualification 'non-unreasonably' is supposed to do the same work as the provision that our care is not unreasonable in (1*). One way of giving a bit more meat to this qualification is to appeal to Arneson's notion of second-best preferences (see Section 1.5). Undoubtedly, this suggestion needs to be developed further – e.g. in relation to things that people do not actually care about but would care about, or want themselves to care about, if they were reasonable – but one basic motivation is that when one's non-instrumental concerns are badly misinformed, e.g. through false empirical beliefs, their satisfaction is not good from the relevant evaluative point of view. However, my main interest here is not in identifying the suitable set of idealized concerns – this issue does not set my account from similar accounts that only apply to self-regarding concerns or preferences – but in defending the view that non-self-regarding concerns matter too from the point of view of luck egalitarian justice.

Because, typically, people care non-instrumentally about their own welfare, typically when we assess outcomes from the point of view of egalitarian justice we should compare people in terms of their welfare. However, many people reasonably care non-instrumentally about things other than their own welfare and inequalities in terms of the degree to which these concerns are realized are unjust when they reflect bad luck. To see this, imagine two persons who enjoy equally good lives. However, one person cares strongly about the preservation for the future of Roman buildings. The other person cares strongly about the preservation for the future of medieval buildings. As it happens, independently of your efforts it is certain that most Roman buildings will be preserved, but certain that no medieval buildings will. Suppose you cannot affect the level of well-being of these two persons. However, you can either ensure that all Roman buildings are preserved or ensure that some medieval buildings are. On standard luck egalitarian accounts, equality is indifferent between whether you do one or the other. However, this seems problematic. Arguably, you do not treat them with equal respect and concern if you decide to make sure that all Roman buildings are preserved. Indeed, in some cases bad luck in terms of one's well-being can be counterbalanced by good luck in terms of one's non-self-regarding preferences such that it need not be unjust that one's life is worse than another person's. Taking account of people's non-self-regarding concerns is a way of respecting them, which only taking into account their self-regarding concerns fails to accommodate.

One worry here might be that no luck egalitarians have actually defended anything like the non-instrumental concern view. However, this might not reflect badly on the view, but simply reflect that much of what people care about non-instrumentally is their own welfare and, thus, reflect that many luck egalitarians have mistaken a proxy for what really matters.

Note also that many of our concerns are valuational in the sense that we can give reasons for why we are concerned with it and in the light of which we see what we are concerned with as valuable. However, in some cases our concerns are brute and while, on my account, brute as well as non-brute concerns matter, one could imagine cases where only non-brute concerns matter from the point of view of egalitarian justice.

4.8. Dworkin's resourcist view

In the previous six sections I have discussed welfarist accounts of the luck egalitarian *equalisandum*. I defended it against a number of objections, but ended up rejecting it in favour of the view that the degree of satisfaction of non-instrumental concerns is the correct metric of equality. Like welfarist metrics, my favoured metric is closely tied to the perspective of individuals, but unlike them it takes proper account of the fact that people are non-instrumentally concerned with things other than their own and that sometimes unconcerned with their own welfare. In the remaining two sections I will assess two alternative and influential accounts of, what people should be equal in terms of starting with Dworkin's resourcist account.

I introduced the essentials of Dworkin's resourcist metric in Section 1.3. Dworkin distinguishes between two forms of resources: internal and external. In the special circumstances of the desert island scenario that I described in Section 1.3, people have equally good bundles of external resources if the envy test is satisfied. Setting aside some reservations that I discussed there, equality of internal resources is brought about if Dworkin's hypothetical insurance scheme is implemented. The fact that Dworkin's account of equality of resources has two separate dimensions raises the question whether equality of resources obtains whenever equality of internal resources and equality of external resources obtains?

If Dworkin did not think that the answer to this question was affirmative, it becomes inexplicable why he saw himself as having offered a theory of equality of resources as opposed to elements that together with other elements might form one. So presumably he did think that equality of internal and equality of external resources implied equality of resources. Yet, once we look at the various things he says of each of the two forms of equality, it seems that they do not apply to overall equality. Take the envy test first. From the fact that I do not envy another person's bundle of external resources and that the hypothetical insurance test mitigates differential luck between us in terms of talents, inborn handicaps, etc., it does not follow that I do not envy another person's bundle of internal and external resources. But if envy in terms of bundles of external resources implies inequality of external resources, why does envy in terms of people's overall bundles of resources not imply inequality of resources overall?

Second, in relation to his argument in favour of the auction and the envy test to determine whether equality of resources obtains, Dworkin writes: '... people should pay the price of the life they have decided to live, measured in what others give up in order that they can do so' (Dworkin 2000: 74). Dworkin thinks that when it comes to external resources the auction and the envy test ensures this. However, he cannot say that the same is true of the distribution of resources overall. For suppose that a tremendously talented person decides to live an idle life of simple pleasures. What others have to give up so that this is possible are the huge amounts of resources that he would have created for the community had he used his talents. Yet, Dworkin's insurance scheme is not adapted to make him pay these costs to others, since, so Dworkin assumes, people would not insure against not being tremendously talented. If they did and if they turned out to be tremendously talented, they would have to spend almost all of their life to produce as much as they can just to cover their insurance premium. This, Dworkin thinks, would amount to a form of slavery of the talent, which, in his view, is objectionable from an egalitarian point of view. This concern – about the slavery of the talented – is his central reason for not offering an account of equality of resources that is not unified in the way that, say, equality of informed preference satisfaction is, but one that is essentially disjunctive and holds that equality of resources obtains, whenever, and only insofar as, both disjuncts are satisfied. This warrants taking a closer look at the slavery of the talented objection (cf. Olson 2010).

To understand the slavery of the talented objection better, suppose that internal as well as external resources are distributed through an auction at which everyone who participates bids and where all have equal bidding power and where the auction is over once no one envies the overall resource bundles of others. Since people have very different skills and talents, talented people can expect that their labour power – essentially their time – will cost much more than the labour power of the untalented. Hence, if I am a talented person who would like some leisure, I will have to bid at the auction for some of 'my own' time; and because, alternatively, I could be very productive in the hours I would like to spend in leisure, others will offer high bids for those hours. Accordingly, I will have to use a lot of my bidding power to ensure that I obtain some leisure time. Similarly, if I am a talented person who wants to spend some of my time in a job I find fulfilling, but for which I do not have any talent and in which I will produce goods that few wish to buy, I will need to use a lot of my bidding power to ensure that this is possible. Indeed, if we allow coalitions of buyers to pool their resources and to buy the labour power of those with talent, I might end up owning none of my time, with the owners of my labour power dictating what I do. This, Dworkin submits, is unfair. The result of the auction, so construed, would be:

> that each would have to spend his life in close to the commercially most profitable manner that he could, or, at least if he is talented, suffer some very serious deprivation if he did not. For since Adrian, for example, is able to produce prodigious income from farming, others would be willing to bid a large amount to have the right to his labor and the vegetables thereof, and if he outbids them, but

chooses to write indifferent poetry instead of farming full time, he will then have to spend a large part of his initial endowment on a right that will bring him little financial benefit. This is indeed the slavery of the talented. (Dworkin 2000: 90)

As a resource egalitarian with real concerns about the slavery of the talented, Dworkin needs to address this problem. He does so by excluding internal resources, e.g. labour, from the auction and the envy test.

For those subscribing to welfarist theories of distributive justice or for that matter my concern-based theory of distributive justice, the slavery of the talented objection is of perverse interest because it poses no problem at all for such theories. Welfarist egalitarians think that people should be equal in terms of welfare, whether understood in terms of (ideal) preference satisfaction or in terms of pleasant mental states. They do not require talented people to have less welfare than others as a result of spending their lives 'close to the commercially most profitable manner'. They might see no injustice in talented people working more (or less) hours than untalented people if, and to the extent that, this is compatible with equality of welfare. Such compatibility might be preserved if, for example, the kind of work talented people do is typically more rewarding than the kind of work untalented people do. However, this hardly qualifies as slavery. Hence, insofar as the slavery of the talented is a problem for egalitarian theories of justice, it is a problem for resource-egalitarian theories only.

Is Dworkin's resourcist metric plausible? One objection that immediately springs to mind is the following. Suppose I happen to prefer goods that many others prefer and accordingly they are very expensive. You prefer goods that few people prefer. As a result I can only reach a lower level of welfare than you can as a result of my bad price luck. Is this not an unjust inequality luck egalitarians should care about? One might think, as I do, that this is the right answer to give. However, it is less clear that appeal to it will serve as a non-question-begging objection to resourcism. After all, its essence consists in pointing out that people with equal amounts of resources might end up with different levels of welfare. But this is a straightforward implication of resourcist egalitarianism and, presumably, one that resource egalitarians accept. This is not to say that the disagreement between those who endorse – Dworkin – and those who repudiate – Cohen – differential price luck is unimportant. As Cohen points out, underlying this disagreement is a disagreement about the justice of the market. While Dworkin thinks that 'the market produces justice insofar as its prices reflect [nothing but: KLR] the play of people's tastes and ambitions', Cohen thinks it plays 'no part in the constitution of justice' and, accordingly, that its outcome 'may be more or less just' (Cohen 2011: 104).

To defeat Dworkin's purely resourcist view, Cohen imagines a person who is very good at controlling the movement of his limbs and very adept at moving them (cf. Section 1.5). So in an important dimension he is more resourceful than the rest of us. The problem is that he experiences pain whenever he moves his limbs. In Cohen's view, this person is worse off than the rest of us in a way that is relevant from the perspective of egalitarian justice. Since he does not have fewer resources than the rest of us – he is very capable of moving his body – and the experience of pain is not a resource, but merely something that affects his welfare, this shows, Cohen argues, that welfare is likewise relevant from the perspective of egalitarian justice. Unlike the abstract appeal to bad price luck, this objection does not seem to beg the question against resourcist luck egalitarians. For one thing, it seems unjust that this person should be worse off than others independently of one's general stance on resource vs welfarist egalitarianism. Moreover, it does not beg the question against Dworkin, because he agrees that it would be unjust for this person to be worse off.

In response to Cohen's objection, Dworkin writes:

> everyone would agree that a decent life, whatever its other features, is one that is free from serious and enduring physical or mental pain or discomfort, and having a physical or mental infirmity or condition that makes pain or depression or discomfort inescapable without expensive medicine or clothing is therefore an evident and straightforward handicap … If the community gives someone money for medicine to relieve pain, it does not do so to make his welfare or well-being equal to anyone else's, but because his physical constitution handicaps his ability to lead the life he wishes to lead. (Dworkin 2000: 297, 491 n.11)

This reply seems deeply unsatisfactory. First, the appeal to the notion of a 'decent life' seems irrelevant to the present dispute between two egalitarians, one reason being that they are not sufficientarians, the other one being that the notion of a decent life can be cashed out in terms of welfare.

Second, even if we describe Cohen's agile person suffering from pain whenever he moves his body, this does not establish that resourcists can accommodate Cohen's putative counterexample. For one might reasonably ask what the relevant handicap consists in and what sort of life Cohen's person is unable to live. The only sensible answers seem to be 'not being able to move one's body without a loss of welfare' and 'a life without constant suffering' and resourcists should be indifferent to this special kind of handicap and ability to live a certain kind of life. Dworkin might respond that Cohen's condition is one that people would want to insure against. However, as Cohen responds: 'a deficit doesn't count as a resource deficit just because people would insure against it' (Cohen 2011: 92). In short, in his reply to Cohen's objection Dworkin expands the extension of 'resources' into the territory of welfarism, thus undermining his claim to rebut Cohen's objection to resourcism in a more restricted sense of that term.

In the previous sections, we used Cohen's case of Tiny Tim as a counterexample to resourcism. However, following Cohen's remark on the loose connection between resource deficits and that which we want to insure against, we can also use it to develop an internal critique of Dworkin showing that Dworkin's auction is sensitive to welfare considerations. Imagine a situation in which talented people do not need to concentrate on what they are doing in order to exercise their talents. Suppose that there are great differences in people's talents and hence productivity, but that exercising one's talents in productive labour is a bit like driving on a deserted road in that it does not require one's attention: thus, for example, a talented brain surgeon can compose and even write down poems while performing surgery. Whether or not they attend to what they are doing, non-talented people cannot perform surgery, but the talented person can do it inattentively without loss of quality or speed in his or her work. The point here is that being at work does not prevent one from doing the things one likes doing or likes doing more than working. Hence, there is no reason for talented people, who put in many hours a day, to envy untalented people, who do not. Of course, talented people do not count as less talented for this reason, or as people who do not command more internal resources than untalented people. Hence, the ground for envy in Dworkin's scenario cannot be that untalented people have more resources than talented ones if labour is put up for bidding at the auction. I have proposed that the envy test registers welfare as well.

So far I have proceeded on the assumption that resource-egalitarian accounts of justice need to avoid productivity-sensitive enslavement. But this is not something that can simply be assumed. Thus, some observers have argued that Dworkin fails to give convincing egalitarian reasons for thinking that talents and labour should not be sold at Dworkin's auction. Miriam Cohen Christofidis pursues this line of argument. In her view, the situation of the talented whose time is in high demand at the hypothetical auction is nothing like slavery in the literal sense (2004: 32). Admittedly, talented people might face a 'severely restricted choice'. They may have to devote most of their purchasing power at the auction to ensuring that they control at least some part of their time. But it is unclear that they end up worse off than others in a sense that ought to trouble egalitarians. That would follow only if all that people cared about, in relation to their jobs, was the number of hours they worked – the fewer, the better. However, people care about other things too, including how fulfilling their working lives are (Christofidis 2004: 36); and since, typically, the jobs of talented people are more fulfilling than those of untalented people, it may well be that hard-working talented people are not envied by much less hard-working untalented people.

In his reply to Christofidis, Dworkin responds that a talented person 'could, if she wished, borrow enough to purchase control of herself' (2004: 351). Others might likewise borrow to purchase control of the talented person, but the talented person could borrow more money than others could 'because it is less expensive to monitor debt service than it is constantly to ensure that an employee is working to the exact limit of her high-production endurance' (Dworkin 2004: 351).

This reply is unconvincing for two reasons. First, it involves an appeal to what is at best a contingent truth about how loan markets and the like function, and it is difficult to see how a fundamental question of justice – to wit, whether labour is to be assessed in the same way as external resources for the purpose of determining whether equality of resources is satisfied – can be determined by such facts. Suppose that technology or the human psyche change in such a way that it becomes more, not less, 'expensive to monitor debt service than it is constantly to ensure that an employee is working to the exact limit of her high-production endurance'. Then Dworkin would have to concede Christofidis' point.

Second, it is ad hoc to introduce the possibility of borrowing money, which can then be used at the auction to bid for resources. If the auction is to serve as a device for ensuring the equal distribution of resources, participants must a have equal buying power. But if participants can borrow extra bidding power on the basis of their talents, an inequality between the participants emerges that under-mines the auction's capacity to model equality of resources.

In sum, Dworkin's resourcism faces some formidable challenges. It does not only offer an unsatisfyingly disjunctive account of equality of resources, its very reason for doing so is a problematic basis for a theory of equality of resources in that, unofficially, it accommodates considerations about welfare.

4.9. Sen's capability metric

Amartya Sen has proposed an alternative and quite influential account of the currency of egalitarian justice, which, so he claims, is distinct from both welfarism and resourcism: the capabilities approach. Sen develops this account in opposition to the views that utility and Rawlsian primary goods are the relevant *equalisanda*. His approach to the currency question has won the favour of many, though perhaps luck egalitarians have been less disposed to endorse the view.

According to Sen, primary goods is an unsatisfactory measure for reasons related to the anti-fetishist argument presented in Section 4.2 above – people have different needs and they will be able to do different things with the same bundles of primary goods and, on Sen's view, it is a 'fetishist handicap' to be non-instrumentally concerned with primary goods, or for that matter any other kind of resource, rather than what these goods '*do* to human beings' (Sen 1980: 218). By way of illustration: in the light of the fact that different individuals have different metabolic rates, it amounts to a form of fetishism to focus on the amounts of food they have as opposed to the level of nutrition that these amounts of food make possible for them.

If one has welfarist sympathies one will be favourably inclined towards this objection to resourcism. However, Sen rejects welfarism though he concedes that it is immune to the fetishism objection. Rather, he rejects it because it is an unsuitable guide to policy (Sen 1985: 21–2, 29; Sen 2009: 282–4; Cohen 2011: 42). The reason this is so is the phenomenon of adaptive preferences. Suppose we take welfare to consist in preference satisfaction. In that case the slave that modifies his preferences such that he only has preferences that, given his poor circumstances, he is likely to satisfy, e.g. a preference for being put to hard work and locked up in a cage, he might have a higher level of welfare than his master, who does not have adaptive preferences. Accordingly, equality of welfare suggests, implausibly, that we should help the master rather the slave.

There are at least two reasons why welfarist egalitarians should not be impressed with this objection. First, it is an objection that not all forms of welfarist egalitarianism are vulnerable to. For instance, if one's rational self would not harbour adaptive preferences, the slave whose actual preferences are satisfied would not on that account have a high level of welfare.

Second, and more importantly, welfarist luck egalitarians do not propose welfare as a guide to policy. Rather they propose it as that dimension, in which the fundamental egalitarian principle requires people to be equal. As Cohen has argued, there is no reason to believe that this dimension will also be that dimension which should guide policies, because policies will have to take into account things such as conflicting values and some people's dispositions to resist just policies (see Section 8.5). Hence, if the capability approach is meant as a proposal for what should guide policy, it should not be seen as a competitor to welfarist or resourcist metrics, because these are proposed for different purposes.

There is an additional aspect of Sen's capability approach that should be highlighted here. While he, in his objection to the Rawlsian metric of primary goods, emphasizes that what is important about resources is what they 'do to human beings', elsewhere he emphasizes a subgroup of the things that resources do to human beings, namely that which they give them the ability and opportunity to do. It is the latter and narrower aspect which makes the label 'capability approach' suitable. To see that resources do more to human beings than confer capabilities to them, return to the example of a person who has plentiful food supplies. The possession of this resource gives him the capability of achieving a satisfactory nutritional level, but it also means that he becomes an attractive object of theft to his less well-fed fellows. This is something that his possession of food does to him and yet it is not an ability or opportunity to do something on his part. Despite his objection to resourcism, it is, as the name of his approach suggests, what resources do to people by way of conferring capabilities on them that Sen thinks matters from the point of view of justice. To understand this focus, we can think of the ascetic who despite having plentiful food freely decides to starve himself and thus is undernourished. Given that his nutritional state does not reflect deficient capabilities on his part, but his free decision regarding how to act given the favourable capabilities that he has, it is plausible that his worse nutritional state is not a concern from the point of view of justice.

While Sen's focus on capabilities, as opposed to outcome, means that his account has some similarities with Arneson's equality of opportunity, the latter has presented a forceful challenge to Sen's account. For even if we agree that the metric of egalitarian justice is capabilities other than capabilities to achieve welfare, that in itself does not tell us which capabilities matter from the point of view of egalitarian justice. Presumably, not all such capabilities do, e.g. unlike you I might not have the capability to watch *Sex and the City* more than forty hours a week. However, given that I have no desire to watch it even for five minutes, and given that perhaps you do not either, this difference in our capabilities does not matter. Accordingly, in order not to be seriously incomplete the capability theory must supply an account of *which* capabilities matter and the worry is that the only plausible way of determining which capabilities matter is to fall back on a theory of welfare – i.e. those capabilities that make a difference to people's welfare – or, as I would suggest, an account of people's rationally permissible non-instrumental concerns. But if that is so, the worry is that the capability approach is not really an alternative to welfarism but rather presupposes an account, whether it be a mental-state, preference-based, or an objective list account.

Responding to worries along these lines, Sen (2005: 158–63) suggests that, perhaps setting aside some very basic capabilities, it is not the task of political philosophers to identify which capabilities matter and how much, but an issue to be decided through democratic deliberation.

This reply, however, is located at a different level from that on which the challenge is posed. First, democratic deliberation is not about basic principles of justice – these are not whatever principles are democratically elected – but about which policies to pursue.

Second, even if, absurdly, people were to decide on basic principles of justice through democratic deliberation, presumably, they will offer arguments for why one metric is better than another and, in principle though perhaps not in terms of sophistication etc., these arguments would be no different from the arguments offered by political philosophers. So the challenge is to say which metric is best supported by arguments and referring to democratic election is simply to avoid answering this question (but see Sen 2009: 241–3).

I conclude that, despite its popularity, the capability approach does not offer a plausible alternative to welfarist and resourcist metric. On reflection, Sen might not even think that it does, since, as noted above, his concern seems to be to propose a plausible guide to policy and, for all I have said in this section, the capability approach might indeed be the best guide to policy.

4.10. Summary

In this chapter I have explored the question of what egalitarian justice requires people to be equal in terms of. This question is a hard one, but it is also one that any account of distributive question must face in some form or another. In Section 2 I presented an argument to the effect that welfare is the most plausible answer to this question, since it seems fetishist to say that something that people care about only instrumentally is that which basic principles of justice requires an equal distribution of. I then defended this argument against a number of challenges, though in the end I proposed to reject welfarism in the light of the non-fetishist objection – what people should be equal in terms of is that which they care about non-instrumentally and not unreasonably so. For most of us our concern about our own welfare is one such concern, but not the only concern of this kind. Admittedly, I have not done much more than sketch this theory, but at least I have shown that an account of this general form is one that coheres best with the anti-fetishist concern that most find very forceful. I then reviewed two competing accounts of the luck egalitarian *equalisandum* – Dworkin's resourcism and Sen's capability approach – offering reasons to reject both of them. The entire discussion in this chapter has rested on the assumption that the site of justice is distributions. This assumption is also embodied in the core luck egalitarian claim that I presented in Section 1.2. However, as we shall see in the next chapter, not all luck egalitarians share this view.

5

Telic and deontic egalitarianism

5.1. Introduction

In previous chapters, I introduced the views of a number of luck egalitarians. Some of them think that it is unjust for the state to treat people unequally and that this is the reason why we ought to bring about an equal distribution. Other luck egalitarians are not particularly concerned with the injustice of state policies, but focus directly on unequal distributions for the purpose of assessing them from the point of view of luck egalitarian justice. By way of illustration: Dworkin thinks the concern for equality is tied to the state's obligation to treat its citizens as equals and, thus, rejects the notion of unjust natural inequalities, i.e. unjust inequalities that exist whatever the state or any other agent does. By way of illustration of the latter view: Larry Temkin thinks that natural inequalities, e.g. that some die young and others old for reasons not in any way connected with state policies, may be unjust. Such inequalities are unjust in virtue of their unfairness.

In an influential lecture in 1991, Derek Parfit introduced a distinction between teleological and deontological egalitarianism – for short, telic and deontic egalitarianism – which is meant to capture this difference. While I will explain the distinction much more fully shortly, at this point it suffices to say that telic egalitarianism is the sort of egalitarian position Temkin represents, while deontic egalitarianism is the sort of position Dworkin represents. As the terminology suggests, in drawing this distinction Parfit probably had in mind the general distinction between consequentialism and deontology even though, as we shall see, the distinction he proposes is different from a mere application of it to equality. Also, one could draw a distinction between telic and deontic versions of the non-egalitarian distributive views discussed in Section 1.7. For simplicity, I shall simply focus on the distinction applied to equality.

Parfit suggests that whereas the concern for equality has, in a way that is attractive, a wider scope on the telic view, deontic egalitarianism has the advantage of being invulnerable to the levelling down objection. Both of these suggestions are widely accepted in one form or another (McKerlie 1996: 280; Nagel: 1997; Temkin 1993: 247–8).

Section 5.2 unpacks the distinction between telic and deontic egalitarianism into three logically independent distinctions. These, I claim, better capture the logical space of possible egalitarian positions. This claim is not intended as a criticism of Parfit. He does not intend the distinction between telic and deontic egalitarianism to provide a logically exhaustive map over egalitarian positions, but to sort typical egalitarians into two types, which draws attention to a number salient differences between the views of some prominent egalitarians. For this purpose, the definitions of the two forms of egalitarianism may well tie together several and logically independent distinctions. Section 5.3 argues, first, that these distinctions are largely neutral with respect to scope. Sections 5.4 to 5.6 show that while some, but not all, forms of telic egalitarianism are vulnerable to the levelling down objection, comparable forms of deontic egalitarianism are vulnerable to an analogous objection. Hence, we cannot choose between deontic and telic egalitarianism on the basis of the levelling down objection or on the basis of considerations about scope. Section 5.7 explores possible luck egalitarian replies to the levelling down objection. My main claims in this chapter are that deontic egalitarianism is vulnerable to an objection quite similar to the levelling down objection if telic egalitarianism is, and that luck egalitarianism is undefeated by the levelling down objection.

5.2. Some distinctions

With an important qualification, to be introduced shortly, Parfit's telic egalitarians claim that:

(1) It is in itself bad if some people are worse off than others. (1998: 4)

Except for the missing bit on bad luck, this claim is close to the core luck egalitarianism claim introduced in Section 1.2. It is less clear what deontic egalitarians claim (cf. O'Neill 2008), but their position is inconsistent with telic egalitarianism. For deontic egalitarians hold that 'it is not in itself bad if some people are worse off than others' (Parfit 1998: 6). While it is often unjust, according to deontic egalitarians, that some people are worse off than others, '[their] objection is not really to the inequality itself. What is unjust, and therefore bad, is not strictly the state of affairs, but the way in which it was produced' (Parfit 1995: 9).

While these claims separate deontic from telic egalitarians, they do not separate deontic egalitarians from non-egalitarians. Like deontic egalitarians, Nozick does not think that inequality is in itself bad. Moreover, he finds certain ways in which inequality may arise unjust, because these involve violations of people's property rights. Yet, he is not in any helpful sense a deontic egalitarian. Accordingly, I take it that deontic egalitarians differ from non-egalitarians in virtue of the distinctive account they give of what makes the genesis of a particular outcome objectionable, e.g. that it involves not treating people with equal respect or concern where that involves something else than simply respecting people's Nozickean entitlements. Unfortunately, Parfit is silent on what such an account must look like.

When Parfit says that deontic egalitarians object 'to the way in which [inequality] was produced', there are two ways to understand this claim. On one reading, it is necessary for the genesis' being unjust in a way deontic egalitarians care about that it led to inequality. Hence, deontic egalitarians do not object to an otherwise comparable genesis of an outcome that for some reason resulted in equality. Suppose that I divide some good between two persons on the basis of my throwing of some deliberately skewed dice intending to favour one of them. On the present reading, if this leads to inequality, then the outcome has been produced in an unjust way. However, if this leads to an equal division, because I improbably end up throwing the same dice for both of the two persons involved, then the genesis of the outcome was not unjust. Call this view *genesis-and-outcome-focused deontic egalitarianism*:

(2) The genesis of an outcome is unjust when it is intrinsically unfair and results in inequality.

On the second reading, it is not necessary for the inequality-producing process' being unjust that it led to inequality. Hence, if an otherwise comparable process led to equality, then this process would be unjust as well and the equal state of affairs would be bad in that the way in which it was produced was unjust. Call this view *pure genesis-focused deontic egalitarianism*:

(3) The genesis of an outcome is unjust when it is intrinsically unfair whether it results in equality or inequality.

Since Parfit writes that it is *often* unjust that some are worse off than others, it is reasonable to understand him as implying that, according to deontic egalitarians, it is *sometimes* not unjust that some are worse off than others. Accordingly, we might take it that on pure genesis-focused deontic egalitarianism, an equal outcome does not imply a just genesis and an unequal outcome does not imply an unjust genesis.

There is logical space for a third deontic position. According to it, certain outcomes are unjust not because they have been brought about in a way that is unjust, nor because the unequal outcome is in itself unjust, but for some other reason. First, at one point Parfit describes deontic egalitarianism as the view that 'we should aim for equality, not to make the outcome better, but for some other moral reason. We may believe, for example, that people have rights to equal shares' (Parfit 1995: 4). This example of a deontic position clearly is outcome-focused: the content of the right is not a right to be treated in a certain way, but a right to a certain outcome. Second, an outcome may be unjust because it matches people's offensive preferences. By way of illustration, suppose that men are much better off than women, that all men desire and value that women are worse off, but that the reason that men are better off has nothing to do with this. Some might say that in this case the inequality is not in itself bad, nor need it have been produced in a way that is unjust. It is unjust because there is a propositional match between men's unjust desires and values and the inequality. We have a reason to eliminate this inequality, if we can, that we would not have had, had men not had such sexist desires. This view would surely qualify as egalitarian. Yet, it does not qualify as telic egalitarianism since it does not imply that inequality is in itself bad. Nor does it qualify as deontic egalitarianism since it does not object to the genesis of the outcome. Let us nevertheless call views such as the ones sketched here *outcome-focused deontic egalitarianism*:

> (4) It is bad if some people are worse off than others provided this inequality violates some people's right to an equal share or matches some people's offensive preferences.

By way of illustration of this view, consider the following: In a discussion of racially discriminatory laws Dworkin rejects these because:

> it is unacceptable to count prejudice as among the interests or preferences government should seek to satisfy ... We concede that laws having exactly the same economic results might be justified in different circumstances. Suppose there were no racial prejudice, but it just fell out that laws whose effect was especially disadvantageous to blacks benefited the community as a whole. These laws would then be no more unjust than laws that cause special disadvantage to foreign car importers or Americans living abroad, but benefit the community as a whole. (1985: 66)

It is testimony to the intuitive appeal of the deontic view entertained here that Dworkin makes his point by imagining a situation where there is no racial prejudice, rather than one in which there is racial prejudice but everyone correctly believes that it played no causal role in the enactment of the law.

The distinction between genesis-and-outcome, pure genesis, and outcome-focused can also be applied to telic egalitarianism. It is clear that there is such a view as *pure outcome-focused telic egalitarianism*. (1) states such a view. However, Parfit also writes: 'We might add [to (1)], "through no fault or choice of theirs"' (1998: 3 n.5). Egalitarians who add this or some such qualification – as luck egalitarians do – care about, but do not only care about, outcomes. Like deontic egalitarians, they – as friends of the core luck egalitarian claim from Section 1.2 – care about the way in which unequal outcomes are brought about, e.g. whether someone is worse off now as a result of what he or she chose in the past. Some egalitarians prefer to state their view as a matter of not whether the worse-off are worse off through no choice or fault of their own, but as a matter of whether they are worse off through no responsibility of their own. As we saw in Chapter 3, there are various ways of specifying the luckist element in luck egalitarianism and at least some of them – the exceptions being the hypothetical choice- and the desert-based accounts – imply that luck egalitarians care about how unequal outcomes came about. Hence, we should allow for *genesis-and-outcome-focused telic egalitarianism*.

If we allow that past choices and faults can be relevant to whether an unequal state of affairs is bad, presumably there could be other historical factors that influence the badness of inequality. For instance, inequality that results from what human agents did or failed to prevent from happening in the past may be thought worse than an inequality that is the result of natural causes. Given this, there seems logical space for a pure genesis-focused telic egalitarianism, i.e. the view that it is in itself bad that an outcome, whether unequal or not, is brought about in a certain way. Call such a view *pure genesis-focused telic egalitarianism*.

So far I have distinguished between three loci of evaluations – outcomes, geneses, and a combination thereof – and between whether these are evaluated in terms of injustice or badness. I have argued that even if telic egalitarians are concerned with badness and deontic egalitarians are concerned with injustice, both of them can adopt each of these three focuses. Deontic egalitarians are not restricted to care about geneses and telic egalitarians are not restricted to care about outcomes.

Some might challenge the use of the distinction between justice and badness to distinguish between telic and deontic egalitarians. After all, to say that something is unjust is to say that it is in one way bad and this is what telic egalitarians say.

In response, it might be conceded that nothing substantial hangs on whether we say that something is bad or whether it is unjust. We might then decide to reserve the label 'deontic egalitarians' for those egalitarians whose focus is exclusively on geneses and use 'telic egalitarians' to refer to those egalitarians whose evaluative focus is also on outcomes or geneses-and-outcomes.

Another, and in my view more attractive, response consists in saying that justice concerns a particular way in which outcomes or geneses of outcomes can be bad, namely one that essentially involves agency or representations (cf. Parfit 1998: 7 n.11). On this account, deontic as well as telic egalitarians may say, for example, that unequal outcomes are bad. However, they will give different accounts of what makes the unequal outcome bad. Hence, we might then say that telic egalitarians are those who think outcomes or geneses can be in themselves bad even if they do not involve agency or representations, while deontic egalitarians are those who affirm this necessary condition for badness. However, telic as well as deontic egalitarians can adopt each of the three loci that I have distinguished between.

A third response which may allow us to distinguish genesis-and-outcome-focused telic egalitarianism from genesis-and-outcome-focused deontic egalitarianism is to say that according to the former view, it is the unequal state of affairs that is non-instrumentally bad provided that it has a certain genesis, while according to the latter view, it is the genesis which is unjust and, thus, bad provided that it results in an unequal outcome. I leave open here whether this is more than a mere verbal difference. Note that even if it is, the two views are extensionally equivalent in the sense that for any genesis-and-outcome-focused telic egalitarian view there is a comparable genesis-and-outcome-focused deontic view that will judge any genesis-cum-outcome unjust, if, and only if, it is bad on the telic view. In any case, this particularistic interpretation does not allow us to distinguish outcome-focused or genesis-focused telic views from outcome-focused or genesis-focused views. Accordingly, I shall ignore it henceforth.

Whether we evaluate in terms of badness or injustice, or whether we are outcome- or genesis-focused egalitarians, we may differ on whether the badness or injustice of inequality or unequal treatment is simply a matter of what actually happens, or whether it is also a matter of what could have happened. *Actuality-focused egalitarians* think that what could have happened is irrelevant, whereas *alternatives-focused egalitarians* think that this is relevant.

In saying that deontic egalitarians may hold an actuality-focused view, I understand the view differently from how one passage suggests Parfit understands it. Quoting Rawls, he writes that the kind of case that most clearly separates deontic from telic egalitarians is that 'in which some inequality cannot be avoided. For deontic Egalitarians, if nothing can be done, there can be no injustice' (Parfit 1998: 7) and, hence, there is no deontic egalitarian objection to the inequality-producing process. I am reluctant, however, to read this passage as implying that on Parfit's view deontic egalitarians have no objections to inequalities that result from the unavoidable and inequality-producing exercise of agency, which may or may not be rare, but which surely is possible. First, the passage from Rawls, to which Parfit refers, as well the example involving inequalities in natural talents, which he uses to illustrate his point, both involve unavoidable inequalities that do not result from the exercise of agency. The Rawls passage concerns the inalterability of the fact that while present generations can do something for future generations, future generations cannot do anything for past generations. Rawls continues: 'What is just or unjust is how institutions deal with natural limitations and the way they are set up to take advantage of historical possibilities' (Rawls 1971: 291). The pertinent fact about intergenerational relations is not only unavoidable, it is also something that does not result from the exercise of agency. Hence, it leaves open that did the fact result from the unalterable exercise of agency, Rawls might consider the question of justice relevant.

Second, consider a case where a sexist employer wholeheartedly discriminates against a female applicant, thereby making her worse off. Surely, the employer treats her unjustly. The discriminatory treatment, however, was unavoidable in the sense that had the employer been inclined not to discriminate, someone or something would have intervened and made him do what he in fact did. Some might think that in order to tell whether the discriminatory treatment was unjust we do not need to know whether the counterfactual intervener could have been absent. Yet, their objection need not be to the resulting inequality in itself. So if they are not deontic egalitarians, we need to introduce a third kind of egalitarians. Hence, given the nature of the present sort of enquiry, it is better to untie the distinction between avoidable and unavoidable inequalities from the distinction between deontic and telic egalitarianism. In saying this, I assume that the issue is whether deontic egalitarians care about unavoidable as well as avoidable inequalities. Hence, if deontic egalitarians care about both, then symmetry between deontic and telic egalitarians is established, i.e. there is no real issue as to whether telic, or for that matter deontic, egalitarians care about unavoidable inequalities only.

Alternatives-focused egalitarians may differ on when a state of affairs is an alternative and on which alternatives matter. With regard to the latter issue, alternatives-focused telic egalitarians may hold that if there are no alternative distributions, where those who are worse off in the alternative are better off than those who are actually worse off, it is not bad that they are worse off. Similarly, alternatives-focused deontic egalitarians may claim that if there are no alternative ways of treating those who suffer unequal treatment – but, for perverse reasons, may end up better off – then their being treated unequally is not unfair. These, however, are not the only positions available to alternatives-focused egalitarians. For instance, they may think that what matters is whether there are alternatives available where those who are actually worse off are worse off or alternatives where those who are better off are better off to a lesser degree than those who are worse off, etc.

With regard to when a state of affairs is an alternative, one issue is whether we should adopt a tracing approach to alternatives. On this approach it might be that although we cannot now act differently such that worse-off people become better off, distributions in which the worse-off are better off is still in the relevant sense a feasible alternative. This is so, if in the past people might have acted differently such that either we could now have made the worse-off better off or the worse-off would have been better off. On a *global tracing approach* something is an alternative, if the world history from the dawn of humankind could have taken a course such that this alternative would have been realized. On a *local tracing approach* something is an alternative, if it could have been realized holding varying past stretches of the world history of humanity constant.

Another issue is whether something is an alternative if it could have been realized had either someone or everyone acted differently or if something is an alternative only if it could have been realized given that some, but not all, e.g. people living within a certain community but not people outside, had acted differently. Call the former view the *global agency approach* and the latter less inclusive view of alternatives, the *local agency approach*. If we adopt the global approach in both dimensions, then inequalities that we have brought about are likely to be inequalities to which, barring fundamental doubts about determinism and the ability to act otherwise, alternative and more equal distributions exist. However, it is still conceptually possible, although perhaps rare, for a certain inequality that has been created by human beings to be one that human beings could not have avoided creating.

To conclude: deontic egalitarians differ from telic egalitarians in that they think that outcomes or geneses of outcomes can be bad only when they involve agency or representations. Deontic and telic egalitarians do not differ in respect of whether they adopt a genesis- or an outcome-focus or whether they adopt an alternatives- or an actuality-focus. Hence, it is better to keep these three distinctions – to wit, outcome/genesis, agency or representations/neither, and alternatives/actuality – separate. I now turn to the issue of what significance the distinction so construed has as well as to how the two latter dimensions, which as we saw were sown into Parfit's distinction between telic and deontic egalitarianism, relate to the issues of scope and levelling down.

5.3. Telic versus deontic and the scope of equality

There are several dimensions in which one may distinguish between narrow and broad-scoped egalitarianism, e.g. time, space, states involving different people, and different kinds of individuals. I explore these scope issues in Chapter 6. Here I focus on a particular scope issue in relation to the distinction between telic and deontic egalitarians.

Call a view according to which equality has the broadest scope possible in all dimensions *unrestricted scope egalitarianism*. Call all other forms of egalitarianism *restricted scope egalitarianism*. On a telic version of the former view, it is bad if two individuals are unequally well off whether they live at different times, in different communities, or belong to different species, e.g. because one is a contemporary, happy fellow citizen whereas the other is a dolphin suffering constant pain at 400 BC (Parfit 1998: 9; cf. Temkin 1995: 72–3 n.2). As this example reminds us, all forms of egalitarianism that have actually been defended have restricted scope in one dimension or other.

Parfit holds that the choice between deontic and telic egalitarianism is likely to affect the scope of equality. Whereas deontic egalitarians may plausibly restrict the scope of equality to people living within the same community, telic egalitarians cannot plausibly do so. Moreover, since there are cases where such restrictions seem counterintuitive, considerations about scope favour telic egalitarianism. (In Section 6.3 I will discuss a case where, initially at least, unrestricted scope seems implausible and to some the example in the previous paragraph will be such an example.) In this section I will argue that neither claim is true. However, before assessing Parfit's two claims about scope in more detail, I want to make two general remarks.

First, suppose that we accept that the ideal of equality is sound and believe that it has the widest possible scope. Suppose, moreover, that injustice requires agency or representations. Finally, suppose that Europeans were better off than Americans prior to the crossing of the Atlantic. Ignoring complications about the global tracing approach, it follows that this inequality is bad but not unjust. Given this and given the construal of deontic and telic egalitarianism proposed in the previous section, this favours the telic over the deontic view, since only the telic view allows us to make this claim. However, this is due simply to the way in which we, and Parfit, have defined the two positions, i.e. that telic egalitarians *may* think that inequalities and geneses of outcomes not reflecting agency or unjust representations are bad, whereas deontic egalitarians deny this. If our definition allowed deontic egalitarians to hold that, say, inequality, in addition to being unjust when involving agency and representations, *may* be bad even when not involving any of these and said that telic egalitarians deny that such inequalities are unjust, then examples of bad inequalities between communities that are not aware of each other's existence have no tendency to favour telic over deontic egalitarianism as such. However, such examples might show that impure deontic positions are preferable to pure deontic positions.

Second, if we build into the distinction that telic egalitarians are concerned with outcomes and deontic egalitarians are concerned with the way in which outcomes are generated, as some of Parfit's formulations suggest, we cannot helpfully say that telic egalitarianism has a broader, as opposed to different, scope than deontic egalitarianism. Accordingly, we must make sure that there are no ways in which an outcome, possibly an equal one, may be generated in ways that involve unjust, unequal treatment, before we conclude that cases such as the divided unequal world is a scope-related, all-things-considered good reason to favour telic over deontic egalitarianism. For if the former sort of cases exist, e.g. wrongful discrimination that unpredictably leads to equality, then these cases counterbalance whatever *pro tanto* reason cases such as the divided unequal world gives us to be telic egalitarians. Considerations about scope, then, would not provide us with a reason to favour pure telic over pure deontic egalitarianism. Rather, they would favour combining the two views.

Consider now Parfit's specific claims concerning the natural scope of telic and deontic egalitarianism. Consider first the claim that telic egalitarianism is most plausibly seen as having the broadest possible scope. Parfit writes: 'If we believe that inequality is in itself bad, we may think it bad whoever the people are between whom it holds' (1998: 8). Accordingly, he thinks that it would be odd for telic egalitarians to hold that inequality is bad only when it obtains between people in different communities: 'If it is in itself bad if some people are worse off than others, why should it matter where or when these people live?' (Parfit 1995: 7).

Unfortunately, this question has force only for people attracted to pure outcome-focused telic egalitarianism. Genesis-and-outcome-focused telic egalitarians do not think that inequality is in itself bad. Consider luck egalitarians who endorse the responsibility clause mentioned by Parfit. They think that an unequal state of affairs is bad only if the worse-off are not worse off through their own fault or choice and this implies that inequalities with certain geneses are not in themselves bad. Presumably, telic luck egalitarians may think that the genesis of a state of inequality may matter in other ways as well. For instance, they may say:

(5) It is in itself bad if some people are worse off than others provided that (i) the worse-off are so through no fault or choice of theirs and (ii) the better-off contributed causally to making or allowing these people to be worse off.

Both (i) and (ii) will in practice imply derivative restrictions in scope, by which I mean restrictions on which inequalities matter from an egalitarian point of view that derive from the genesis of the inequalities. Suppose that prior to the crossing of the Atlantic people in America were worse off than people living in Europe through a fault of their own. In that case this would not in itself be bad, because the unequal state of affairs fails to satisfy either of the two requirements concerning geneses.

It might be replied that from the fact that genesis-and-outcome-focused egalitarians endorse restrictions in scope that derive from conditions pertaining to the genesis of unequal states, it does not follow that they must accept restrictions in scope not derived from a concern with the proper genesis. This is indeed true. But note, first, that the focus of almost all egalitarians would suggest that either they think that the scope of equality is restricted to human beings – Parfit uses the term 'people' – or that while they think that human beings fall within the scope of equality they have no view on whether non-human animals fall within that scope as well. Hence, almost all egalitarians that Parfit would classify as telic egalitarians do, as a matter of fact, accept non-derived restrictions in scope. This reminds us that Parfit's appeal to the fact that telic egalitarians think that inequality is in itself bad can do no work. For even if we say that, we still need to say whom we think of when we say that it is bad if some are worse off than others. Moreover, if it could do real work here, presumably it would follow that telic egalitarians cannot restrict the scope of equality to people who are not responsible for being worse off. If inequality is bad in itself, why should it matter whether the worse-off are responsible for so being?

This leaves us with Parfit's claim that it seems a 'strange coincidence' if inequality is bad only if it obtains between members of the same community (1995: 7). However, in itself this hardly provides a reason for rejecting the view, although it may point to the fact that its subscribers can offer no reason to accept it. I conclude that while there is a form of telic egalitarianism which is unrestricted in scope, it has not been shown to be the only reasonable telic view.

Consider next the plausible scope of deontic egalitarianism. Deontic egalitarians object to inequalities with a certain history or to geneses of a certain sort whether they lead to inequalities or not. It is natural to assume the history of a certain outcome can be objectionable, only if it involves some human agent conducting himself in an objectionable manner. As Parfit writes: on the deontic view, inequality is unjust and 'injustice is a special kind of badness, one that necessarily involves wrong-doing ... Deontic Egalitarians are concerned only with what we ought to do' (Parfit 1998: 7; see also McKerlie 1996: 280–1). Note that I can be concerned with what we ought to do from the point of view of equality and yet not be concerned with the genesis of the present state of affairs. For instance, I may think that we should always act in such a way that we maximize future equality. On that view, it is irrelevant how it came about that some are worse off than others. Accordingly, the concern for how a certain state of affairs was (or will be) produced is different from a concern for what we ought to do (or ought to have done).

So far I have largely followed Parfit in assuming that injustice necessarily involves wrong-doing on the deontic egalitarian view. I insert the qualification 'largely', because I allowed for injustice due to a propositional match between unjust desires and values, on the one hand, and an outcome or genesis on the other. It is, however, logically possible and not implausible, as I shall now argue, to think that a certain genesis is unjust even if it involves no wrong-doing, i.e. no people acting in a way that they ought not to act.

On many people's view, including Parfit's, it is possible for an outcome to be unjust or unfair, even if it does not result from, nor could have been prevented by, the exercise of agency (Parfit 1998: 7 n.11). But if so, why could not a genesis of a certain outcome be unjust even if it did not result from agency, nor was under the control of agency?

In reply, it might be conceded that this is possible albeit not plausible. However, this is too hasty assuming that natural injustice in outcomes is possible. Suppose two persons, each living on a deserted island, are busy tending to their scarce crops. For strange reasons the occurrence of hurricanes on the islands is influenced by two naturally formed, indeterministic quantum-mechanic devices, the effects of which are magnified such that there is a great probability of hurricanes sweeping the first person's island and a slight probability of hurricanes sweeping the second person's island. Just prior to harvest time a hurricane destroys the first person's crops. However, it also washes ashore several barrels of corn – an event that, even given the occurrence of a hurricane, is very improbable – thereby compensating the loss caused by the storm. Might we not say here that although there is no natural injustice in outcome, the genesis of the outcome is naturally unjust, i.e. that it was naturally unjust that the two persons ended up equally well off through a series of improbable events and that one of them had so much better prospects than the other?

We might deny this, because we think justice concerns outcomes only: because no agency, whether human or non-human, was involved in the genesis of the outcome; or because we think that what the example shows is simply that a particular kind of outcome is bad, i.e. inequalities in prospects. The first objection is beside the point, because the present issue is whether, on the assumption that genesis matters, we can meaningfully speak of natural injustice in the genesis of an outcome.

The second objection is also beside the point, because it does not establish a difference between deontic and telic egalitarianism. If injustice requires agency, then there can be natural injustice neither in outcome, nor in genesis, and for present purposes we have already granted natural injustice in outcomes.

In response to the third objection, we might say that although this is one interpretation of the example, it is also possible to insist that what matters is how well off people actually end up being and the justice of the way in which their levels of well-being are produced.

In support of these replies consider that, according to Temkin, a state of affairs is naturally unjust if it is such that 'if someone *had* deliberately brought it about she would have been perpetrating an injustice' (1995: 76). If one accepts this view about the injustice of outcomes, then it is hard to see how one could deny that a genesis of an outcome, even an equal one, could not be unjust, too. Surely, if someone had deliberately made the fate of the two individuals in my previous example depend on the imagined indeterministic devices, this would be seen by many as unjust even if no unequal outcome resulted.

Suppose that, despite what has been said so far, we reject natural injustice in geneses despite accepting the possibility of natural injustice in outcomes. In that case, a genesis can be unjust only if it somehow involves agency or representations. On a broad deontic account, any genesis that results from or could have been relevantly different through the exercise of agency may be unjust. Thomas Nagel seems to adopt this position when he denies that there is any morally relevant distinction between inequalities that the state produces and inequalities the state merely allows, i.e. the state is negatively responsible for inequalities (Nagel 1991: 84, 99–102, 107–8). On a narrow deontic account, only geneses that result in a certain way from or could have been relevantly different through a particular kind of exercise of agency, e.g. the inequality was intended and not merely foreseen or brought about and not merely allowed to arise, may be unjust. It may be the case that any inequality that is bad on a telic account and that is avoidable is unjust on a broad deontic account. Hence, whenever an unequal outcome is bad on a telic account and not unjust on the deontic account, then the inequality is unavoidable, in which case the difference between the two positions is merely nominal in the sense that it never gives rise to conflicting recommendations. At least, this is so on the assumption that if something is bad, then there is a reason to avoid it (if one can).

Parfit writes that deontic egalitarianism may connect with the traditional deontological doctrines of doing and allowing and the doctrine of the double effect: '[deontic egalitarianism] may cover only inequalities that result from acts, or only those that are intentionally produced' (1998: 8). Since Parfit writes that deontic egalitarianism *may* cover only such inequalities, this is not contrary to the view taken here. At least this is so, unless it is implied that telic egalitarians may not consider inequalities that are brought about rather than simply allowed to exist or inequalities that are countenanced intentionally rather than merely countenanced as a foreseen side-effect as worse. However, given that telic egalitarians endorse a responsibility clause, it is hard to see how they can simply dismiss that other facts about the way in which an unequal outcome was brought about may be relevant for its badness.

In conclusion, the distinction between deontic and telic egalitarianism is much more loosely connected with the choice of scope than is commonly assumed. First, it is not the case that whereas deontic egalitarians may plausibly restrict the scope of equality to people living within the same community, telic egalitarians cannot plausibly do so. Second, considerations of scope do not favour one view over the other. In the next section, I turn to the second issue in relation to which Parfit thinks it makes a difference whether one is a deontic or a telic egalitarian.

5.4. The levelling down objection

In recent years many have expressed scepticism about egalitarianism by appealing to the levelling down objection. Most assume that, unlike deontic egalitarianism, telic egalitarianism is vulnerable to the levelling down objection. In this section, I explain this objection. Section 5.5 challenges the view that all forms of telic egalitarianisms are vulnerable to the levelling down objection. Section 5.6 argues that at least some forms of deontic egalitarianism are vulnerable to the levelling down objection, if some forms of telic egalitarianism are. Together these claims imply that, unlike what is commonly assumed, telic and deontic egalitarianism are symmetrically positioned relative to levelling down objections. This makes it even more urgent for luck egalitarians to respond to the levelling down objection, so Section 5.7 surveys some of the main responses to the objection.

To see the force of the levelling down objection, suppose we can bring about either one of the following two alternative distributions:

E: Everyone at some level.
I: Some at this level. Others better off. (Parfit 2002: 111)

In I there is inequality, but this inequality is bad for no one, since everyone is at least as well off in I as in E. However, if one holds, as telic egalitarians do, that inequality is unjust in itself, at least when resulting from differential luck, then one seems committed to the view that I is worse than E in one respect at least, i.e. from the point of view of egalitarian justice.

Deontic egalitarians might respond to the levelling down objection by pointing out that their view does not commit them to any claims about which of the two outcomes is better. All they claim is that justice requires that people are treated equally and this in itself does not commit them to the view that I is in any respect worse than E.

While this reply seems cogent, it gets deontic egalitarians off the hook too easily. Are they not committed to saying that in bringing about I rather than E one does not treat people equally and, if so, is this implication not just as problematic as the telic egalitarians' assessment of I being bad in one respect? I return to this question in Section 5.6, but to see its force suppose we can bring about two variants of I: one where one half of the population is better off and another where the other half of the population is better off. Suppose we cannot choose between these two variants through a lottery device, but must simply decide which people we should make better off. Is it not plausible to say that deontic egalitarians are committed to the view that we do not treat the people whom we do not make better off equally and, thus, in one respect unjustly? And is this commitment not implausible given that the alternative to making some people better off is to make no one better off?

Return to telic egalitarians. They need not say that I is *all things considered* worse than E. It seems fanatical to hold that the goodness of outcomes is only determined by the degree of inequality they involve. Such a view would imply, for instance, that it is better if all of us suffer constant torture, but equally so, than if all of us live blissful lives though some of us are slightly better off than the others. Accordingly, telic egalitarians are pluralists about the goodness of outcome. They think that values other than equality bear on the value of outcome. For instance, they might think that it is better the more well-being an outcome contains. If so, they can say that while I is in one respect worse than E, it is all things considered, i.e. in view of the increase in welfare and inequality that it involves, better than E.

Hence, their view may not even indirectly support the claim that, all things considered, we ought to bring about E rather than I.

The present two-value view – equality as well as welfare are good-making features of an outcome – has the advantage that the more inequality we eliminate by levelling down, the more welfare we lose. Roughly, if there is a lot of inequality some will have a lot more well-being than others and, thus, levelling down will result in the loss of a lot of well-being. Hence, telic egalitarians can say with some plausibility that, in fact, there is no possible form of levelling down which, from their point of view, will result in an improvement of the outcome, all things considered.

There is an additional reason why telic egalitarians are not committed to the claim that we ought to bring about E rather than I. As telic egalitarians they might also subscribe to deontological constraints. Specifically, they might subscribe to a deontological constraint against making some people worse off, when that benefits no one. Hence, even if they thought that (2) was, all things considered, a better outcome than (1), they might still deny that we ought, all things considered, to bring about (2).

At this point one might ask why the levelling down objection is that, i.e. an objection, and not simply a straightforward mapping of some of the implications which telic egalitarians are obviously and self-consciously committed to in virtue of their view. There are at least two reasons why this is so.

First, many theorists who have thought of themselves as egalitarians have not thought through what their view implies in relation to levelling down situations (but see Section 5.7). Pointing out to them that equality implies a commitment to levelling down being in one respect good forces them to reconsider their views and ought in many cases to lead them to see that what they are really committed to is not egalitarianism but some other view. Parfit mentions Thomas Nagel as 'one writer who sometimes uses the language of equality, when he is really appealing to the Priority View [i.e. what I called prioritarianism in Section 1.7: KLR]' (Parfit 2002: 108). For instance, Nagel imagines a case where 'he has two children, one healthy and happy, the other suffering from a painful handicap. He could either move to a city where the second child could receive special treatment, or move to a suburb where the first child would flourish'

(Parfit 2002: 81). To make the case a test for equality Nagel supposes that:

> the gain to the first child of moving to the suburb is substantially greater than the gain to the second child of moving to the city … If one chose to move to the city, it would be an egalitarian decision. It is more urgent to benefit the second child, even though the benefit we can give him is less than the benefit we can give to the first child. (Parfit 2002: 81)

Parfit believes that Nagel's test case is flawed, because prioritarianism might give the same answer as egalitarianism (but see Otsuka and Voorhoeve 2009). Moreover, he conjectures that Nagel thinks that it would be just as urgent to benefit the handicapped child if he had no sibling and, thus, benefiting him would not reduce inequality. Indeed, Nagel seems to 'conflate equality' and prioritarianism when he writes: 'To defend equality as a good in itself, one would have to argue that improvements in the lot of people lower on the scale of well-being took priority over greater improvement to those higher on the scale' (Parfit 2002: 107). So Nagel, it seems, is one whom the levelling down objection can alert to the fact that, really, he does not accept egalitarianism, but prioritarianism. Presently, as a result of Parfit's writings on the levelling down objection most contributors to the debate about distributive justice are well aware of the objection. This makes it much less likely than it was when Parfit set out the objection that it will help anyone to see that what they are really committed to is prioritarianism, not egalitarianism.

Second, independently of our views about the value of equality many often appeal to a person-affecting view: 'if an outcome is worse for no one, it cannot be in any way worse' (Parfit 2002: 114). This view, Parfit suggests, might be defended by 'appeal to some view about the nature of morality, or moral reasoning' (Parfit 2002: 114). For instance, Parfit suggests a 'contractualist view about moral reasoning … may lead' to the person-affecting view. Here Parfit has in mind Thomas Scanlon (Parfit 2002: 114). However, it is unclear which line of reasoning Parfit has in mind here. Scanlon has famously suggested that 'an act is wrong if its performance under the circumstances would be disallowed by any set of principles for the general regulation of behaviour that no one could reasonably reject as a basis for informed, unforced general agreement' (Scanlon 1982: 153). One reason why it is not immediately clear how one could get from this contractualist formula to the person-affecting principle is that Scanlon's principle concerns the wrongness of acts, not the badness of outcome. However, if we assume an analogous principle regarding the badness of outcomes, presumably Parfit's idea would be that any principle regarding the value of outcomes that no one could reasonably reject implies that inequality is not in any way worse than levelling down. Presumably, those who would be worse off under equality could, given that their so being would benefit no one, reasonably reject principles which imply that inequality is in some way worse than levelling down.

An alternative way of supporting the person-affecting principle is by showing that it underlies some of our other moral commitments. Take, for instance, Nozick's use of the Wilt Chamberlain example in his critique of egalitarianism (Nozick 1974: 161–3; see also Section 8.2). Nozick asks his anti-libertarian opponent to choose an initial distribution which the opponent deems just. He supposes that the opponent finds an equal distribution of all (external) resources just. Nozick then imagines that, from this equal point of departure, a lot of people make a deal with Wilt Chamberlain – a gifted basketball player – that each of them will pay him a small amount of money to see him play basketball. Everyone is happy about the arrangement and yet a new and unequal distribution in Wilt Chamberlain's favour will result. However, since the initial distribution was assumed to be just and since what took us from the initial, just distribution to the new, unequal one was 'capitalist acts between consenting adults' (Nozick 1974: 163), Nozick thinks that no one can complain about the new and unequal distribution on grounds of injustice. It is plausible that at least part of the force of the example derives from something like the person-affecting principle, i.e. that part of why it may appear difficult to pattern-upsetting capitalist acts between consenting adults is that the resulting unequal state of affairs is worse for no one – indeed, it is better for everyone – than the initial equal one.

While the particular initial pattern selected in the Wilt Chamberlain example might give the impression that egalitarianism is vulnerable to the levelling down objection, because of its commitment to equality, it is important to see that the levelling down objection applies to a broader range of distributive views. Equality is a matter of a distributive relation between people and that views endorsing other distributive relations than equality are vulnerable to the levelling down objection as well. Consider a relational version of sufficientarianism according to which it is unjust if some people have less than half the average level of well-being (cf. Section 1.7). Unlike non-relational sufficientarianism, which is the version of sufficientarianism that is most common, this version holds that to determine whether someone has enough we have to know what others have. For present purposes the important point is that this version of sufficientarianism is no less vulnerable to the levelling down objection than egalitarianism is. To see this, suppose that Adam is at 200 and Beatrice is at 50. This situation is unjust according to the proposed view because Beatrice has less than 65.5, which is 50 per cent of the average. If, however, we were to level down by reducing Adam to 100, the outcome would in one respect be better from the point of view of relational sufficientarianism, since Beatrice would now have more than 50 per cent of the average level, i.e. 37.5. This suggests that the feature of egalitarianism that makes it vulnerable to the levelling down objection is that it is a view which ascribes moral significance to relations between individuals. Since there are other views that do the same, egalitarianism is not the only view which is vulnerable to the objection.

Unfortunately, the situation is not that simple. Non-relational views are vulnerable to the levelling down objection too. Take absolute sufficientarianism and suppose we have a choice between two outcomes. One involves a number of people living lives that are just better than good enough. The second outcome involves the same number of people living equally good lives but also some additional people, all of whom live lives that, although they are quite well worth living, fall slightly below the threshold level. According to standard non-comparative sufficientarianism (cf. Section 1.7) the latter outcome is in one respect worse than the former. However, there is no one for whom the latter outcome is worse. Hence, even non-relational sufficientarianism is vulnerable to the levelling down objection too. More generally, in order to be vulnerable to the levelling down objection a view need not be comparative across individuals. It seems that all it requires is that it ascribes positive moral significance to features other than individual well-being. Since many moral views do that, the levelling down objection is not a problem for egalitarianism in particular, it is a problem for a wide range of moral views. As we shall see in Section 5.7, this might to some degree undercut the force of the levelling down objection.

5.5. Telic egalitarianism and the levelling down objection

Telic egalitarians believe that, justice-wise, it is in itself bad if some are worse off than others. Does this imply that inequality is always bad according to telic egalitarians?

In an exploration of a possible egalitarian response to the levelling down objection, Andrew Mason points to the relevance of two different distinctions. The first distinction is between instrumental and non-instrumental value. Something has non-instrumental value if it has value for its own sake, whereas something has instrumental value if it has value as a means to something else. The second distinction is between intrinsic and extrinsic value: 'The intrinsic value of a thing is any value it possesses that is grounded entirely in its intrinsic properties, where its intrinsic properties are those which do not depend, even in part, on the existence or nature of something else' (Mason 2000: 247–8). These two distinctions diverge. Something may have non-instrumental value in virtue of its extrinsic properties. It might have non-instrumental value to have written the best poem ever, but being the best poem ever is an extrinsic property of the poem, since it depends on how it compares with other poems. When this distinction is clearly set out, it seems that although telic egalitarians say that inequality is in itself bad, what they really mean is that inequality is non-instrumentally bad (Parfit 1998: 5; cf. McKerlie 1996: 287–8; Temkin 1993: 248).

Mason exploits the difference between these two distinctions to propose two forms of telic egalitarianism that are immune to the levelling down objection. Although both of them hold inequality to be non-instrumentally bad, neither of them implies that it is in one way better to level down. According to the first form of what he calls conditional egalitarianism:

(6) Inequality is extrinsically and non-instrumentally bad provided that it harms some.

This position qualifies as egalitarian because it holds inequality to have non-instrumental disvalue. Moreover, it accommodates the levelling down objection because inequality has no disvalue on this view when no one is harmed by it and exactly this is the case when the only alternative to, say, half at 50 and half at 75 is everyone at 25.

Unlike me, Mason states conditional egalitarianism in terms of a claim about the value of equality and not in terms of a claim about the badness of inequality. Thus, the relevant counterpart to (6) is:

(6*) Equality is extrinsically and non-instrumentally good only when at least some people benefit from it.

It is reasonable to hold that equality is valuable only if no one is harmed by it rather than only if some benefit from it. For suppose there are two possible states of affairs. In both states people are equally well off and they are equally well off across these states. The two states differ in terms of properties that do not affect people's levels of well-being. Surely, egalitarians would want to say that these states of equality are valuable even if no one benefits from, nor is harmed by, equality.

To this form of conditional egalitarianism, Mason adds another form of telic egalitarianism, which appeals to a particularist conception of intrinsic value:

(7) Inequality is intrinsically and non-instrumentally bad provided that it harms some.

The positive counterpart to (7) is: equality is intrinsically and non-instrumentally good provided that it benefits at least some. The idea here is that the disvalue of inequality depends on the context. This is no different from (6). But unlike (6), defenders of (7) will not say that a state of inequality is disvaluable in virtue of the fact that people are unequally well off and that some are harmed by it. Instead, they will say that a state of inequality is bad in virtue of the fact that people are unequally well off. However, in their view inequality does not always possess intrinsic disvalue. It does so only when it harms someone.

The general idea here is that something may be necessary for something's being good or bad and yet not be something in virtue of which the latter is good or bad. Some, of course, would argue that the difference between saying that the fact that inequality harms some is something that enables inequality to be in itself productive of disvalue and saying that this fact together with the fact of inequality is productive of disvalue is merely verbal. Even if this is right, it remains a fact that a form of conditional egalitarianism is invulnerable to the levelling down objection.

It may seem odd that the disvalue of inequality is conditional. However, in reality, Mason's conditional egalitarianism differs from standard telic egalitarian views not in being conditional, but in virtue of the content of the condition invoked, i.e. that inequality harms some and not that the worse-off are not responsible for so being. I have several things to say about Mason's conditional forms of egalitarianism. First, I want to make a taxonomical observation. Conditional egalitarianism raises the question of where exactly to draw the line between egalitarian and non-egalitarian positions. Consider the following position:

> (8) Welfare is non-instrumentally good provided that people are equally well off. Nothing else is non-instrumentally good.

On the one hand, this seems an (implausibly) extreme egalitarian position. Nothing is good if people are unequally well off. On the other hand, this position does not claim that equality has non-instrumental value (or that inequality has non-instrumental disvalue). It is just that equality is a necessary condition of anything having non-instrumental value. In view of this, the fact that this position does not claim that equality has non-instrumental value is by no means a decisive argument for disqualifying it as egalitarian. Note also that this position is (extremely) vulnerable to the levelling down objection: if half is at 75, the other half at 74, then there is nothing good about this outcome. However, if we were to level down to 1, then not only would this state be in one respect better, presumably it would be all things considered better! Hence, if we refuse to call (8) an egalitarian position on the ground that it does not take inequality to be non-instrumentally bad, then we must concede that some telic, non-egalitarian positions are vulnerable to the levelling down objection. This is significant, because many are inclined to see vulnerability to the levelling down objection as a reliable test, if not a criterion, for a view's constituting telic egalitarianism.

Whereas Mason's line of argument suggests that it is not clear that egalitarians need even claim that equality has non-instrumental value, it is also not clear that one qualifies as an egalitarian simply because one accepts (6) or (7). Endorsing either of these positions is consistent with believing that inequality has intrinsic, non-instrumental value given a particular type of context. For instance, the view that inequality is intrinsically valuable provided that it matches people's differential, libertarian entitlements seems an anti-egalitarian view. Accordingly, I suppose that at least in some contexts it would be counterintuitive to call someone who endorses this view in addition to (6) or (7) an egalitarian. I say 'some contexts' because in some contexts it may not, e.g. a context in which people are differentially responsible. While conditional egalitarianism is an egalitarian *view*, holding an egalitarian view does not make *you* an egalitarian, for you may consistently with so doing hold an anti-egalitarian view. What is at stake here is not simply a matter of the well-known fact that egalitarians may be pluralists and subscribe to non-egalitarian values, but that inequality may be both non-instrumentally bad and non-instrumentally good given different features of the situation in which it obtains. In sum, Mason's considerations complicate considerably the business of distinguishing egalitarians from non-egalitarians at a theoretical level at least.

It might be replied to the claim that not all forms of telic egalitarianism are vulnerable to the levelling down objection that this point is, although true, rather insignificant, since those putative forms that are not are either utterly implausible for different reasons, or not really egalitarian views at all. While for the purpose of establishing my main claim, i.e. that there is no relevant asymmetry between telic and deontic egalitarianism as far as the levelling down objection is concerned, I could concede this point, I want to respond to it by addressing two reasons why one may be attracted to this reply.

First, suppose we have a state of inequality. There is an empirically possible alternative state of affairs in which people are equally well off and some are better off than they are in the actual state of affairs. In this case, the actual, unequal state of affairs is bad from the point of view of conditional egalitarianism. But now suppose that anti-egalitarians render the alternative state of affairs impossible. In that case, the actual and unequal state of affairs is no longer bad from the point of view of conditional egalitarianism. This is implausible. If egalitarians were to try to render the alternative state of equality possible again, it would seem reasonable for them to say that they do so in order to improve the situation from the point of view of equality. Suppose they can make the alternative state of equality possible without cooperation, but cannot make it actual without cooperation from some they know will not cooperate. Conditional egalitarianism implies that they should not render the equal state possible for in so doing they would make the world worse. Most will reject this implication. Whilst I concede that this implication is unattractive, conditional egalitarianism can accommodate it by adopting a suitable version of the tracing approach to the identification of alternatives. On such a version, the mere fact that we cannot realize a certain state of affairs now does not imply that it is not an alternative in the relevant sense, since it may be the case that we could have acted differently in the past such that this state of affairs would have been realized.

Second, it might be objected that while standard forms of telic egalitarianism are, indeed, forms of conditional egalitarianism due to the common responsibility clause and while the forms of telic egalitarianism that meet the levelling down objection are concerned with relativities, the latter cannot be defended in terms of the underlying rationale for egalitarianism, i.e. that it is unfair that some are worse off due to bad luck. Hence, when we consider the underlying rationale for conditional egalitarianism we see that it is not an egalitarian view after all (cf. McKerlie 1996: 288).

While I am sympathetic to this account of the underlying rationale for egalitarianism (cf. Section 2.7), it is not uncontroversial, and other views which are commonly regarded as egalitarian cannot be motivated by this rationale, e.g. that social inequalities are worse than natural ones. Hence, I do not think that appeals to underlying rationale are decisive in the present context (cf. the luck-neutralizing account of luck egalitarianism in Chapter 3). Moreover, appealing to underlying rationales in the present context seems inappropriate in any case. These are at a different level than the level at which we distinguish between forms of egalitarianism according to which inequality is non-instrumentally bad and those according to which it is not. Here I focus on this distinction and ask if, at this level, there is any relevant asymmetry between these two views as regards the levelling down objection.

I conclude that not all forms of telic egalitarianism are vulnerable to the levelling down objection and that those that are not cannot be immediately dismissed as extremely implausible versions of telic egalitarianism or as non-egalitarian views.

5.6. Deontic egalitarianism and the levelling down objection

I shall now argue that some, but not all, forms of deontic egalitarianism are vulnerable to an objection comparable to that of the levelling down objection. Consider, first, a deontic egalitarian position according to which it is unjust to treat people unequally, where that means treating one more favourably than another without there being any good reason for treating this person more favourably than the other. Suppose that I can give either Adam or Beatrice, but not both, 70 – the other will then get 25 – or alternatively that I can give both 10. Since I have no good reason to give Adam instead of Beatrice or Beatrice instead of Adam 70, I shall be treating them unequally if I go for the first option. The mere fact that I have a good reason to give one of them 70 does not imply that there is a good reason for me to give one rather than the other 70. Hence, I shall be acting unjustly on the proposed deontic view if I give one of them more than the other. However, was I instead to treat them equally, then both of them would end up worse off. This might prompt one to ask: how can it be unjust to treat people unequally, when treating them equally requires treating everyone worse and benefits no one in any respect? Arguably, this question has the same force as the similar one asked about the goodness of outcomes in situations involving levelling down.

One initial reaction to this deontic version of the levelling down objection is that most who think about the goodness of outcomes are inclined to accept the person-affecting principle discussed above or, as Larry Temkin has called it, the Slogan:

(9) If one outcome is worse than another in any respect, then it is worse for someone in some respect.

Yet many are inclined to think that the justice and wrongness of actions are not similarly constrained. Indeed, many see the goodness of outcomes to be explained in terms of benefits to people, see justice as a deontological constraint and, hence, accept that in some cases justice requires acting in a way that prevents us from bringing about the best outcome. Hence many would, one might think, reject the following parallel to the Slogan as having no comparable intuitive appeal:

(10) If an act or omission is *pro tanto* unjust or *pro tanto* wrong, then there is someone for whom it would have been better in some respect had this act or omission not taken place.

As Temkin notes, the Telic Slogan may be used against those deontic egalitarians who think that 'other things equal an outcome where one has acted wrongly will be worse than an outcome where one has acted rightly' (1993: 254 n.17). A similar consideration applies to those deontic egalitarians who think that equality produced through treating people equally is just and, thus, good. The Deontic Slogan may be used not only against these egalitarians, but also against those who deny that an outcome is bad in one respect, if someone has acted wrongly, or good if someone has acted justly.

To distinguish this slogan from the Slogan discussed by Temkin, I shall call the former slogan the Deontic Slogan. I now want to argue that the Deontic Slogan is no less attractive than the Slogan, i.e. the Telic Slogan. Since my aim is to defend this comparative thesis and not to defend the Deontic Slogan as such, my line of argument is not threatened by putative counterexamples to the Deontic Slogan, e.g. the view that it would be unjust to benefit sinners thereby making them better off than saints even if there is no one for whom not doing so would be better in any respect. Incidentally, Temkin appeals to proportional justice to raise an analogous objection to the Telic Slogan (1993: 262).

Temkin believes that the levelling objection is forceful. He believes that '[i]t is the Slogan that gives the [levelling down objection its] powerful rhetorical force'. While the Slogan along with the levelling down objection ultimately must be rejected in Temkin's view, he carefully shows how the Slogan is 'implicitly involved' in a number of influential arguments in moral philosophy (Temkin 1993: 249). However, of the seven examples he gives, six of them are best seen as implicitly involving the Deontic rather than the Telic Slogan. These examples are: (i) it would be 'wrong, not to' turn a non-Pareto optimal situation into one that is; (ii) *pace* some formulations of Rawls' difference principle, gains to the better-off might be 'permissible' even if they do not benefit the worse-off; (iii) Nozick's celebrated Wilt Chamberlain argument for why no one can 'complain on grounds of justice' against voluntary exchanges draws force from the assumption that there is no one for whom such exchanges are worse; (iv) on Locke's theory of appropriation one can justly acquire an unowned, external thing only when one does not worsen the situation of others; (v) Scanlon implies that rights can only be justified 'by appeal to the human interests their recognition promotes and protects'; and (vi) standard objections to rule-utilitarianism, virtue ethics, and deonto-logical theories often appeal to cases 'where no one benefits and some are harmed, or where some benefit and no one is harmed, if only one does or doesn't (a) follow the rule, (b) act virtuously, or (c) do one's duty' (Temkin 1993: 249–55). In all of these cases what is directly at stake is not the comparative goodness of different outcomes, but whether a piece of conduct that harms no one really can be said to be, e.g. impermissible, wrong, or to violate someone's rights. Hence, to the extent that some deeper principle underlying the views mentioned by Temkin constitutes our underlying reason for finding the levelling down objection forceful – and I certainly think that he does identify some crucial considerations in this respect – we should find the Deontic Slogan, thus, and the analogous levelling down objection to deontic egalitarianism at least as forceful as the Telic Slogan and the levelling down objection to telic egalitarianism.

While this is not a compelling argument in favour of the equivalence of the Telic and the Deontic Slogan, it is striking that Temkin's discussion of the Slogan offers no reason to think that while the Slogan with regard to the goodness of outcomes is intuitively very attractive, no such thing can be said for a comparable Slogan with regard to the rightness or justice of actions. If anything, it is the reverse. And since this Slogan commits us to an objection to Deontic egalitarianism, which is comparable to the levelling down objection to telic egalitarianism, it suggests that telic and deontic egalitarianism are symmetrically vulnerable to considerations about levelling down.

There is a further reason why the Deontic Slogan may actually appear in Temkin's reasoning. Suppose we have a choice between two states, A and A+. In A everyone is at 100. In A+ twice as many people exist, half of them those that would otherwise exist in A. Suppose, moreover, that the former would still be at 100 in A+, while the latter would be at 50. Temkin seems to think that the inequality in A+ is objectionable although A+ would not, all things considered, be worse than A and that this supports telic egalitarianism. This is so, because the worse-off people cannot claim to have been treated unjustly by being caused to exist, when the alternative for them would be not to exist at all (Temkin 1993: 253–4 n.15).

In response to this, some might simply say that Temkin's examples are misleading. They might insist that treating people unequally when the alternative is to treat everyone worse is not unjust and for that reason deontic egalitarians do not object to unequal treatment in such cases. Deontic egalitarians object to unequal treatment when and only insofar as this involves unjust treatment.

This response is flawed. First, while deontic egalitarians might say that treating people unequally is unjust only when treating them equally does not harm everyone, this establishes no asymmetry between telic and deontic egalitarianism. This position would simply represent the deontic counterpart to the forms of conditional telic egalitarianism discussed in Section 5.4.

Second, if we disregard conditional telic egalitarianism and allow deontic egalitarians to endorse unequal treatment in some cases and do not allow telic egalitarians to endorse inequality in comparable ones, we compare logically heterogeneous positions. While we insist that telic egalitarians are concerned with relativities, we allow that deontic egalitarians, to a certain extent, are not. But then the resulting asymmetry of telic and deontic egalitarianism with regard to levelling down is due not to the structural differences between telic and deontic egalitarianism, but to certain idiosyncratic additional clauses built into our definition of these two positions, as I shall now explain more fully.

We need to distinguish between egalitarian and non-egalitarian accounts of just treatment. On the one extreme, accounts that say that treating people justly (and, for that matter, equally) is to respect their Nozickean entitlements or to maximize the sum of welfare are clearly non-egalitarian accounts (Kymlicka 2002: 37–45, 121–7). On the other extreme, an account that says that treating people justly is to make sure that they are equally well off is clearly an egalitarian account.

In between these two extremes are views such as the view that treating people equally is to act in such a way that people have equal prospects for well-being or, if doing so implies giving no one better prospects, to act in such a way that the worse-off have prospects for well-being that are as good as possible. A similar intermediate view, modelled on the prioritarianism, says that to treat people equally is to maximize (or aim at maximizing) the weighted sum of individual prospects where the weighting is such that increases in prospects at lower levels counts for more. We might call such intermediate views forms of deontic egalitarianism just as the telic version of the priority view is often called an egalitarian position. Suppose we do the former and that we define telic egalitarianism restrictively such that, e.g. the priority view is not an egalitarian view. In that case it is hardly very interesting to conclude that whereas telic egalitarianism is vulnerable to the levelling down objection, deontic egalitarianism is not vulnerable to any comparable challenge. This asymmetry is not due to the fact that, say, the focus of deontic egalitarians is on unjust geneses and not on the badness of unequal outcomes, but due to the fact that to count as a telic egalitarian you must be concerned with relativities, whereas to qualify as a deontic egalitarian you need not.

A similar reply is available to counter those who would like to press the objection that Dworkin distinguishes between treating people as equals and treating them equally, where, in his view, none implies the other and the former is what he thinks governments are obligated to do (Dworkin 1986: 190). While Dworkin's requirement is in one way concerned with relativities, clearly it is so in a way that is different from standard telic views. For one thing, being treated as unequals is a moralized notion – we need to know how it is befitting for equals and unequals to be treated to tell if some are not treated as equals – where being unequally well off in the way that telic egalitarians are concerned with is not. A telic view, which is comparable to Dworkin's, says that it is bad if through no choice or fault of their own some people have less than what is befitting given that all are equals. Presumably, if Dworkin can avoid the deontic levelling down objection by saying that giving some more when the only alternative is to leave some worse off and no one better off is compatible with treating these people as equals, then so could the proposed telic view avoid the corresponding telic levelling down objection.

Third, at least some deontic egalitarians subscribe to views that would suggest that they are vulnerable to the deontic version of the levelling down objection. Consider for instance Dworkin's diachronic envy test. According to Dworkin, a test of whether a certain distribution has treated everyone with equal respect and concern is whether anyone prefers anyone else's bundle of resources, because he lacks unchosen endowments that the other person has (Veen 2002: 55–67). If, in my deontic levelling down objection, I choose to give Cecil the prospect of gaining 70 rather than giving everyone 10, then Dorothy may reasonably envy Cecil's prospects for these are indisputably better. Hence, insofar as the diachronic envy test is seen as a reliable indicator about the nature of Dworkin's view about what constitutes equal treatment, then at least one paradigmatic deontic egalitarian has a view that is vulnerable to the deontic levelling down objection.

In a reply to Robert van der Veen, Dworkin insists that treating people with equal concern is best understood as implying equality of resources *ex ante* (Dworkin 2002: 120–5). This suggests a rejection on Dworkin's part of the diachronic envy test. However, in my view this test does form part of his earlier view at least (see Dworkin 2000: 85, 89, 91). Also, other deontic egalitarians have endorsed the diachronic envy test (see Kymlicka 2002: 81).

What lurks in the background of the present discussion is probably the thought that the deontic concern for equality takes the form of a deontological side-constraint, e.g. that we cannot treat people unequally even if that brings about a better outcome. However, nothing in the discussion above implies that it must take this form. Deontic egalitarians may be consequentialists. They may think that it is bad from an agent-neutral point of view if persons are treated unjustly and think that we should maximize the sum of moral value, which in some cases may require treating someone unjustly to prevent more cases of people being treated unjustly.

Moreover, telic egalitarianism is simply a claim about what is in itself bad. As such it is consistent with consequentialist as well as deontological moral views on what one ought to do. For instance, one could be a telic egalitarian and hold that it is impermissible for us to bring about an unequal outcome even if it is the best outcome. Such a deontological constraint would operate not on the genesis of the unequal outcome, but on the outcome in itself.

This is not to deny that it might be useful to draw a distinction between deontological and consequentialist egalitarians (in the standard sense). Deontological egalitarians, on this view, think that there is at least one moral restriction on our conduct such that there could be circumstances under which bringing about the best outcome (-cum-genesis) would be morally impermissible, because it would require treating someone in a way that violates egalitarian justice. Moreover, this constraint might be agent-relative, e.g. it would forbid members of a given society from bringing about the best outcome because doing so requires their not treating someone unequally. But it could also be agent-neutral, e.g. because it forbids all of us from treating someone unequally or allowing someone to be treated unequally even if doing so would bring about a better outcome. Consequentialist egalitarians think that inequality is in itself bad or that it is bad if people are treated unjustly and that we should maximize overall moral value. Since it would be implausible to claim that only equality has intrinsic value, they would have to admit that in some cases bringing about the best outcome would require bringing about an unequal outcome or treating someone unjustly. 'Teleology', unlike 'consequentialism', is not taken to imply an agent-neutral ranking of states of affairs. But if teleological egalitarians think that inequality is in itself bad, then inequality is bad for anyone and for everyone there is a reason to eliminate it.

While I have not shown that it might not turn out, say, that deontic egalitarians are better equipped, at the end of the day, to meet the deontic levelling down objection than are telic egalitarians vis-à-vis the telic levelling down objection, at least I have shown that there is a prima facie case to be made for symmetry in this respect. Not only do the examples invoked by Temkin in favour of the Telic Slogan in fact better support the Deontic Slogan, the assumption that deontic egalitarians are invulnerable to the levelling down objection may stem from irrelevant features, e.g. that we stipulate that telic egalitarians necessarily are concerned with relativities and make no similar stipulation in the case of deontic egalitarians. Hence I conclude that insofar as we want to be either deontic or telic egalitarians (and cannot be both), we cannot base that choice on considerations of scope or levelling down. This makes it even more urgent for egalitarians to respond to the levelling down objection.

5.7. Egalitarian responses

So does the levelling down objection amount to a knockdown argument against egalitarianism whether telic or deontic? I do not think so. Egalitarians have responded in various ways to the objections and the force of these responses, when considered together, seems sufficient to deny that we must reject the value of equality.

First, John Broome (1991: 165) has suggested that inequality is bad in one respect for the worse-off people in levelling down situations, i.e. it is bad in that they suffer unjust inequality and this badness detracts from what Broome calls the personal goodness of this individual. Now, insofar as this is bad for the worse-off people it is bad in a special way. To see this, suppose that Adam is worse off than Beatrice. We can either level down thereby benefiting Adam in Broome's justice-related way, i.e. by making it the case that he does not suffer unjust inequality, or we can benefit Adam in a non-justice-related way, e.g. by eliminating some pain of his, satisfying some of his preferences, or by making him enjoy more by way of objectively valuable goods. Plausibly, if we should act out of a concern for Adam, it seems we should do the latter. But this suggests that if Broome is right that inequality is bad for the worse-off, this simply shows that the person-affecting principle, which underlies the levelling down objection, is one that does not apply to the sort of harm involved in being unjustly worse off. Accordingly, it is simply a matter of specifying this principle correctly and once we do that we can state a revised version of the levelling down objection which seems no less forceful than the original one and one to which the present Broomean reply is irrelevant. Hence, this first line of response is unconvincing.

Second, another response to the levelling down objection is to hold, as we saw Andrew Mason do in Section 5.5, that equality is non-instrumentally valuable, but that it is so only on condition that it benefits someone (Mason 2001: 246–54). While this move has some merits it also has its problems. One is that one would need to supply an explanation for why inequality is bad only when its elimination could benefit those who are worse off. Obviously, prioritarians could explain this because, for them, it is benefits to people, weighted according to how badly off they are, that count morally, but it is less clear what egalitarians could say. Second, some egalitarians do want to say that inequality is unjust even when its elimination would benefit no one. Obviously, they are barred from subscribing to conditional egalitarianism.

Third, values other than equality imply that one outcome can be better than another, even if it is better for no one in any respect. From a retributivist perspective on criminal justice, for instance, a world in which criminals are justly punished might be assessed as better than one in which they are not, even if this is better for no one because punishment has no deterrent effect. Hence, if the Slogan that 'One situation *cannot* be worse (or better) than another *in any respect* if there is *no one* for whom it *is* worse (or better) *in any respect*' (Temkin 1993: 248) obliges us to reject a wide range of values other than equality, perhaps the intuitive cost of rejecting it is lower than the intuitive cost of rejecting equality, desert and all the other values that offend against the Slogan (Temkin 1993: 261).

Fourth, at least some of those who reject egalitarianism in response to the levelling down objection are not really in a position to do so (Persson 2008: 295–303). Consider prioritarianism. On this view, if we transfer one unit of well-being from a well-off person to a badly-off person this will result in an increase in moral value. But where does this increase come from, one might ask? *Ex hypothesi*, the decrease in well-being experienced by the source is exactly as great as the increase in well-being experienced by the recipient of the well-being. Accordingly, the extra value the transfer brings into existence seems to be unconnected to the sum of well-being. This suggests that prioritarianism, like egalitarianism, is committed to the idea that values are not tied to well-being for individuals, in which case it is less clear that they can appeal to the person-affecting principle which underlies the levelling down objection (cf. Segall 2014). Commonly those who canvass the levelling down objection against egalitarianism adopt prioritarianism. Hence, this reversal of the attack has considerable bite.

Finally, as I hinted above, some egalitarians take a bullish stance. They insist that, because it follows straightforwardly from strict equality – provided they do not endorse Mason's conditional egalitarianism – that a state in which everyone is worse off, but equally well off, is in one respect – though not all things considered – better than one in which everyone is better off, though unequally so, this implication is something they were aware of that they were committed to all along. Accordingly, the levelling down objection cannot play the dialectical role of an *objection* – it does not point to an implausible implication to which egalitarians are committed and of which (until the alleged objection was presented to them) they were unaware. Ironically, in view of Parfit's formulation of the levelling down objection, it is probable that more egalitarians now will take this attitude than would have done so thirty years ago.

5.8. Summary

This chapter has examined and critically reconstructed Parfit's distinction between telic and deontic egalitarianism. I have argued that the distinction has less significance than Parfit ascribes to it in that it does not imply any differential commitments on the issue of the scope of equality, nor are telic and deontic egalitarianism asymmetrically vulnerable to the levelling down objection as it is commonly held. While many views other than egalitarianism might be vulnerable to the levelling down objection, this makes it urgent for egalitarians to respond to the levelling down objection. In the previous section I surveyed some plausible luck egalitarian responses to the levelling down objection which to my mind shows that whether or not luck egalitarianism should be ultimately rejected, levelling down objection is, while powerful and well worth exploring in depth, not the knock-down argument some take it to be.

6

The scope of luck egalitarianism

6.1. Introduction

Recall my initial statement of luck egalitarianism from Section 1.2:

> (1) It is unjust if some individuals are worse off than others through their bad luck.

While useful in many ways, in itself this statement does not tell us anything about the scope of this principle, i.e. who are the individuals between whom luck-based inequalities are unjust (cf. Knight 2009: 5). In this chapter, I address some of the most pressing issues in relation to the question of scope. I connect these with the claims that I have made in the previous chapters, including my claim in Chapter 2 that fairness is the value that underlies the presumption in favour of equality. Section 6.2 discusses whether equality concerns people's whole lives or comparable segments thereof. Section 6.3 reflects on whether the scope of equality extends in time beyond the present generation to past and future generations. Section 6.4 asks if equality is concerned with relations between individuals only, or also take into account groups. Section 6.5 reflects on whether equality concerns only relations between co-citizens or, cosmopolitan-style, also concerns relations between individuals per se. Section 6.6 explores whether equality extends beyond human beings or persons to non-human animals. On many, but not all issues, I defend broad-scoped versions of equality.

6.2. Whole lives

Until recently, egalitarians assumed that equality applies to people's whole lives (e.g. Dworkin 2000: 89). On this view, there need not be anything unjust about two persons being unequally well off at some point in time provided that this inequality is counterbalanced by inequalities favouring the worse-off person at other times. Thomas Nagel for instance contends: 'the subject of an egalitarian principle is not the distribution of particular rewards to individuals at some time, but the prospective quality of their lives as a whole, from birth to death' (Nagel 1991: 69).

Recently it has been contended that equality is more demanding than that. Here is an example by Dennis McKerlie:

[I]magine that the same city block contains a condominium complex and a retirement home. The residents of the complex are middle-aged, affluent, and happy. The retirement home is old and overcrowded. Its residents have adequate medical care but little dignity or happiness. Our first reaction is that this inequality raises an issue of justice. Age inequality is especially troubling because, like racial inequality, it is rooted in a factor for which people are not responsible ... However, there is an obvious difference between age inequality and racial inequality. Native Americans do not become Caucasians, or vice versa. But the young do grow old, and the very old were once young. So let us also suppose that the people in the condominiums will end up in such a place as the nursing home, and that the people in the home used to be as fortunate as their neighbors now are. When we think about the past and the future as well as the present ... the present inequality does not disappear, but it might seem to lose its moral importance. The example presents us with a puzzle. In one way the question about fairness is pressing. But when we think about the same case from a different perspective it is not clear that there is a concern of justice at all. (McKerlie 2001: 152–3)

McKerlie, like Temkin, thinks that, in the end, non-lifetime inequalities are a concern from the point of view of justice.

Suppose that we go along with McKerlie and reject the lifetime view. Which are the alternatives then? One is to say that for all individuals and all moments in time, if one individual at one time is worse off than another individual at the same or another time, this involves injustice. For instance, justice-wise it is better if both of us go to the dentist today rather than that I do so today and you do so tomorrow. As this example brings out, such a view is strongly counterintuitive. If we are to reject the lifetime view, we must avoid this extreme.

People do so in two ways. First, instead of focusing on equalities at any given moment, they focus on inequalities between segments of people's lives. Obviously, it is a difficult issue to delimit such segments non-arbitrarily and those who reject the lifetime view tend to use vague terms such as 'adolescence', 'adulthood', 'old age', etc., to label segments without really taking an informed stance either on why, say, adolescence is a segment which bears significance from the point of view egalitarian justice, or on how exactly the different segments are to be distinguished from one another. Second, instead of rejecting the lifetime view altogether they say that it should be supplemented. That is, lifetime equality matters, but it is not the only inequality that matters.

Which, then, are the segments of people's lives, in addition to their lives as a whole, to compare to assess the situation from the point of view of justice? The two main proposals in the literature are simultaneous segments and corresponding segments. To see the difference between these two views, return to McKerlie's example. Here there is simultaneous segment inequality, even if there is no corresponding segment inequality, since those who are middle-aged now will end up being as badly off as those who are old now, and those who are old now were as well off as those who are middle-aged now, when they were middle-aged. To the extent that we share McKerlie's assessment of his example, it could be – though I will return to this shortly – influenced by the simultaneous segment view. This leaves us with the task of offering an example of a situation which is unjust from the point of view of corresponding segment egalitarianism but neither bad from the point of view of whole lives egalitarianism nor from the point of view of simultaneous segment egalitarianism. Imagine the situation where there are two generations, one born in 1960 and the other one in 1990. From 1960 to 1990 only the first generation exists and it enjoys a level of well-being of 120. From 1990 to 2020 both generations exist and both enjoy a level of well-being of 80. From 2020 to 2050 only the second generations exists and its members enjoy a level of well-being of 120. In this situation there is no simultaneous inequality, no lifetime inequality, but corresponding segment inequality, e.g. the first generation is worse off when old than the second. If you think that there is something bad about this situation, justice-wise, this might reflect that you subscribe to the corresponding segment inequality view.

Should we give up on lifetime egalitarianism? There are at least three reasons why examples such as McKerlie's do not justify our doing so. First, consider a Robinson Crusoe island situation with only one person. Suppose there are two possible outcomes – one where the person is equally well off at each day of her entire life and one where her level of well-being varies from day to day though life as a whole is exactly as good in terms of well-being as in the first outcome. Suppose that this person suffers from a very rare disease. If on Monday she wakes up with the body and interests of a 20-year-old, she will wake up on Tuesday with the body and interests of a 60-year-old. On Wednesday she will revert to her 20-year-and-one-day-old self, and so on and so forth. Unless we think, implausibly, that age in itself – that is, irrespective of what age does to people – is a concern from the point of view of justice, this person's youth and old age overlap. Hence, in the second scenario we have inequalities between simultaneous and corresponding segments of this person's life. However, it is implausible to claim that this raises a matter of concern from the point of view of justice. Assuming that this is so, the question is: why does this scenario not raise an issue of justice? The obvious reply is that it is the same person who is involved and that in the second scenario, where this person's level of well-being varies from day to day, the deficiency that this person suffers from on below-average days is compensated for by the above-average levels that the person enjoys on good days. Accordingly, there is no injustice in the situation. However, this reply is available only to the friend of a whole life view. Friends of the two segment views that I have described cannot avail themselves of this answer because they are committed to the view that compensation within a life does not eliminate injustice. This might seem fine in situations such as McKerlie's that involve interpersonal comparisons and where there is some intuitive attractiveness of the view that whole lives are not all that matters. However, if in order to explain why intrapersonal inequalities do not matter, justice-wise, we have to appeal to the view that compensation within a life eliminates injustice, then it seems prohibitively costly to reject the lifetime view.

This brings me to my second point. As McKerlie concedes, there are strong arguments in favour of the lifetime view. What speaks in favour of rejecting or supplementing it are intuitions such as the one generated by his condominium example. But this means that if we can explain these intuitions in ways other than by rejecting the lifetime view, we have a strong case against rejecting it. Unfortunately, McKerlie does not consider such 'error theories'. Indeed, the way in which he describes the example is one that might easily lead us to assess it in terms other than egalitarian justice. For instance, he says that old people in his example lack 'dignity' and he compares (and contrasts) it to racial inequality, the injustice of which is not normally seen to consist simply in some kind of distributive injustice. This raises the suspicion that what we are really responding to when we find his scenario objectionable is the sort of social relations or the lack of communal relations that exist between middle-aged and old people in his example rather than to some kind of inegalitarian injustice, distribution-wise. Indeed, there is a suspicion that the injustice that McKerlie focuses on, to the extent that it obtains, is of the sort that social relations egalitarians are concerned with. I shall say more on this in Chapter 7 (cf. Bidadanure forthcoming).

Third, on some views about what matters in identity from the prudential point of view are relations of psychological connectedness and continuity. Since these tend to weaken over time, this view could motivate a rejection or supplementation of the lifetime view (cf. Navin 2011: 543–5). However, McKerlie thinks the lifetime view should be rejected without any appeal to any such reductionist view about what matters in identity. But this creates a problem regarding how responsibility can be combined with a segment view. To see this, suppose that people should be equally well off in corresponding segments and suppose that Adam is better off than Burt when they are middle-aged, while Burt is correspondingly better off than Adam when they are old. This segment inequality between them is a result of their choices, let us suppose – they could have chosen to act in such a way that they would have been equally well off in both segments. In that case, it seems implausible to hold that the relevant segment inequality is unjust. Indeed McKerlie seems to agree: 'like racial inequality, [age inequality] is rooted in a factor for which people are not responsible. We cannot blame people for growing old and experiencing the problems that old age bring' (McKerlie 2001: 153). So when old Adam complains that it is unjust that he should be worse off than old Burt, we can say to him that this is not unjust, because this a result of something he knowingly chose to do when middle-aged. Old Adam might retort that he cannot see how it can be just that he should be worse off now just because of a choice he made thirty years ago. To this one would like to say that this is just, because he is the same person as the one who made the relevant choice thirty years ago. However, this is a reply that it is unclear that segment egalitarians can give. After all, when it comes to compensation across time they do not think identity over time enables counterbalancing benefits in one segment to eliminate the injustice of disadvantages in another. If so, it is in need of an account of why identity over time transfers responsibility for an act in one segment to responsibility for a foreseen effect in another segment.

In sum, while McKerlie has identified some important intuitions that need to be explained, these need not derive from egalitarian justice. Moreover, insofar as we care about inequality because we care about fairness, then, setting aside reductionist views about what matters in personal identity over time, equality over lifetimes is what we should be interested in.

6.3. Generations

There is another consideration about scope that relates to time, which is different from the lifetime versus life-segments issue that we addressed in the previous section (Gosseries and Meyer 2009). Suppose that we accept the lifetime view and suppose that we compare two generations that are separated by many generations and of which it is therefore true that none of its members existed when at least one member from the other generation existed. By way of illustration we can compare the generation of Frenchmen that were born around the time Jeanne d'Arc was burned for heresy in Rouen (1431) with the generation of Frenchmen that were born around the time François Mitterrand took office as the twenty-first president of France (1981). Whichever metric is the metric of egalitarian justice, on average members of the latter generation are much better off than members of the Jeanne d'Arc generation. For instance, life expectancy in medieval Europe was around thirty years. Frenchmen born in 1981 can expect to live lives that are three times as long. Is this just from the point of view of luck egalitarianism?

Obviously, those Frenchmen born around the time of Jeanne d'Arc were in no way responsible for having been born at this not so favourable time in French history. Accordingly, it seems that they were worse off than those Frenchmen born under Mitterrand through their bad luck. Yet, when people complain about unjust inequalities they hardly ever have in mind the inequalities between distant generations (but see Segall forthcoming) and they certainly do not worry that it would be unjust of the present generation of Frenchmen to do something that improves their situation on the ground that this would make the inequality between their generation and the Jeanne d'Arc generation even greater (cf. Section 5.3). Hence, either luck egalitarianism is implausible or its scope is narrow such that only inequalities between members of the same or overlapping generations are unjust.

Initially, this dilemma seems to put luck egalitarians in an impossible position. However, on reflection we can see that at least one of the horns of the dilemma is not damaging. Let me start with the second horn of the dilemma. This horn seems not so threatening, if only luck egalitarians could argue that it is not bad luck that the Jeanne d'Arc generation were born when they were, rather than at the time of the Mitterrand generation. If so, they might be worse off than the latter generation but it is not a result of luck. Arguably, there is a way which they could defend this position. According to origin essentialism, it is an essential property of me that I developed from the sperm and ovum from which I developed. If at the time I was conceived another sperm had fused with the ovum from which

I developed (and vice versa), this might well have led to the development of a person, but that person would not have been me. In this sense my origin is an essential property of me. Perhaps I could have been conceived at a different moment from which, in fact, I was conceived but there is a pretty strong sense, short of logical impossibility, in which I could not have been conceived almost six hundred years later than the time at which I was in fact conceived. Hence, there is a pretty strong sense in which it is not as a result of bad luck that the Jeanne d'Arc generation was conceived much before the Mitterrand generation and, thus, is much worse off. At least, this is so if for an outcome to be bad luck for someone, there has to be a possible alternative outcome which is better for that person (cf. Section 3.7).

While this reply to the second horn of the dilemma holds some promise and may succeed in showing that there is at least one way in which the inequality is not a result of bad luck, it may at best yield a partial reply. For instead of saying that the bad luck of the Jeanne d'Arc generation consists in their not having been conceived later, we could say that their bad luck consists in the low level of technological, industrial and scientific prowess at the time of their conception. The fact that this is their bad luck is unthreatened by origin essentialism and, accordingly, the purported response to the second horn of the dilemma achieves a very limited success at best. Alternatively, we can say that 'luck' simply means something for which one is not responsible – recall the responsibility-based notion of luck in Chapter 2 – in which case the time at which one is born is a matter of luck even if it was not possible that one was born at a different time.

There is another reply which addresses the second horn of the dilemma that should be mentioned but, so I think, ultimately rejected. As we saw in the previous chapter, Parfit entertains the possibility that inequality is bad only when it holds between relevantly related groups. Since fifteenth- and twentieth-century Frenchmen are not relevantly related, the inequality between them is not unjust. Parfit finds this form of conditional egalitarianism implausible, since he thinks that it would be a 'strange coincidence' if inequality would be unjust only when it obtained between relevantly related groups. It is more plausible to say that if we are attracted to conditional egalitarianism this just shows that we are not concerned with distributional equality as such, but that we are concerned with something else, e.g. that communal relations have a certain egalitarian nature (see Chapter 7). I agree with Parfit's conclusion here. Not because conditional egalitarianism as such is implausible. As we saw in Chapter 5, luck egalitarianism is a form of conditional egalitarianism, i.e. inequalities are unjust only when they reflect bad luck on the part of the worse-off. Rather, what makes it implausible to restrict the scope of equality to individuals who are related is that what makes the latter form of inequalities unjust is the unfairness they involve. Unfairness explains why inequalities for which the worse-off are responsible are not unjust – no unfairness is involved – but it cannot explain why only inequalities between related individuals are not unjust – it is unfair that some generations face extreme scarcity while others do not. We know this commitment from the way in which we think of the moral issue involved in global warming, where most think it would be unfair of us to make future generations suffer from disastrous climate change. Hence, I think that only the first of the two responses to the second horn of the dilemma has some, though not much, force.

Turning now to the first horn of the dilemma, let us suppose that it is indeed bad luck that the Jeanne d'Arc generation is worse off. In that case, it seems that the fairness rationale for equality that I defended in Chapter 3 does indeed imply that the relevant inequality is unjust. So perhaps luck egalitarians should face the first horn of the dilemma directly by arguing that, on reflection and despite our initial reaction, intergenerational inequalities are indeed unjust. In my view, this is the right response to our present dilemma.

Here is one way that luck egalitarians might try to persuade us that intergenerational inequalities can be unjust. When people think about the Jeanne d'Arc case they tend to assume that the present generation of French people can do nothing to improve the situation of the long-deceased members of the Jeanne d'Arc generation. However, at least on some theories of welfare this need not be the case. For instance, on some such theories how good a person's life was might be affected by what happens after this person has ceased to exist. For instance, if a person wants his family to live well after he has ceased to exist, it makes his life worse if, after his death, his family suffers. Obviously, such theories of welfare are quite controversial, but let us suppose they are true. Moreover, suppose that members of the Jeanne d'Arc generation had strong concerns that the churches they built were preserved for as long as possible. Suppose, finally, that the present generation of Frenchmen can either spend some resources on something about which they are concerned, letting fifteenth-century churches be steadily destroyed by the wear and tear thereby further increasing the inequality in welfare between the two generations, or alternatively spend the resources on preserving those churches, thus making themselves somewhat worse off but still much better off than members of the Jeanne d'Arc generation. In this case, the thought that egalitarian justice requires them to do the latter seems perfectly intelligible. Hence, the first horn of the dilemma looks weak.

In response, it might be said that even if it is conceded that, on the assumption that what we do now can affect the degree to which the concerns of the deceased generations are met, there is some case for the scope of equality including all generations, this assumption is controversial. A satisfactory response to the scope objection should proceed – so the response continues – on the plausible assumption that there is nothing we can do now to improve the situation of fifteenth-century Frenchmen. So could luck egalitarians deny that their view has counterintuitive implications on this assumption?

There are two things they might say here. First, they might say that the present objection really is no different from the levelling down objection which I discussed in Chapter 6. The levelling down objection normally involves imagining a situation where some contemporary worse-off people are not made better off in any way by a move towards greater equality. However, in principle it could be formulated using deceased worse-off people. The relevance of being deceased, it might be argued, is that once one is deceased one is not benefited in any way by greater equality between oneself and people who exist later. The fact that one is deceased does not, once we set this fact about non-affectability aside, in itself make any moral difference. That much was shown two paragraphs above, where we imagined that we could affect the level of well-being of deceased people. Of course, being deceased might be relevant in relation to other values. For instance, it might be said that we do not stand in

the same communal relations to deceased members of past generations, if we stand to them in any communal relations at all, as to
contemporary members of our own generation. Hence, insofar as we
care about communal relations having a certain egalitarian character,
this is a reason to care about members of the present generation
which does not apply to members of past generations. Perhaps
this is why egalitarians are much more exercised about inequalities
between contemporaries than about inequalities between fifteenth-
and twentieth-century Frenchmen and not because they deny that,
given the 'short, nasty, brutish' lives of past generations, there is
a fairness-based reason why in one respect it is unjust that better-
off present and future generations get even better off. In sum: the
present scope objection reduces to the levelling down objection,
which I responded to in Section 5.7. In view of this, I contend that
the most plausible view holds that the scope of egalitarian justice
extends across all generations. Admittedly, introducing the value
of egalitarian communitarian relations to accommodate the present
intuition and the value of welfare to avoid embracing levelling down,
all things considered, alongside the value of luck egalitarian equality
means ending up with having to balance three values against one
another. Unfortunately, no one has proposed any clear principles
for how this should be done. However, this predicament may
simply reflect moral truth or, at least, amount to the best account of
considered beliefs about distributive values.

6.4. Groups

I now turn to a third issue in relation to the scope of inequality. The
canonical formulation of luck egalitarianism says that it is unjust
if some people are worse off than others through their bad luck.
This formulation is ambiguous in two ways. First, it does not itself
tell us whether we should be concerned with inequalities between
individuals or inequalities between groups. Second, it does not tell us
whether individual choice or group choice undermine luck. I believe
the best way to understand equality implies that it is concerned with
inequalities between individuals and individual choices only.

Starting with the first issue, if all individuals are equally well off, there can be no inequalities between groups, assuming that groups consist entirely of individuals. However, if there are inequalities between individuals there might or might not be inequalities between groups. If equality is concerned also or only with inequalities between groups, the latter situation, i.e. one in which relevant groups are unequally well off, is worse than the former, i.e. one in which there are no group inequalities but no less inequality between individuals than in the former situation, all else being equal.

By way of illustration, suppose that men and women are the only two groups inequality between which matters from the point of view of justice. If groups matter, which groups do so – clearly not all groups, e.g. the group of people whose surname starts with an 'F' or an 'M', matter – is a complicated issue in itself, but for present purposes we can set it aside. Suppose that in one situation all men are at 100 and all women at 50. In another situation half the men and half the women are at 200 while half the men and half the women are at 0. In both situations there are inequalities between individuals. Moreover, in the latter situation the overall inequality between individuals seems much greater because the gap between the best-off and the worst-off individuals is much greater. However, in the latter situation there is no inequality between the two groups – or, at least, there is no such inequality if a comparison of group averages is what determines whether there is any inequality between the two groups (cf. Lippert-Rasmussen 2013a). If group inequality is all that matters, and men and women are the only relevant groups, the latter situation is not bad in any way justice-wise. However, this seems very implausible and suggests that insofar as group inequalities matter justice-wise they matter in addition to inequalities between individuals.

It is doubtful whether group inequalities play even this more limited role, i.e. as something that matters in addition to inequalities between individuals. For suppose that there is a trade-off between greater equality between individuals and greater equality between groups, e.g. that the only way to make men and women more equal involves increasing inequalities between individuals, e.g. by making the worst-off men and women even worse off such that the worst-off women under the distribution, which involves no inequality between men and women, are worse off than the worst-off men under the distribution, which involve inequality between men and women. Insofar as we are not willing to make this trade-off, this suggests that group inequalities matter only instrumentally. We might add that under normal circumstances reducing group inequalities reduces inequalities between individuals and, thus, normally is a good proxy for reducing inequalities that matter non-instrumentally.

Some may resist a purely instrumental view of group inequalities because they think that group inequalities reflect social structures – often of an oppressive nature – and that inequalities between individuals are natural inequalities and because they think that justice is concerned with social inequalities only (e.g. Anderson 1999a). Obviously, luck egalitarians reject the latter claim, since on their view differential, purely natural, bad brute luck can result in unjust inequalities.

Even if we reject the luck egalitarian stance on natural, differential brute luck, the exclusive concern with social inequalities does not motivate an exclusive focus on group inequalities. First, group inequalities could result from non-social causes (cf. Lippert-Rasmussen 2013a). Suppose a society consists of two equally well-off ethnic groups. A new strain of malaria spreads and in a way that is unpreventable and, due to some otherwise insignificant genetic variation between the two groups, results in one group ending up worse off than the other. Second, individual inequalities might have social causes. Difference in the length of lives of different individuals is an important source of inequality. While it is affected by bad brute luck it is also affected by social structure. If, for instance, we have greater socioeconomic equality there will be less overall inequality between individuals in terms of their lifespans. I conclude that egalitarian justice concerns relations between individuals not groups.

I now turn to the second matter of ambiguity that I described initially – the one that pertains to what I shall call the distinction between individual choice and group choice. To get a grasp of what is the relevant issue here, imagine a situation where people in general have 100 of whatever is the relevant metric of egalitarian justice. However, Adam and Beatrice will end up at 50 unless Adam transfers a benefit of 50 to Beatrice and Beatrice transfers a benefit of 50 to Adam. If both make the transfer both will end up with 100 like everyone else. Suppose that for selfish reasons neither transfers the benefit to the other as a result of which they end up worse off than the rest. In that case, both of them could claim that they are worse off than others through no choice or prudential fault of their own, and that they are therefore worse off as a result of bad luck. Of each it is true that had they acted otherwise, i.e. made the transfer, they would have been no better off. Compare the situation of Adam and Beatrice with that of Claire and Derek. Each of them is at 50 and has the opportunity to help themselves to an additional 50 – an opportunity which they do not avail themselves of, so now they are as much worse off than others as Adam and Beatrice. The question is whether the situations of the two pairs are different from the point of view of luck egalitarian justice.

Initially, one might say that while Adam and Beatrice are worse off as a result of bad brute luck, because it is true of each of them that had he or she acted differently he or she would still have been worse off than others, the same is not true of Claire and Derek. Hence, while it is unjust that Adam and Beatrice are worse off, the same is not true of Claire and Derek. However, the view that there is a difference between the two pairs that is relevant from a luck egalitarian point of view seems implausible. Why should luck egalitarians be more concerned about the situation of selfish Adam and Beatrice than about negligent Claire and Derek?

In response luck egalitarians might say that Adam and Beatrice are worse off as a result of what *they* did. It is true of each of them that had they both acted differently they would not have been worse off than others and this is why their being worse off is not bad luck. Accordingly, their situation is not different justice-wise from that of Claire and Derek.

There is another reply, however, which they might give and which I find more attractive. In Chapter 3 I distinguished between various notions of luck and mentioned one according to which one has bad luck to the extent that one is worse off than others who from the point of view of equality are no more deserving than oneself. On this view, one could be less deserving from the point of view of equality by not availing oneself of an opportunity to make oneself as well off as others, but one could also be less deserving by failing to make someone else as well as off as others. On this view, Adam, Beatrice, Claire and Derek are all equally less deserving from the point of egalitarian justice. This is so not because of the significance of group choice, but because, luck-wise, individual choices should be assessed not simply in terms of how beneficial they are for the chooser, but also in terms of whether they promote equality. This seems desirable given that group choice is beyond the control of its individual members and, thus, group choice has a more problematic relation to luck than individual choice.

In view of the arguments above, I conclude that the relevant ambiguity in relation to the canonical formulation of luck egalitarianism should, on both dimensions, be resolved in favour of individualistic readings, i.e. that neither group inequalities nor group choices matter from the point of view of luck egalitarian justice (cf. Lippert-Rasmussen 2011a; 2011b). This is a respect in which I do not favour a luck egalitarian account with the broadest possible scope.

6.5. States

One issue concerning scope, which has received much attention in recent years, is whether the scope of egalitarian justice stops at the borders of states – call this *statist egalitarianism* – or whether it is cosmopolitan such that inequalities between citizens from different states are just as bad as inequalities between citizens from the same state – call this *cosmopolitan egalitarianism.*

A number of prominent egalitarians have assumed or defended statist egalitarianism. Below I briefly mention the view of three such theorists, but obviously this far from constitutes a complete review of the literature (e.g. cf. Blake 2001: Sangiovanni 2007). John Rawls – who, as noted in Chapter 1, is an egalitarian in a broader sense of the term – famously thought that the difference principle applies only within states and not across states. This is not to say that no principles regulate the relation between states, but these principles – the laws of peoples (Rawls) – are different and nowhere nearly as demanding as the difference principle. Specifically, Rawls thought socioeconomic differences between different states were mainly to be explained by differences in terms of the qualities of their political institutions and, thus, that the main obligation states had to other states is to help them establish well-ordered political institutions. More generally, at various places Rawls contends that justice is a matter of a fair distribution of the benefits from social cooperation. On the assumption that such cooperation takes place within states but not between members of different states, this suggests that justice is a feature of relations between members of the same states (cf. Caney 2008).

Ronald Dworkin is another egalitarian with what appears to be an anti-cosmopolitan view. He derives his egalitarian principles from the assumption that the state has to treat *its* citizens with equal concern and respect. This leaves open whether states need to treat citizens of other states with the same concern and respect as its own citizens, but suggests that they do not.

Finally, Thomas Nagel thinks that egalitarian justice obtains only within states. This is so because any political coercive structure has to be justified to each of its members, in whose name its laws are imposed, in order to be legitimate. States constitute such structures, but there is no comparable global political structure. Moreover, according to Nagel this demand for justification can only be met if a state adheres to something like luck egalitarian principles of justice. Because there is no similar requirement of justification at stake at an international level, Nagel thinks that no egalitarian principles of justice apply at an international level.

Some luck egalitarians, e.g. Kok-Chor Tan, however, have defended cosmopolitan luck egalitarianism and, as will become apparent shortly, this is where my sympathies lie as well. However, before proceeding to an assessment of the two views, it should be noted that, at a practical level, how we resolve this question of scope is very important. Inequalities between members of different states, e.g. Niger and Kuwait, are even more striking than inequalities within states, e.g. Sweden. Accordingly, from the perspective of most people living in wealthy states, cosmopolitan egalitarianism might well be hugely more demanding than even the most radical egalitarian policies that aim at redistribution within those states.

Let me start by explaining why the fairness-based view of egalitarian justice implies that cosmopolitanism is the right view and then critically assess some of the arguments that have been offered in favour of statist luck egalitarianism. If what makes inequalities unjust is the fact that some people are worse off than others through no fault or choice of their own, it is hard to see how international inequalities could fail to be unjust assuming that they do not reflect – possibly collective – choices or faults. People in Niger are not worse off than people in Kuwait because of choices they made. Accordingly, they seem to be worse off for the same luck-related reasons that some members of Kuwait are better off than others, e.g. they happen to be born into wealthy families.

In response to this it might be conceded that, normally, when we explain why it is unjust for someone to be worse off than others simply as a result of being born into a poor family, we do not also mention that what makes this fact unjust is that it obtains between co-citizens. But the real underlying view is that differential luck is unfair only when it obtains between members of the same state. At this point, cosmopolitan luck egalitarians might press statist egali-tarians to explain why differential luck is unjust only when it obtains between members of the same state. Offhand, this seems not very plausible. First, it does not seem intuitively attractive that when learning of two persons who are unequally well off due to differ-ential luck we must withhold forming a view about the injustice of this inequality until we know whether they are co-citizens (cf. Caney 2011: 514).

Second, it seems unfair that one person is worse than another through bad luck, because the former is just as morally important as the latter. But if so, and assuming that statehood does not affect equal moral standing, it is unclear why the unfairness of relations of differential luck depends on co-citizenship (see however Sangiovanni 2011).

At this point it might be worthwhile to look at two of the main justifications for statist egalitarianism. The first justification appeals to the Rawlsian idea that justice is a matter of distributing the benefits of cooperation fairly.

In response to this argument cosmopolitan egalitarians can either attack the empirical assumption – that social cooperation is mostly intrastate rather than international – or the moral assumption – that justice is a matter of sharing the benefits of social cooperation fairly – or they can do both. The former type of attack – i.e. the attack on the relevant empirical assumptions – can take two forms. Perhaps in some states there are isolated communities that do not interact with other citizens of the state or interact more with people outside the state. In such a case, the scope of justice is narrower than the borders of the state. Also, one can argue – as Thomas Pogge (2008) (cf. Beitz 1975) – that there is an international structure under which social cooperation between states take place involving a huge social surplus which, however, is distributed very unequally.

While these two arguments imply that the relevant distinction to make does not coincide with state borders, they do not establish cosmopolitan egalitarianism. To get there, one needs to attack the normative premise that relations of justice obtain only between people who cooperate to bring about a social surplus. Arneson (1999a) imagines a scenario that is intended to support this conclusion. Suppose a number of people each live alone on different islands. All of them are stuck on their island and accordingly there can be no social cooperation between them. Those who live on the lush islands can, however, load barrels with goods, throw them into the ocean, where currents will then reliably transport the barrels to islands that are arid. On the view that justice requires social cooperation there would be nothing unjust about people living on lush islands not helping people living on arid islands. Yet, this is not plausible according to Arneson. On the assumption that it is purely a matter of luck whether one is stuck on a lush or an arid island, intuitively, it is unfair that some people are better off than others.

This argument is unlikely to convert many to cosmopolitanism. One reply, which it is bound to be met with, is that while it might be that people living on lush islands are morally required to help people living on arid islands they do not have a duty of justice to do so. For instance, Nagel takes this view. This reply threatens to transform what appears to be a substantive disagreement into a difference in terminology – that is, one that involves apparent discussants using the term 'justice' in different ways. In Section 8.6 I will return to this problem sketching different things people might have in mind when they use the term justice. While I share Arneson's assessment of his examples, I suspect that it adds little to the above-mentioned appeal to the fairness rationale for equality.

The other main justification for statist egalitarianism is Nagel's appeal to the coercive structure embodied in states. According to Nagel, states exercise coercive authority over their citizens and do so in their name. No international institutions do that. On his view, if an institution exercises coercive authority over people this exercise must be justified to them. According to Nagel, such justification can only be given if the state complies with luck egalitarianism. Citizens have an equal standing and, thus, arbitrary difference is something they have a standing to reject.

Again a cosmopolitan luck egalitarian may respond to this argument in different ways. She might attack the empirical assumption that no institutional institutions exercise coercive authority over citizens (Caney 2008: 498–504) or she might argue that states exercise coercive authority over non-citizens, e.g. by denying them entry (cf. Abizadeh 2007). If the former claim is true, all individuals have a standing to reject arbitrary differences between them. If the latter claim is true, states must be justified not just to their citizens, but also to non-citizens.

Alternatively, or additionally, the luck egalitarian might attack the assumption that individuals are owed a justification that they are not owed when coercive authority is not exercised over them. For instance, they might argue that an individual is owed a justification if state policies causally affect her even if no coercive authority is exercised over her (cf. Goodin 2007). On this view, people affected by global warming not living in China might be owed a justification for Chinese climate-relevant policies even though none of these policies involves the exercise of coercive authority over non-Chinese citizens.

Finally, cosmopolitan luck egalitarians might say that luck egalitarianism does not simply derive from the duty to justify policies to citizens. There could be reasons why luck egalitarianism applies to relations between individuals other than their being subjected to the same institution exercising coercive authority in their name. At best, the coercive structure argument is an argument for why luck egalitarianism applies to some relations, e.g. relations between co-citizens, not an argument for why it does not apply to others, e.g. relations between fellow human beings or persons.

At this point some might object that luck egalitarianism is too demanding. Imagine that we were to discover that Mars is inhabited by a large number of people who are worse off than we are through bad luck. On cosmopolitan luck egalitarianism this is unjust and if we could make Martians better off by transferring some of our resources to them, this would be what justice requires. Moreover, since Mars might not be the only planet inhabited by persons who are worse off than us, luck egalitarianism seems to commit us to open-ended sacrifices for the worse-off, wherever in the universe they are (cf. Fabre 2006). However, this shows according to some that luck egalitarianism is too demanding.

In response to this objection, Kok-Chor Tan contends that global brute luck inequalities form unjust inequalities if, and only if, global institutions turn them into 'actual social advantages and disadvantages' (Tan 2014: 153). This implies, Tan believes, that his position is immune to the present *reductio* (Tan 2014: 158), since it denies that 'our distributive duties to be without end and predictability' (Tan 2014: 166).

However, it is unclear that he is entitled to this dismissal. He says that his luck egalitarianism is not 'overly harsh' (Tan 2014: 169) because it can recognize duties of humanitarian assistance, different from duties of distributive justice, to assist badly-off extraterrestrial aliens. However, in principle such a humanitarian duty to assist extraterrestrials with basic needs deficits involves the same, though admittedly mitigated, open-endedness and lack of predictability that is his ground for denying duties of distributive justice to worse-off extraterrestrials. Accordingly, luck egalitarians should deny that the present implication is an implausible one, adding that insofar as it is, it is one that constitutes a reason to reject many other principles such as sufficientarianism and prioritarianism. To the extent that our intuitions are that we should not compensate extraterrestrials, this might simply reflect speciesist bias or a failure to take fully on board that the relevant extraterrestrials are persons.

Tan might reply that there are independent reasons for thinking that the site of egalitarian justice is institutional. According to Tan, institutional luck egalitarianism is reasonable given value pluralism. Individuals are committed to ends that are not defined by justice, and the value of their pursuit of these ends is one value along with the value of justice. Institutionalism reconciles these 'two potentially competing demands … [P]ersons have the duty to establish and support just institutions, but within the rules of these institutions persons may freely pursue their ends' (Tan 2014: 28).

This defence of institutionalism raises two questions. First, suppose one holds that justice requires that the worst-off be made as well off as possible. Suppose, moreover, that this requires, Cohen-style, that people seek to benefit the worse-off in their everyday life. It is unclear why the institutional approach is not then simply a way of weighing justice against a competing, non-justice value, i.e. the value of personal pursuit of ends. Admittedly, for Tan the goal of the institutional approach is *not* 'to maximize social equality ... Its purpose is to make it possible for persons to live meaningful and worthwhile separate lives consistent with the demands of social justice given the assumption of value pluralism' (Tan 2014: 34). However, a response to the present question that appeals to this fact assumes that the substantive demands of social justice cannot be determined independently of which institutions can accommodate individuals' pursuit of their ends. But some luck egalitarian value pluralists reject this assumption.

Second, if the institutional approach is uniquely justified as a reconciliation of the two values in question, there is no other equally attractive way of reconciling them. However, as Tan acknowledges, combining trans-institutionalist act egalitarianism – 'Always act in such a way that you make the worst-off as well off as possible' – with a personal prerogative to give greater moral weight to pursuing one's own ends to the detriment of the worst-off is another way of achieving the relevant reconciliation. Tan dismisses this suggestion claiming that it 'merely restates the very problem that the institutional approach is supposed to solve' (Tan 2014: 31; cf. Section 8.3). It does not 'answer the basic question: how do we determine in a principled manner legitimate personal prerogatives?' (Tan 2014: 31). Here Tan seems to make two claims. The first – the mere restatement claim – is false. The act egalitarianism-cum-prerogative approach describes the contours of a solution to the reconciliation problem and, surely, offering an admittedly incomplete solution to a problem goes beyond restating it.

In response to Tan's second claim – the no principled manner response – friends of the act egalitarianism-cum-prerogative approach might assert, *tu quoque*, that a similar problem afflicts the institutional approach. On this approach, the justice parameters within which agents can pursue their ends can be more or less constraining and any fixing of these parameters will be unprincipled in the same way as the fixing of the personal prerogative parameters. For instance, under non-ideal circumstances 'the space for personal pursuits has to be recalibrated' (Tan 2014: 81), but Tan offers no principled account of what a suitable recalibration amounts to.

While Tan's exploration of the institutional approach is insightful, it is inconclusive. One wonders whether the core issue separating Tan and trans-institutionalists is really value holism, not pluralism, about justice, i.e. whether justice is determined in part in the light of non-justice values. Cohen is a value pluralist, but he rejects value holism regarding justice, i.e. he thinks that the demands of justice are independent of how realizing these demands affects the realization of other values. Tan rejects this view and his favoured institutional approach 'takes it as a given from the very outset that a conception of justice has to be attuned to these matters of personal pursuits' (Tan 2014: 72). I return to the difference between value pluralism and value holism in Section 8.6.

As a final objection to cosmopolitan luck egalitarianism, I want to consider the objection that it is incompatible with national, or at least state, self-determination. An underlying idea here is that the wealth of states depends on the collective choices of their citizens. Accordingly, inequalities between members of different states are, let us suppose, solely a result of different collective choices. If we furthermore assume that these collective choices are democratic such that, arguably, all citizens are responsible for the collective choices made by their state even when they opposed them, it seems that global luck egalitarianism is incompatible with national self-determination (cf. Miller 2008: 68–75). Suppose that one state decides to invest in its future while another consumes most of its income. Over the years the former grows increasingly better off than the other. At one point members of the latter state are worse off than members of the former and each member can say that this is a result of bad luck. Hence, it seems that there is a case for luck egalitarian redistribution across the two states. But that would in effect deprive states of the option of making different collective decisions regarding the distribution across investment and consumption.

In response, it should be noted that the objection is structurally similar to that which Dworkin gives for why it would be unjust for the state to tax individuals who enjoy good option luck to benefit those who suffer bad option luck. Doing so would, in effect, deprive people of the option of gambling. However, this also shows us that the present objection is not an objection to luck egalitarianism as such, but an objection to forms of luck egalitarianism that simply apply to individuals and their individual choices. As noted in Section 6.4 on group inequalities and group choices, there are forms of luck egalitarianism that ascribe significance to group as well as individual choices. One such group choice is collective decisions by members of a state. Accordingly, the objection from national self-determinism is not an objection to luck egalitarianism as such and to the extent one finds it persuasive one should broaden the range of choices that one considers relevant from the point of justice rather than reject luck egalitarianism. I conclude that global luck egalitarianism is better grounded than statist luck egalitarianism.

6.6. Individuals who are neither persons nor human beings

In the previous sections I have assumed that the relations of inequality that luck egalitarians are concerned with are relations between people like you and me or groups of people like you or me – that is, human beings who are persons. However, not all individuals are like us (surprise, surprise!). Many human beings are not persons – that is, they do not enjoy rationality, self-consciousness, and awareness of themselves as extended over time. Foetuses, severely demented, irreversibly unconscious individuals and newly born infants, for example, are not persons. Some of them might have the potential to become persons, while others have not. Some individuals are not human beings. Some of them might be persons – as some argue that chimpanzees are – and some of them are not persons – e.g. mice.

The existence of such individuals raises at least four questions. First, does the scope of egalitarian justice include all human beings, including human beings who are not persons and perhaps even human beings who do not even have the potential to become persons and may not even be sentient? Second, do persons who are not human beings – e.g. extraterrestrials who have all the defining features of persons – fall under the scope of egalitarian justice? We touched upon this question in the previous section. Third, do non-human animals who are not persons, and perhaps, as is probably almost always the case, do not even have the potential to become persons, fall under the scope of justice such that it is unjust that they are worse off than human beings who are persons? Fourth, do inequalities between non-human animals who are not persons fall under the scope of inequality such that it is unjust if some of these animals are worse off than others. Is it, for instance, unjust that some mice live long lives while other mice do not? Since mice are not responsible for anything, to the extent that some are worse off than others we can safely assume that such inequalities are unjust provided they fall within the scope of egalitarian justice.

How we answer these question has very significant implications. Take for instance the third question. Mice are much worse off than persons – one pretty indisputable reason for this being so is that their lives are radically simpler and shorter than the lives of human beings – and, accordingly, if inequalities between animals, who are not persons, and persons are unjust, then the injustice of inequalities between persons might seem tiny compared to the former. If one was worried about these implications in relation to intergenerational justice, e.g. in relation to demandingness, one should be terrified about the view that all sentient beings fall under the scope of equality.

The issues raised by these questions are daunting and I shall not try to answer them adequately here. I shall limit myself to two observations. The first one is that, as we saw in Chapter 3, while the issue of scope is a very serious problem for luck egalitarians, they are not alone in facing this challenge. Take for instance prioritarianism. On this view, one could argue that, almost always, benefits to mice count for more, morally speaking, than benefits to human persons, because the former are almost invariably much worse off. Similarly, one might assume that all mice live lives the quality of which falls below the sufficientarian threshold. Hence, it seems sufficientarianism implies that justice requires that we give priority to improving the situation of mice rather than the situation of human persons who have enough.

Admittedly, sufficientarians might reply that, on their view, sufficiency is only concerned with human persons, or persons in general, or that sufficiency is only concerned with individuals having what is sufficient for a being of their kind, where it is understood that what is sufficient for mice is much less than what is sufficient for human persons. My point here is not to assess these replies, but simply to point out that sufficientarians, as well as friends of other distributive views, do not avoid the present kind of questions that luck egalitarians must answer. Rather, these replies are taking a stand on the pertinent issues. Moreover, it is reasonable to assume that if one finds it problematic to restrict the scope of egalitarian justice to human persons, then, with some qualifications, one will find it similarly problematic to restrict the scope of sufficiency to human persons. More generally, the present problem is not distinctive of luck egalitarianism and insofar as one wants to reject a particular version of luck egalitarianism on account of how it delimits its scope in relation to non-human animals, etc., this reason is probably not a reason to reject luck egalitarianism as such, but rather a reason to reject a whole range of theories of distributive justice most of which are not luck egalitarian (cf. Vallentyne 2006b: 216).

The other observation I want to make concerns the possibility of a certain intermediate luck egalitarian position. Before I introduce it, let me mention two extreme views of the scope of egalitarian justice. One extreme view – the *maximalist view* – holds that any relation of inequality between individuals who have interests counts, and counts as much as relations of inequality between persons, from the point of view of equality. So on this view, it is just as bad that two mice are unequally well off as that two human persons are unequally well off. Also, an inequality between two human persons is just as bad, all other things being equal, as an inequality between a mouse and a human person. The maximalist view seems very counterintuitive even though, perhaps, it is not as maximalist as it could be, because it does not include human beings who have the capacity for sentience, but are not actually sentient. The fact that no actual luck egalitarian has expressed qualms about inequality relations such as those just mentioned attests to this fact. Admittedly this might simply reflect prejudice or insufficient reflection on the matter, but at least it suggests that we should consider whether it is possible to defend a version of luck egalitarianism with a narrower scope.

One such view is the *minimalist view*. On this view, only inequalities between human persons fall within the scope of egalitarian justice. So on this view, if we discover a planet populated by persons who are not *Homo sapiens*, justice is indifferent about whether they are worse or better off than we are, whereas if we discover a planet populated by persons who are *Homo sapiens*, say, descendants of our ancestors at a now-forgotten time of technological advancement, justice would be concerned with whether we are as well off as they are, even if everything else is identical to the case of the first planet. Also, on this view, if a world populated with 10 billion mice all of which are equally well off is no better than a world with the same amount of mice half of which suffer terribly and the other half of which live very good mouse-lives such that the overall sum of welfare in the two worlds are the same, we should be indifferent between these two worlds. Neither of these implications is particularly attractive.

Presumably, there might be moral principles that apply only to persons. For instance, assuming that it is possible to promise something to an animal, it may still be the case that an animal cannot be wronged by one's breaking one's promise to it, because the moral force of the promise requires that the promisee is capable of understanding that he or she has been given a promise by the promisor. However, personhood is not required for suffering bad brute luck. Admittedly, this does not in itself imply that differential bad brute luck endured by non-persons is of concern from the point of justice, because perhaps relations of differential brute luck are unjust only when they obtain between persons even if it is not clear why absence of personhood should render differential brute luck not unjust.

At this point it is worthwhile introducing an *intermediate position*. On this view, inequalities between all individuals matter. However, inequalities between persons matter more from the point of view of justice than otherwise comparable inequalities between non-human animals. Also, inequalities between persons matter more than inequalities between persons and non-human animals. This view has the merit of accommodating the moral intuitions in the light of which I suggested that the maximalist and the minimalist positions are implausible. However, it is not immediately clear what the rationale for such a view could be.

Specifically, with regard to the proposal I described in Chapter 2 on why all human beings are equal, it is clear that if the present intermediate position is accepted, this rationale will have to be supplemented. On this suggestion all human beings ought to be treated equally in virtue of their capacity to be non-instrumentally concerned with things in a distinctive way, e.g. one that involves long-term planning. Since some non-human beings do not have this capacity and since, on the intermediate view, inequalities between such individuals do matter from the point of view of egalitarian justice, this suggestion cannot provide a complete rationale for egalitarian justice. Indeed, providing a rationale for the intermediate view seems an even more daunting task than providing one for the view that all human beings are equal.

In view of this some might be tempted to go for the minimalist view. Frances Kamm (cf. 2013: 312–14) suggests something like the following argument for doing so. On her view, levelling down might be in one respect good when we are talking about persons. However, levelling down to create equality between non-persons is not good in any respect. If we share this view, this is some argument for the minimalist view. Note also that if we take this view, we will need to say something about why the presence or absence of personhood makes a difference to the injustice of inequality. Probably the explanation that comes to mind first is that only persons have the capacity to see themselves as being (unjustly) worse off than others. However, this explanation is one that telic egalitarians cannot avail themselves of, since it is hard to reconcile it with the view that inequality is intrinsically unjust. Indeed, it suggests that the badness of inequality lies in a whole of inequality and its perception. Admittedly, this leaves open the possibility that inequality is non-instrumentally unjust. However, it seems not to be what egalitarians have in mind, e.g. when they object to intergenerational inequality (see Section 6.3 above). Accordingly, I must end this section on a somewhat inconclusive note. Luck egalitarians must decide whether they favour an intermediate or extreme position on the scope of egalitarian justice. However, this choice will constrain them, e.g. in relation to their account of what makes inequality unjust.

6.7. Summary

Luck egalitarianism says that it is unjust if some individuals are worse off than others through their bad luck. This statement is silent on its scope, i.e. on who are the individuals, luck-based inequalities between whom are unjust. In this chapter I critically discussed various scope-based issues. Section 6.2 argued that egalitarian justice concerns equality of people's lifetimes. Section 6.3 contended that egalitarian justice is concerned with equality between individuals who are members of different, even temporally very distant, generations. Section 6.4 defended the view that equality is concerned per se with relations between individuals and individual choices as opposed to inequalities between groups and group choices. Section 6.5 took – perhaps unsurprisingly given the view on intergenerational justice defended earlier – the view that egalitarian justice is cosmopolitan in nature. Finally, Section 6.6 explored the intriguing question of whether the scope of egalitarian justice extends beyond human beings and/or persons without really committing itself to any particular view on this matter. In any case, this issue is a challenging one and, as I argued, the main alternatives to luck egalitarianism face a similar challenge.

7

Social relations egalitarianism versus luck egalitarianism

7.1. Introduction

Over the last fifteen years social relations egalitarianism has appeared as an important competitor to the luck egalitarian account of justice. People who subscribe to social relations egalitarianism include Elizabeth Anderson, David Miller, Thomas Scanlon, Samuel Scheffler and Iris Marion Young. Negatively, they are united in a rejection of the view that justice is a matter of eliminating differential luck. On their view, some people can be worse off than others through no responsibility of their own and yet this need not be unjust. Similarly, they think that justice is compatible with people being equally well off despite the fact that some have made great efforts and others have not. Positively, they subscribe to the following view:

(1) A society is just if, and only if, individuals within it relate to another as equals.

For social relations egalitarians the site of justice – that is, that to which principles of justice apply – is society, not distributions.

Section 7.2 elaborates this general characterization of social relations egalitarianism, while Section 7.3 describes the most influential version, i.e. Elizabeth Anderson's democratic egalitarianism. Section 7.4 responds to two of the most important challenges pressed against luck egalitarians by social relations egalitarians. Section 7.5 argues that many of the concerns that are adduced in support of social relations egalitarianism can be accommodated by luck egalitarianism. Section 7.6 critically assesses an attempt by Elizabeth Anderson to identify the source of the disagreement between luck and social relations egalitarians. Overall, this chapter defends luck egalitarianism against the challenge from social relations egalitarianism.

7.2. Social relations egalitarianism

When do individuals relate to one another as equals (see Cohen 2013: 193–200)? In response to this question we can easily offer paradigmatic examples of social relations, where individuals do not relate to one another as equals. Generally, whites and blacks did not relate to one another as equals in South Africa under Apartheid, and, generally, women and men do not relate to one another as equals in Saudi Arabia, e.g. women need the permission of a male member of their family if they want to travel abroad, whereas the reverse is not the case (cf. Fourie 2012: 107–8). But once we move beyond a handful of paradigmatic examples things become much less clear. Take, for instance, the relation between parents and young children. Offhand, these relations do not seem to be relations between equals. So, one might ask: do relations between children and adults exist in the sort of society favoured by social relations egalitarians? Similar questions might be asked about many other social relations, e.g. between prisoners and prisoner guards, professors and students, charismatic political leaders and their followers (cf. Scheffler 2005: 17–18).

Social relations egalitarians might respond by saying that their ideal only enjoins egalitarian social relations in particular spheres of society, e.g. in the political sphere. This would not address the example of the relation between charismatic political leaders and their followers. Moreover, it raises the question of why their ideal is restricted to particular spheres. One might doubt that there are social relations to which the ideal of relating to one another as equals does not speak at all. For instance, there is a huge difference between seeing children as the private property of parents and seeing children as individuals with an independent moral status who are owed justification of how one treats them. It would be surprising if social relations egalitarians thought justice did not speak to which of these two social relations are preferable.

Alternatively, social relations egalitarians might retract to a very undemanding notion of relating to one another as equals such that, say, the relation between prison guards and prisoners is compatible with relating to one another as equals. However, doing so raises the obvious question whether some of the hierarchical relations which social relations egalitarians consider objectionably inegalitarian might be compatible with the ideal of relating to one another as equals so construed. If the relation between a prison guard and a prisoner can be one that embodies the ideal of equality of social standing despite the fact that the prison guard has authority over the prisoner in all sorts of ways, why cannot the relation between a patriarchical husband and an obedient wife, who after all may have more freedom of discretion than the prisoner, be one that is compatible with standing to one another as equals? These issues show that, however forceful the phrase 'a society of individuals who relate to one another as equals' is as a slogan, it needs to be spelled out much more for us to get a clear grasp of what it really amounts to. To put this point positively: social relations egalitarianism comes in many different species and what makes them form a genus is their endorsement of the claim that a society is just if, and only if, individuals within it relate to one another as equals. Different social relations egalitarians give different accounts of when individuals relate to one another as equals as well as which individuals justice requires should relate to one another as equals.

It is fair to say that so far social relations egalitarians have offered accounts of their ideal that are more sketchy and incomplete than one might have wished for. Moreover, just as different luck egalitarians give different accounts of egalitarian justice, so do different social relations egalitarians give different accounts of a society of equals. David Miller, for instance, contends that a society of equals 'is not marked by status divisions such that one can place different people in hierarchically ranked categories, in different kinds of classes' (Miller 1998: 23). When the social ideal of equality is realized, people 'regard and treat one another as equals' (Miller 1998: 23). The objection to inequality, then, is that it creates 'social divisions'. For example:

those whose incomes fell below one-half of the mean income (say) were very likely to feel alienated and excluded from social life, would experience an immense social gulf between themselves and those living a comfortable middle-class lifestyle ... *our society should not be like that.* In objecting to inequality, we are objecting to social relations that we find unseemly – they involve incomprehension and mistrust between rich and poor, for instance, and arrogance on one side and forelock-tugging on the other. (Miller 1998: 24)

Miller at no point defines a society in which everyone regards all others as equals, but he provides a thumbnail sketch:

Where there is social equality, people feel that each member of the community enjoys an equal standing with all the rest that overrides their unequal rankings along particular dimensions. This is expressed in the way people interact: they use common modes of address ... they shake hands rather than bow, they choose their friends according to common tastes and interests rather than according to social rank. (Miller 1998: 31)

In a society of equals condescension cannot be seen as a virtue, since this would mean that some people enjoy privileges of superiority of the sort that make it possible, in condescending, to waive a right to deference (Miller 1998: 32).

Samuel Scheffler – another prominent social relations egalitarian – briefly describes a 'social and political ideal of equality' resembling the one set out by Miller (Scheffler 2003a: 22). The ideal, Scheffler notes, is 'opposed ... to oppression, to heritable hierarchies of social status, to ideas of caste, to class privilege and the rigid stratification of classes, and to the undemocratic distribution of power' (Scheffler 2003a: 22). As a moral ideal it holds that 'all people are of equal worth'; as a social ideal, that 'a human society must be conceived of as a cooperative arrangement of equals'; and finally, as a political ideal, that one has 'a right to be viewed simply as a citizen, and to have one's fundamental rights and privileges determined on that basis, without reference to one's talents, intelligence, wisdom, decision-making skill, temperament, social class, religious or ethnic affiliation, or ascribed identity' (Scheffler 2003a: 22). While the ideal of equality rightly construed is an ideal 'governing the relations in which people stand to one another', it has certain 'distributive implications' (Scheffler 2003a: 21). For instance, a society in which everyone's basic needs are not met, or in which there are 'significant distributive inequalities' that generate 'inequalities of power and status that are incompatible with relations among equals', cannot be a society of equals (Scheffler 2003a: 23; cf. Scanlon 2000: 52).

These characterizations of a society of equals could be expanded and otherwise improved. However they are so expanded and improved, an obvious question arises – namely: does anything prevent luck egalitarians from accepting social relations egalitarianism? As we saw in Chapter 1, luck egalitarianism states a sufficient condition for a distribution being unjust. However, doing so leaves it entirely open for them to accept that there are other sufficient conditions and, more specifically, that for a society to be just people have to relate to one another as equals. This is where the social relations egalitarians' negative contribution – i.e. the critique of luck egalitarianism – comes into the picture.

Negatively, social relations egalitarians reject the luck egalitarian view that egalitarian justice requires that no one is worse off than others through no responsibility of her own. Rather than equality they think that just distributions are distributions where everyone has enough, where 'enough' means enough to participate in social and political life on an equal standing. As we saw in the case of Scheffler, this does not means that social relations egalitarians are indifferent to inequalities in well-being or, for that matter, in terms of any other *equalisandum*. However, they think such inequalities matter, from the point of view of justice, only instrumentally through their effects on the egalitarian character of social relations. In principle, social relations egalitarians could think that, as a matter of fact, all inequalities corrupt social relations, but, as a matter of fact, social relations egalitarians do not think so.

7.3. Anderson's democratic equality

Having given a broad-brushed characterization of social relations egalitarianism in the previous section, I now want to take a closer look at the position of Elizabeth Anderson in this and the following two sections. Anderson accuses luck egalitarians of misconstruing the point of equality. Polemically, she asks: 'If much recent academic work defending equality had been secretly penned by conservatives, could the results be any more embarrassing for egalitarians?' (Anderson 1999a: 287). Apparently, her answer is 'no'. Before proceeding to present her reasons for this assessment, however, I should mention a feature of Anderson's critique, which determines the merits to which it can lay claim.

In effect, Anderson's critique is theorist-, not theory-, focused. By that I mean that while she offers a broad sketch of luck egalitarian justice, her critique is not based on a definition of the position she attacks or, for that matter, of the position she defends. Rather, she pinpoints various counterintuitive views held by, or implied by views held by, a number of theorists whom she labels luck egalitarians. Admittedly, her selection is largely well motivated and her critique points to some important problems with these views, e.g. how they tend to ignore the situation of dependent caretakers and the claim to compensation of people who make prudentially bad, but morally required or supererogatory, choices. But this form of criticism has its limitations. On the assumption that the selected luck egalitarian theories do not exhaust the logical space of luck egalitarian theories, her critique does not impugn luck egalitarianism *as such*.

Anderson writes that the basic flaw of luck egalitarianism is that it construes 'the fundamental aim of equality' as a matter of compensating 'people for undeserved bad luck', when the 'proper negative aim of egalitarian justice is to end oppression, which by definition is socially imposed' (Anderson 1999a: 288–9). Moreover, the proper positive aim 'is … to create a community in which people stand in relations of equality to others' (Anderson 1999a: 288–9). Like that of other social relations egalitarians, her critique has two components: a negative one offering various reasons for why luck egalitarian justice is counterintuitive, and a positive one sketching an alternative egalitarian view, i.e. democratic equality.

The basic thrust of the negative part is to show that luck egalitarianism does not express 'equal respect and concern for all citizens', and the 'most fundamental test' which any egalitarian theory must meet is that it has this expressive feature. The term 'test' suggests something that can play a well-defined role in Anderson's argumentation. However, this is not the case. First, the requirement is vague, as Anderson herself acknowledges (Anderson 1999a: 295). For instance, it is syntactically ambiguous, viz. does 'equal' qualify 'respect' as well as 'concern'? If 'yes', it is unclear how the test coheres with the sufficientarian component in Anderson's democratic equality. If 'no', it becomes murky how the test favours egalitarianism as opposed to other distributive principles. However this issue is resolved, it is far from straightforward whether a certain item involves treating with or expressing equal concern and respect. Moreover, it is unclear whether the 'equal concern and respect' test is a test of the relevant theory's egalitarian credentials, or of the theory's plausibility as an account of justice.

Second, there is a sense in which any theory of justice must – and almost all do – meet the requirement that it implies that all persons have the same moral status (Kymlicka 1990: 5). Thus, for luck egalitarianism to fail Anderson's test it must be much more specific and, thus, cannot derive any support from this truism – for instance, many would deny that the plausibility of moral principles depends on what they, or rather actions informed by them, express (Adler 2000). But then the test itself – unlike the uncontroversial test, which, along with most other theories, luck egalitarianism passes – requires an argument, if it is to be employed to adjudicate between competing views of egalitarian justice.

Due to these considerations, it is warranted to focus not on Anderson's test, but on the various putatively counterintuitive luck egalitarian views she enlists. She sorts these into two groups. First, in cases involving bad option luck, luck egalitarianism implies that justice does not require, or even forbids, coming to the assistance of people who ended up badly off, e.g. luck egalitarianism allows letting a motorcyclist who had a head injury in a traffic accident die when she knowingly took the risk of driving without a crash helmet (cf. Fleurbaey 1995: 40–1; Voigt 2007).

Second, in cases involving bad brute luck it fails 'to express concern for everyone who is worse off' and 'the reasons it offers for granting aid to the worst off are deeply disrespectful to those to whom the aid is directed' (Anderson 1999a: 303). The reason for this is that worse off people have a claim to compensation, according to luck egalitarianism, not in virtue of being equals, but in virtue of their inferiority (Anderson 1999a: 306). So in compensating people for their bad brute luck for luck egalitarian reasons, one expresses pity, which 'is incompatible with respecting the dignity of others' (Anderson 1999a: 306). To support this claim Anderson imagines what sort of appalling justifications a luck egalitarian state could offer people whom it compensates for bad brute luck, e.g. people with low intelligence or who are deemed unattractive. Despite her opening polemics about conservatives penning the work of luck egalitarians, she even quotes Hayek approvingly to the effect that luck egalitarianism 'requires the state to make grossly intrusive, moralizing judgments of individuals' choices' (Anderson 1999a: 310).

While Anderson's substantive criticism of luck egalitarianism focuses on *victims* of bad luck, she does not criticize luck egalitarians for adopting excessive *softness* (assuming this is the opposite of harshness) towards beneficiaries of option luck, who get to keep their windfall benefits, and for branding beneficiaries of good brute luck as being *superior*. However, from the perspective of democratic equality it appears no less problematic to, say, stamp some as being superior to others than to stamp some as being inferior. Both acts clash with persons' standing in relations of equality to one another. Hence, some of the force of Anderson's critique derives from sources other than democratic equality and to the extent that one concurs, it is unclear that the proper response is to endorse democratic equality.

I now move on to Anderson's positive characterization of democratic equality. Democratic equality seeks to construct 'a community of equals' that 'integrates principles of distribution with the expressive demands of equal respect. Democratic equality guarantees all law-abiding citizens effective access to the social conditions of their freedom' (Anderson 1999a: 289). While democratic equality is not concerned with the distribution of individual goods per se, it is instrumentally concerned with it insofar as an unequal distribution might cause inequality in social relations, e.g. scraping of the poor in front of the rich. Negatively, one can characterize a society organized along the lines of democratic equality as one in which there are no 'relations between superior and inferior persons' (Anderson 1999a: 312). A society realizing democratic equality manifests the 'equal moral worth of persons' where this involves, negatively, a denial of 'distinctions of moral worth based on birth or social identity' and, positively, 'that all competent adults are equally moral agents: everyone equally has the power to develop and exercise moral responsibility, to cooperate with others according to principles of justice, to shape and fulfil a conception of their good' (Anderson 1999a: 312; Anderson 2010b: 89–11).

These characterizations cast little concrete light on democratic equality. Many non-egalitarians subscribe to the claims about equal moral worth Anderson mentions, e.g. right-libertarians like Nozick. However, Anderson supplies some hints of how these characterizations are to be interpreted. For instance, she refers to Young's notion of five faces of oppression and notes that real-life egalitarians are opposed to the six 'inegalitarian ideologies of racism, sexism, nationalism, caste, class, and eugenics' (Anderson 1999a: 312; cf. Young 1990). Unfortunately, this list is not very helpful either, since presumably, to qualify as a democratic egalitarian it does not suffice that one opposes the six inegalitarian ideologies she mentions. For instance, Nozickean libertarians oppose such ideologies to the extent that they think that property rights do not depend on race, sex, nationality etc. Let us look at each of them separately.

While racist ideologies and ideologies of caste involve a denial of equal moral worth, not everyone who opposes racism and caste is a democratic egalitarian. Eugenics in its racist forms belongs to the list, but one can be committed to the improvement of future generations, e.g. health-wise, without being committed to the unequal moral worth of persons (Glover 2006: 32–6).

Extreme nationalists may deny the equal moral worth of persons, but few nationalists subscribe to anything stronger than liberal nationalism, which involves no such denial (e.g. Miller 1995; Tamir 1993). Anderson might respond that while nationalism articulated at a theoretical level is compatible with equal moral worth, lived nationalism is not. For instance, many people think that *our* soldiers need not accept small risks to avoid imposing much greater risks on *their* combatants or civilians (McMahan 2010). However, if that is her thought, it is strange that soldiers form one of Anderson's favourite examples of workers in dangerous occupations that luck egalitarians abandon.

Finally, it is unclear what Anderson has in mind when she refers to ideologies of class. For sure, there are people who think that a just society may consist of different classes in some sense, but unless Anderson by 'equal moral worth' means something such that one denies it if one holds that it is not unjust per se for people to be divided into, say, workers and capitalists, there are hardly any contemporary ideologies of class that deny the 'equal moral worth of persons'.

Anderson also mentions relations where 'some people dominate, exploit, marginalize, demean, and inflict violence upon others' as social relations that are incompatible with democratic equality (Anderson 1999a: 313). Several questions are in order here. First, one wonders if her list is meant to be complete. Specifically, why are relations where some coerce, manipulate, ignore or deliberately misunderstand others not on her list? Second, of those relations that she mentions one wonders if all of them are incompatible with relating to one another as equals. Do cases of mutual exploitation – such as those involved in at least some forms of sugar-dating – really involve a denial of something as basic as equal moral worth?

Among the examples Anderson gives of equal social relations are the political relations that we have to one another in virtue of the one-person-one-vote principle and 'open discussion among equals' where 'no one need bow and scrape before others or represent themselves as inferior to others as a condition of having their claim heard' (Anderson 1999a: 313). However, the scope of democratic equality extends beyond the state to civil society and, for instance, is incompatible with hierarchical social relations in the marriage. This completes my presentation of Anderson's ideal of democratic equality. I have not offered a concise formulation of it, but, in part at least, this reflects that Anderson does not offer any such formulation.

7.4. Humiliation and harshness

In this section I assess Anderson's criticisms of luck egalitarianism. First, I consider her objection that luck egalitarianism commends the abandonment of victims of bad option luck: this is the *harshness* objection. I then turn to examine her view that luck egalitarianism expresses pity towards victims of bad brute luck: this is the *humiliation* objection.

The harshness of objection presupposes that people can act in such a way that, according to luck egalitarianism, they deserve, or are responsible for, their own hardships. It may be that there is nothing in standard formulations of luck egalitarianism to rule this out, and indeed some formulations, such as Dworkin's, require us not to offset disadvantages resulting from bad option luck. However, nor do luck egalitarians *have* to agree that people sometimes deserve to end up very badly off (Olsaretti 2009, 2013; Vallentyne 2002). Thus standard formulations of luck egalitarianism rule out the idea that people who have bad option luck should end up worse off than people, acting in a similar situation, who have good option luck (Christiano 1999). For example, the luck egalitarian view that justice requires people's relative positions to reflect nothing but their relative exercises of responsibility does not imply that someone who drives a motorcycle not wearing a crash helmet deserves to end up dying, while someone who wears a helmet deserves to survive. In fact this formulation rules out the view that two motorcyclists, both of whom drive dangerously, should end up unequally well off.

This reply might be taken to show that luck egalitarianism is an indeterminate position. In a fully worked out development of it, the conditions under which people's relative positions reflect their relative exercises of choice would be specified. But to say that a theory is under-specified is not equivalent to saying that it has counterintuitive implications. Moreover, the indeterminacy at issue here does not affect my core point: the harshness objection fails to establish that egalitarianism *as such* should be rejected; at most, it demonstrates that we should reject variants of egalitarianism specifying what it is for people's relative positions to reflect their relative exercise of responsibility in such a way as to imply that harsh outcomes of the sort Anderson has in mind are just. Even here there is room for counterargument. Assuming we cannot help everyone, it seems unjust to disregard how people ended up in dire straits (Albertsen and Knight 2015; Arneson 1999b; Arneson 2000a: 343–4; Christiano 1999; Sobel 1999).

Anderson mentions G. A. Cohen and John Roemer as two theorists who question the 'structure of opportunities generated by markets' and may therefore be less vulnerable to the harshness objection. She concedes that their views avoid the 'worst outcomes generated by laissez faire capitalism', but she notes that as 'theorists from the Marxist tradition' they neglect the situation of 'non-wage-earning dependent caretakers' (Anderson 1999a: 300). However, she does not write that 'as luck egalitarians' Cohen and Roemer fail to consider 'non-wage-earning caretakers', and it is clear that she is not minded to connect the neglect here with luck egalitarianism. While she might be right that luck egalitarianism *as such* does not impose any constraints on the structure of opportunities generated by free markets, for the reason just given it is also true that it is compatible with such constraints being imposed. Assuming, for instance, that individuals are aware in advance of how the state will shape market outcomes (e.g. to secure a certain social minimum), nothing clashes with people's relative positions reflecting their relative exercise of responsibility. Hence, the present objection is at best an objection to a certain form of luck egalitarianism, not to luck egalitarianism as such.

Second, democratic equality is vulnerable to something like the harshness objection. Suppose that infectious diseases ensure that all of the citizens of a poor republic live in harsh conditions, and that as a result of this everyone stands in relations of equality to one another. Suppose next that a philanthropist – a Bill Gates-like billionaire – offers to fund a one-off, free vaccination programme for everyone. Participants will irreversibly enjoy much better conditions. Suppose finally that if most but not all citizens decide to be vaccinated, this will unavoidably introduce hierarchical social relations. Assuming that there is a small minority of citizens who refuse, say, for religious reasons, democratic equality implies that it would be unjust if the majority were to get themselves vaccinated and thereby escape their harsh conditions. To make this point more vivid, assume that this minority also forms a racial minority, and that its members' refusal of the vaccination will predictably result in stigma attaching to being a member of the relevant racial minority group, e.g. because the relevant diseases drain people of their energy and their motivation to participate in politics. If it is an objection to luck egalitarianism that it recommends abandoning the imprudent, it seems no less objectionable that in cases of the sort just described democratic equality condemns the prudent majority for escaping their harsh conditions.

Let me turn now to Anderson's humiliation objection. The first thing to note is that there is a question about whether this objection sticks. As the title of Anderson's 1999 article suggests, her concern differs from that of at least some of her luck egalitarian opponents. On Cohen's view equality does not *have* a point in the sense that, say, anti-discrimination laws have a point, namely to reduce unjust discrimination. Rather, equality is what justice requires, and this claim simply states a truth which, like the truth that *modus ponens* is a valid form of inference, has no point as such, even if there might be a point in stating or defending it. By contrast, part of Anderson's worry is that various luck egalitarian writings on issues such as the requirement of justice to support lazy able-bodied surfers put egalitarians in a vulnerable political position. She therefore deploys phrases such as 'invites the charge', 'feeds the suspicion', 'bolster the objection', rather than contending straightforwardly that the views with which she is concerned are false (Anderson 1999a: 287–8). Similarly, when Anderson charges that luck egalitarian principles 'stigmatize the unfortunate' or give 'individuals an incentive to deny personal responsibility for their problems,' what she has in mind is acting in accordance with these principles, not the principles themselves. However, a true principle as such neither stigmatizes anyone, nor gives anyone an incentive to do one thing rather than another – and Cohen takes the issue to be what, exactly, these principles are (Anderson 1999a: 311; Cohen 2008: 271; Arneson 2000a: 345).

Anderson thinks that egalitarian philosophizing should not be too far removed from real-life efforts to promote equality. However, because many real-life egalitarians *are* concerned about socioeconomic inequality, this theoretical plea may in fact favour luck over social relations egalitarianism. Cohen thinks a gap between the philosophizing and the reality of equality is tolerable, because, and insofar as, real-life egalitarians are obliged to take into account much else besides what egalitarian justice requires. (I discuss his distinction between fundamental principles of justice and rules of regulation in more detail in Chapter 8.) For instance, their concerns must also be shaped by competing values and by what they can realistically hope to bring about. It would be an error to require a priori that the concerns of the egalitarian political philosopher do not diverge from those of the activist.

Second, setting aside my first response, is it true, as Anderson contends, that luck egalitarianism locates the ground of people's compensation in their inferiority? Obviously, it is true, trivially, if we treat bad luck as something that *confers* inferiority. However, according to the luck egalitarian the victim of bad luck also makes a claim to compensation in virtue of her equality with others, insisting that she has the same claim not to be worse off as others have unless, say, differential exercises of responsibility lie at the root of an unequal outcome. Once this distinction is made, it is unclear that grounding claims for compensation in inferiority of the first kind is objectionable.

Third, the humiliation objection focuses in part on the morally objectionable attitude of *pity* expressed by someone who, acting on luck egalitarian principles, compensates another for bad brute luck. However, here is a simple counterargument to this pity-based objection:

> (2) If it is an objection to a moral principle as such that in acting on it one expresses a morally objectionable attitude, then, necessarily, in acting on that principle one expresses a morally objectionable attitude.
> (3) Of no moral principle is it true that, necessarily, in acting on that principle one expresses a morally objectionable attitude.
> (4) Hence, it is not an objection to a moral principle as such that in acting on it one expresses a morally objectionable attitude.
> (5) Luck egalitarianism is a moral principle and pity is a morally objectionable attitude.
> (6) Hence, it is not an objection to luck egalitarianism as such that in acting on it one expresses pity.

The premises entail the conclusion, so the question is whether they are true. I have my doubts about the second conjunct of (5) (the first conjunct is uncontroversial), but these are irrelevant here since Anderson needs it to be true if her humiliation objection is to go through. To see the kind of consideration that lies behind (3), imagine John. Acting on a luck egalitarian principle, John seeks to compensate people for their bad brute luck, because he has promised to do so. Presumably, however, in doing so he expresses his belief that one ought to keep one's promises, which does not amount to expressing a morally objectionable attitude – far from it. In response, Anderson might say that John is not concerned with no one's being worse off through no responsibility of her own *for its own sake*. Accordingly, John does not act *on*, though he acts *in accordance with*, a luck egalitarian principle in the relevant sense. The problem here is that a person who is motivated by such a concern need not be motivated by pity. For example, her concern about equality might be entirely impersonal (cf. Barry 2006: 97). Hence, in making this reply Anderson would undermine her humiliation objection to luck egalitarianism.

Premise (2) is true. One can act on any moral principle in a way that expresses a morally objectionable attitude – e.g. one could act on the principle of democratic equality thereby expressing a morally objectionable, unthinking deference to the views of Anderson. But, surely, this is no objection to these views. Perhaps a premise could be formulated which is weaker than (2), congenial to Anderson's objection, yet stronger than a revision that reads: 'If it is an objection to a moral principle as such that in acting on it one expresses a morally objectionable attitude, then, *possibly*, in acting on that principle one expresses a morally objectionable attitude'. However, the burden of proof here rests on friends of democratic equality.

Fourth, is democratic equality immune to the humiliation objection (assuming it is an objection)? According to Anderson, one has a claim to have one's capability set improved where, and only because, that set is worse than those available to others such that one stands in a relation to other citizens as an inferior. But then it is hard to see why this is not to have a claim in virtue of one's inferiority. Moreover, democratic equality only indemnifies individuals for those losses that impair their 'functioning as a free and equal citizen and avoiding oppression'. Accordingly, it will provide treatment to a smoker who has developed lung cancer, but it will not compensate this individual for 'the dread that she feels upon contemplating her mortality' (Anderson 1999a: 327). Anderson is right that normally dread of one's mortality does not interfere with one's 'functioning as a free and equal citizen'. However, some people's dread of mortality affects them more seriously than the rest of us, and they become unable to function as free and equal citizens as a consequence. Democratic egalitarians would want to provide assistance to them, but presumably any potential beneficiaries of such assistance would have to document their abnormal dread in order to receive additional resources. Anderson focuses on capabilities and not actual functionings. Given this, to implement democratic equality, one has to 'check who lacks a functioning through choice and who lacks it through lack of capability'. This means that Anderson endorses 'conditional benefits', and accordingly that, if luck egalitarians are burdened with the problem of humiliation involved in 'shameful revelations', i.e. having to reveal sometimes very intimate or personal facts about oneself which are in themselves shameful, or in a way, that is shameful, so is democratic equality (Wolff 2010: 348; cf. Firth 2013; Kaufman 2004: 828).

This concludes my assessment of Anderson's two main lines of attack on luck egalitarianism. They seem inconclusive at least: in part because they are misdirected or otherwise weak, in part because even if they were not, democratic equality would be vulnerable to similar criticisms.

7.5. What is at stake?

The social relations egalitarian critique of luck egalitarianism raises many issues. These can be fruitfully teased apart and considered separately. In this section I consider nine issues that Anderson and others present as matters of contention between luck egalitarians and friends of democratic equality (I label these (a)–(i)). In each case I argue that luck egalitarianism and democratic equality do not necessarily diverge over the matter at stake and that the concern she raises can be accommodated by luck egalitarianism.

(a): Anderson objects to the luck egalitarian's narrow focus on 'the distribution of divisible, privately appropriated' or 'privately enjoyed' goods such as income and wealth, as opposed to goods like the freedom of gays and lesbians to 'appear in public' without 'shame or fear' (Anderson 1999a: 288; cf. Young 1990). Objections of this kind to narrowness of focus are objections not to a theory, but its theorists. In point of fact, the canonical formulation of luck egalitarianism leaves it entirely open whether the freedom of gays and lesbians to 'appear in public' without 'shame or fear' and similar goods are to be included in the relevant *equalisandum*. Thus, Cohen's formulation of luck egalitarianism – that a difference in people's advantages is 'just if and only if it accords with a certain pattern in the relevant people's choices' – is compatible with the notion that the relevant 'advantage' includes the ability to appear in public without shame or fear (Cohen 2011: 117). Indeed, given how strongly inhibiting such shame or fear can be, it would seem very strange for Cohen – or indeed for any other luck egalitarian, including a friend of the account of the egalitarian *equalisandum* that I have proposed in Chapter 4 (cf. Arneson 2000a: 341–2) – not to regard this as a form of disadvantage that matters from the point of view of justice.

(b): In a related contrast, it might be said that whereas democratic egalitarians are concerned with social relations, luck egalitarians are concerned with other entities (cf. Wolf 2010: 358). However, this need not be so. Consider the good of having social standing that is equal to that of another. Mary and John have equal amounts of this good, *ceteris paribus*, if, and only if, they relate to one another as equals. Mary has more of this good than John has, *ceteris paribus*, if, and only if, John relates to Mary as a superior individual to an inferior individual and *vice versa*. The luck egalitarian view that it is unjust if some are worse off than others in terms of social standing unless this reflects their differential exercise of responsibility certainly overlaps, in terms of its locus of concern, with democratic equality. Consider Anderson's claim that 'democratic equality is sensitive to the need to integrate the demands of equal recognition with those of equal distribution' (Anderson 1999a: 314). On the present proposal this contrast is misleading. While recognition may be a feature of social relations between individuals, some individuals may enjoy more recognition than others and, for that reason, luck egalitarians could sensibly object to unequal distributions of recognition that do not reflect differential exercise of responsibility. Note, finally, that Anderson appeals to Sen's capability approach 'to identify goods within the space of equality that are of special egalitarian concern' (Anderson 1999a: 316). But, surely, *one* member of the luck egalitarian family, at least, says that people should be equal in terms of the relevant 'sets of functionings [they] can achieve, given the personal, material, and social resources available to [them]' (Anderson 1999a: 316).

(c): Occasionally Anderson gives the impression that whereas luck egalitarians think that differences in welfare and differences in all kinds of resources are relevant from the point of view of justice, democratic egalitarians take only a restricted range of goods to matter and expect individuals 'to take personal responsibility for the other goods in their possession' (Anderson 1999a: 289). For instance, Anderson emphasizes that democratic equality does not require *equality of functionings*. It requires only 'effective access to levels of functioning sufficient to stand as an equal in society ... Democratic equality does not object if not everyone knows a foreign language, and only few have a Ph.D.-level training in literature' (Anderson 1999a: 318–19). These remarks are misleading. To begin with, the first sentence ignores the possibility that 'standing as an equal' requires not just *effective access* to a certain level of functioning, but the *actual enjoyment* of this level of functioning: for example, the requirement is not just for effective access to a certain level of education, but for people actually to have that level of education. By ignoring this possibility Anderson avoids the inconvenient – given her hostility towards paternalism and the state telling people how to run their lives – question of what democratic equality implies about the practice of nudging, incentivizing or even forcing people who are unwilling to get an education to do so.

Second, the target of the comment about foreign language mastery and the possession of a PhD is a straw man: at any rate, no luck egalitarian holds the view contrasting with democratic equality here. Finally, as we saw in Chapter 4, luck egalitarianism can coherently be combined with various kinds of *equalisanda*. One could have a very narrow opinion about what goods fall within the scope of egalitarian justice and remain luck egalitarian. Arguably, there are limits to this narrowness. For example, the view that it is unjust if, and only if, some people have lower levels of welfare on their eighteenth birthday or weaker constitutional rights than others through no responsibility of their own might not qualify as luck egalitarian, but this point, while true, is compatible with my present criticism.

(d): The two views might be thought to differ in terms of their scope in the following way. Democratic equality governs the relations between citizens presently living in the same nation state, whereas luck egalitarianism extends to all individuals across the borders of states and time. However, this contrast is misleading in several ways. First of all, as we saw in Section 6.5 at least two of the luck egalitarian theorists Anderson criticizes – Dworkin and Nagel – do not adopt luck egalitarianism with global scope, and in fact standard formulations of luck egalitarianism do not specify scope in this regard.

Second, although democratic equality, as Anderson states it, concerns relations between citizens, she must recognize that democratic equality with global scope would be a close cousin of her view. It is not clear, for instance, why democratic egalitarians should not be in favour of non-co-nationals standing in equal social relations to one another. More generally, one could certainly imagine cosmopolitan versions of social relations egalitarianism, versions that might indeed seem more attractive than state-bound ones in the light of globalization (cf. Schemmel forthcoming).

(e): Anderson's harshness objection appeals to the fact that responsibility plays a significant role in luck egalitarianism. In view of this, and given her positive proposals, one might assume that a key difference between luck egalitarians and democratic equality theorists is that the former take responsibility to justify some being worse off than others and the latter deny it. However, this is a misunderstanding although, admittedly, there is a possible variant of social relations egalitarianism which is identical to Anderson's ideal of democratic equality except for the fact that it ascribes no role whatsoever to responsibility. As a democratic equality theorist, Anderson thinks a situation in which citizens who do not abide by the law are worse off than others in terms of 'effective access to the conditions of their freedom at all times' (Anderson 1999a: 289) is not thereby unjust. Admittedly, her reason for thinking so might not be responsibility-based. She asserts, however, that 'egalitarian principles should uphold the responsibility of individuals for their own lives without passing demeaning and intrusive judgments on their capacities for exercising responsibility or on how well they have used their freedoms' (Anderson 1999a: 314). Presumably, this view is what motivates her position on the just deficiencies in functioning involved in just punishment. Similarly, she thinks that lazy able-bodied surfers can, justly, be much worse off than others on the ground that they could get a job if they wanted (as we assume). Finally, she emphasizes that democratic equality 'guarantees not actual levels of functioning, but effective access to those levels' (Anderson 1999a: 318). Hence, on Anderson's view there is nothing unjust about someone who has effective access to functionings necessary for standing as an equal within civil society as well as within the state, but who refrains from accessing these functionings. This strongly suggests that democratic equality ascribes significance to substantive responsibility (cf. Brown 2005: 334).

(f): In response to the previous paragraph one might wonder whether it is possible that, although both luck egalitarians and democratic equality theorists ascribe a role to responsibility, the two views differ over *what* that role is. However, it is unclear even that this more modest claim is true. Anderson writes: 'Effective access to a level of functioning means that people can achieve that functioning by deploying means already at their disposal, not that the functioning is unconditionally guaranteed without any effort on their own part' (Anderson 1999a: 318). To paraphrase: there is no injustice in a person not enjoying the relevant level of functioning when this reflects the person's refusal to make any effort to do so. Something like this thought underlies luck egalitarianism, since if someone has the means at his disposal to make himself as well off as others, then in all likelihood insofar as he is worse off than others he is responsible for so being. However, democratic equality requires individuals, irrespective of their irresponsible choices in the past, always to have effective access to the functionings necessary for standing as an equal, whereas standard luck egalitarianism imposes no limits on how badly off one might permissibly end up as a result of irresponsible choices. The relevant threshold requirement might be an implausible one, but whatever its credentials are, it is not one that luck egalitarians are *obliged* to reject. It is all a question of which set of options they think people should face in a just society. This reply ignores cases of extreme scarcity in which not everyone can have effective access to the functionings necessary for standing as an equal. Possibly, but perhaps not plausibly, luck egalitarians might say that when individuals fall below a certain threshold no inequality between them can reflect their differential exercise of responsibility. Friends of democratic equality and luck egalitarianism might give different accounts of what makes a situation in which everyone falls below a threshold line unjust, but here I focus on luck egalitarianism and democratic equality as views about *when* a society or distribution is just, not views about *what makes* them so (recall Section 1.2). It is true that luck egalitarians have failed to consider many of the issues that Anderson helpfully raises, but this is not due to inherent limitations in luck egalitarianism.

(g): Another contrast that occasionally surfaces in Anderson's critique relates to morally praiseworthy, but imprudent or risky choices. Anderson considers 'workers in dangerous occupations', an example being soldiers who risk their lives defending their country. If soldiers are aware of the risks associated with their occupation and could have chosen alternative employment, the harms they risk are, if things turn out badly, a matter of bad option luck, and thus they have no luck egalitarian claim to compensation.

This case involves a complication that Anderson's other counter-examples of people unjustly suffering from bad option luck do not involve – namely, that here other citizens benefit from the risky choices of workers in a dangerous occupation and might even have been the intended beneficiaries of an arrangement in which workers take up risky occupations. Many luck egalitarians construe responsibility for being worse off as a matter of whether one has made the most prudent choice. However, responsibility can be interpreted in various other ways in the luck egalitarian framework. Substantive responsibility could be specified in such a way that it is absent when one's being worse off is the result of acting as one was morally required to act, or acting in a supererogatory way (e.g. one enters a burning building at a high risk to one's own life, saves the child, but suffers severe burns that make one worse off than others) (Eyal 2007; Kaufman 2004: 826; Lippert-Rasmussen 2011a, 2011b; Temkin 2003(b)). Indeed, as we saw in Section 6.4 luck egalitarianism based on an account of luck which ties luck to moral deservingness will have no problems accommodating this particular criticism.

(h): The previous contrast is close to another alleged difference between the two theories: that luck egalitarianism seeks to tailor distribution to *desert*, while desert plays no role in democratic equality. This suggestion is doubly mistaken. First, consider the following passage: 'Yet a society that permits its members to sink to such depths, due to entirely reasonable (and, for dependent caretakers, even obligatory) choices, hardly treats them with respect. Even the imprudent don't deserve such fates' (Anderson 1999a: 301). The second sentence here can only support the first if Anderson's notion of respectful treatment requires people to be treated in such a way that their fates correspond to what they deserve. But if that is so, desert has a role to play in democratic equality. Second, very few egalitarians ascribe a role to desert as such. For Cohen and Temkin, to mention two influential luck egalitarians, it is responsibility, not desert, that really lies at the core of the luck egalitarian's commitments (Hurley 2003: 191–5, 197–8).

(i): It may be suggested that luck egalitarians and democratic equality theorists are raising different questions. The luck egalitarian asks what a just distribution is. Anderson is asking what a just state or society is like. 'Democratic equality applies judgments of justice to human arrangements, not to the natural order' (Anderson 1999a, 336), she says; and she further contends that the 'distribution of natural assets is not a matter of justice', but that 'what people do in response to this distribution is' (Anderson 1999a, 331). Does this mark an important difference in the topics of luck egalitarianism and democratic equality? Undoubtedly, there is a difference here, and I will return to it in Section 8.6. Perhaps what looks like a disagreement really is a matter of responding to different questions? Be that as it may, some luck egalitarians certainly address themselves to Anderson's question. For instance, this is true of Dworkin, for whom the core question is what it takes for a state to treat its citizens with equal concern and respect. More generally, deontic luck egalitarians, in Parfit's sense, will agree that justice concerns human arrangements (Parfit 1998: 6–9).

In the light of the considerations stated above, I conclude that many objections that are made to luck egalitarianism do not really separate social relations and luck egalitarians. Even if they point to concerns that are relevant from the point of view of justice, these are concerns that luck egalitarians can accommodate – either because they can be incorporated into luck egalitarianism as such or because luck egalitarians can accept that there are other justice values than those articulated by luck egalitarianism.

7.6. The source of the disagreement between social relations and luck egalitarians?

So far in this chapter, we have looked at a number of objections to luck egalitarianism on account of some of its specific implications. More recently, however, Anderson has argued that the basic source of the disagreement between social relations egalitarians and luck egalitarians about the requirements of egalitarian justice is a disagreement that concerns the standpoint from which principles of justice are justified. According to Anderson:

> Luck egalitarians follow a *third-person* conception of justification. In a third-person justification, someone presents a body of normative and factual premises as grounds for a policy conclusion. If the argument is valid and the premises are true, then the conclusion is justified. The identity of the person making the argument and the identity of her context are irrelevant to the justification. By contrast, most relational egalitarians follow a *second-person* or *interpersonal* conception of justification. This follows from their contractualism ... In a second-person justification, a claim of justice is essentially expressible as a demand that a person makes on an agent whom the speaker holds accountable. Justification is a matter of vindicating claims on others' conduct. Vindication involves demonstrating that the claims are addressed to those properly held substantively responsible for the conduct in question, by persons entitled to the moral authority or standing to hold them to account. (Anderson 2010a: 2–3)

This account of the deeper disagreement underlying the (putative) disagreement regarding the contours of justice seems to rule out any attempt to defend a pluralist version of egalitarian justice, according to which a just society is one in which the distribution complies with luck egalitarianism and people relate to one another as equals. After all, if Anderson is right, these two components rest on conflicting ideas of justification. Fortunately, worries about the coherence of such an ecumenical position can be dismissed, as we shall now see.

Anderson's characterizations of the two justificatory perspectives do not match. Her description of the third-person conception of justification says: 'In a third-person justification, someone presents a body of normative and factual premises as grounds for a policy conclusion. If the argument is valid and the premises are true, then the conclusion is justified' (Anderson 2010a: 2). The matching characterization of the second-person conception of justification would then say that it is insufficient, to justify a policy conclusion, simply to present a valid argument for it invoking only true normative and factual premises. However, this is not how she describes this conception. Instead, she writes that second-person justifications are a matter of 'vindicating claims on others' conduct' (Anderson 2010a: 3). This heterogeneity is problematic.

First, it implies that there are more than two conceptions of justification in play. Let us call justifications that conform to Anderson's characterization of third-person justification 'context-insensitive' and those that do not 'context-sensitive'. Moreover, let us call justifications meeting Anderson's characterization of second-person justification 'conduct-claim dependent' and those that do not 'conduct-claim independent'. These two distinctions cut across one another such that four different positions are possible: (a) justification is context-insensitive and conduct-claim independent; (b) justification is context-sensitive but conduct-claim dependent; (c) justification is context-insensitive but conduct-claim dependent; and (d) justification is context-sensitive and conduct-claim dependent. The first two views are the ones which Anderson focuses on in her reconstruction of the disagreement between luck egalitarians and social relations egalitarians; (a) corresponds to her view of third-personal justification, whereas (b) corresponds to her model of second-personal sort of justification. However, (c) and (d) are possible as well.

According to the context-insensitive, conduct-claim dependent view of justification, i.e. (c), a distribution of goods, say, is unjust only if it results from some people not fulfilling the demands others can reasonably make on them, and these demands can be given a context-insensitive justification. Hence, unavoidable inequalities are not unjust on this view, because they do not satisfy the former condition.

According to the context-sensitive, conduct-claim independent view of justification, something might be unjust even if it does not result from some people not fulfilling the demands others can reasonably make on them, and if these demands can be given a context-sensitive justification. According to this view, unavoidable inequalities might or might not be unjust, since it might be impossible to give a context-relative justification for their injustice. Suppose all involved parties deny that natural inequalities are unjust. Given this supposition, and given that one cannot justify a certain view by appealing to a principle that one rejects, *they* (as opposed to people who subscribe to no such principle) cannot justify, or demonstrate, to others the injustice of such inequalities to one another. Rawls might gesture at a context-sensitive conception of justification in relation to a different topic: 'A person's right to complain is limited to violations of principles he acknowledges himself' (Rawls 1971: 217).

Second, in her critique Anderson fails to offer an example of a justification that is context-sensitive. Admittedly, she discusses some justifications that she thinks involve unreasonable demands and fail for that reason. However, the relevant justifications fail – if indeed they do – irrespective of perspective and this makes her claim about the source of the disagreement between luck egalitarians and social relations egalitarians dubious. By way of illustration, consider her discussion of Salieri's complaint that Mozart has a greater natural musical talent than he does (Anderson 2010a: 10). According to Anderson, the injustice of relevant inequality cannot be established from a second-person point of view. However, her contention does not rest on an appeal to context-sensitivity. Instead, it rests on the contention that it 'is unreasonable to demand that people do things beyond human capacities' (Anderson 2010a: 10). Her argument goes as follows:

(7) A state of affairs is unjust only if it involves a person's failure to comply with a reasonable demand another person can make.

(8) A state of affairs involves a person's failure to comply with a reasonable demand another person can make only if the person failing to comply can prevent that state of affairs from obtaining.
(9) If it is beyond human capacities to prevent a certain state of affairs from obtaining, no person can prevent it from obtaining.
(10) It is beyond human capacities to prevent Mozart's natural musical talents from being greater than Salieri's.
(11) Thus, no person can prevent Mozart's musical natural talents from being greater than Salieri's (from 9 and 10).
(12) Thus, it is unreasonable to require any person to prevent Mozart's natural musical talents from being greater than Salieri's (from 8 and 11).
(13) Thus, it is not the case that the state of affairs of Mozart's musical talents being greater than Salieri's is unjust (from 7 and 12).

Whatever the merits of this argument if it is sound, then *anyone* can employ it to justify *to anyone*, e.g. Beyoncé can employ it in a discussion with Madonna about the justice of Mozart's musical talents being superior to those of Salieri just as, second-person style, Mozart can offer it to Salieri. Imagine, then, that Mozart affirms (7)–(9), and continues:

(10*) It is beyond human capacities to prevent *my* natural musical talents from being greater than *yours*.
(11*) Thus, no person can prevent *my* musical natural talents from being greater than *yours* (from 9 and 10*).
(12*) Thus, it is unreasonable to require any person to prevent *my* natural musical talents from being greater than *yours* (from 8 and 11*).
(13*) Thus, it is not the case that the state of affairs of *my* musical talents being greater than *yours* is unjust (from 7 and 12*).

There seems no reason why this would not work as a justification when offered by Mozart to Salieri, if it works when offered by Beyoncé to Madonna.

I should like to end this section with an ironical twist to the criticism just made. G. A. Cohen, whom Anderson thinks of as a main representative of luck egalitarianism, has offered a much-discussed critique of incentives-based arguments for inequality. This critique is built on the so-called 'interpersonal test', i.e. a test where justifications for policy proposals are uttered by different groups of individuals to other groups. If the justifications do not work irrespective of who are the justifiers and who are the recipients of the justification, the justification fails the interpersonal test. This is ironical because, *qua* luck egalitarian, Cohen is supposed to take a third-person perspective on justification and yet context-variation plays an essential role in this critique of the incentive argument for inequality.

In Cohen's critique of incentives-based arguments for inequality, he argues that an unequal distribution is unjust precisely because, while incentives-based justifications might work when untalented people justify to other untalented people the need for incentives to talented people ('We should be made as well off as possible and unless they get incentives this won't happen'), they do not work when talented people justify why they should be given incentives to untalented people ('You should be made as well off as possible and unless we get incentives this won't happen'), despite the validity of the argument and despite the truth of its premises. The reason for this context-sensitivity is that in the latter, but not the former, context, it is those who offer the justification that make its empirical premise true – i.e. that unless the talented get incentives the untalented won't be made as well off as possible – and they cannot justify doing so. At least, they cannot do so given the Rawlsian view – Rawlsian according to Cohen, at least – that having inferior talents is a matter of having had bad luck in the natural and social lottery.

As I will return to in the last Section 8.4, it is unclear if this critique reflects non-luck egalitarian commitments on the part of Cohen – e.g. his commitment to a certain kind of justificatory community whose relation to luck egalitarian justice is unclear. Whatever is the right view on this matter, it is strange that Anderson's characterization of a third-person justification, and therefore her implicit characterization of a second-person justification, in large part overlaps with, if indeed it is not adopted from, Cohen's exposition of his interpersonal test and how it implies context-sensitivity of justification (2008: 35–41, 64–8). While there is much more to be said about Anderson's disagreement source claim than I have said here, including much more positive things (see Lippert-Rasmussen forthcoming), what has been said should suffice to cast significant doubt on her analysis of the nature and depth of the disagreement between social relations and luck egalitarians.

7.7. Summary

Since Elizabeth Anderson's influential 1999 article on the point of equality, social relations egalitarianism has emerged as a strong competitor to luck egalitarianism. In this chapter I have argued that the former does not succeed in rebutting luck egalitarianism and, indeed, that it is unclear to what extent the two theories are incompatible. I have argued the former point in Sections 7.3 and 7.4 by showing how Anderson's ideal of democratic equality is under-specified and unattractive in various respects and by rebutting the humiliation and harshness objections. In response to the latter point – the one about incompatibility – I have argued that pluralist luck egalitarians might simply allow that egalitarian social relations is another determinant of justice in addition to the one captured by luck egalitarianism (cf. Chapter 8). Also, as shown in Section 7.5, many of the concerns expressed in Anderson's critique of luck egalitarianism are accommodated by certain forms of luck egalitarianism – forms that perhaps have not been defended by any actual luck egalitarians but forms that would certainly qualify as such on the definition of luck egalitarianism offered in Chapter 1. Plainly, this observation leaves us with the substantive task of determining what kind of luck egalitarian theory we should accept, but this issue is one that separates various members of the luck egalitarian family from one another, not one that refutes luck egalitarianism as such. Hence, the conclusion of this chapter is that while social relations egalitarians might have identified some aspects of justice luck egalitarian theorists have tended to ignore – e.g. the issue about compensation for morally praiseworthy actions that are prudentially bad for the agent – luck egalitarianism should not be rejected in the light of the critique from social relations egalitarians.

I concede that in this chapter I have focused on a particular version of the social relations egalitarian critique of luck egalitarianism – that of Elizabeth Anderson. This focus, however, is warranted to the extent that, arguably, it is the most influential version thereof and that many components of social relations egalitarianism that are found in the work of others correspond to elements in her account. I have not shown that there could be no form of social relations egalitarianism – other than that of democratic equality – which is indeed incompatible with luck egalitarianism, nor that there could not be social relations egalitarian objections to luck egalitarianism that are more successful than, say, the harshness and the humiliation objections. Still, as the debate stands presently it seems fair to conclude that luck egalitarianism survives social relations egalitarianism and, indeed, may in many ways be combinable with or incorporate it (cf. Schemmel forthcoming).

If they are combined in a pluralist account of egalitarian justice in this way, the question arises whether the different components can be grounded in the same way. In Section 2.7 I suggested that luck egalitarianism is grounded in a concern for fairness. However, it is not clear if people relating to one another as equals can be similarly grounded. One suggestion here, which I will simply suggest, but not develop or defend, is that it is grounded in fairness, like ordinary distributive equality, tough in a different way. Agents who do not relate to one another as equals – at least, when this is what they are – do not have the virtue of being fair, and a hierarchical society is one in which people relate to one another in an unfair manner.

8

Other values

8.1. Introduction

In the previous chapters, we explored the nature of and justification for egalitarian justice. More specifically, and with the exception of Chapter 7, we looked at *luck* egalitarian justice. In this chapter, I will assume that luck egalitarian justice should be understood and justified roughly as set out in previous chapters. The question I shall address in this chapter is how this ideal relates to other ideals – especially ideals that in recent discussions have been said to refute or clash with luck egalitarian justice. The question of how equality relates to other values is important because, as we saw in relation to the levelling down objection in Chapter 6, it is highly implausible to claim that *only* equality is valuable. If it were, a world in which everyone suffers and equally so would be better overall than a world in which everyone lives blissful lives, but some slightly more so than others.

If there are other values than equality, then, in principle, there are two possibilities. Either it is the case that, despite the fact that there are different values, all of them can be realized at the same time, or not all of them can be realized at the same time. The former possibility would be truly surprising. If several distinct values exist, we would expect them to be realized by different states of affairs. If so, it seems possible that different values might be in conflict with one another in the sense that we cannot realize all of them to a maximum degree. This will mean that we have to weigh them against one another. For instance, we would have to say whether a great reduction in equality is worth more than a small loss of privacy (to refer back to Cohen's discussion of objections to equality that are not objections to the proposed *equalisandum*). On the view, which I will take for granted until the last section in this chapter, pluralism about values is true. That is, there is a plurality of values, not all of them can be realized at the same time, and there is no lexical ranking of them such that for any pair of values, a loss in one of them, however small, will always be worse than a loss in the other, however great.

As many have noted, weighing different values against one another is difficult and in what follows I shall not say anything about how much weight exactly should be given to luck egalitarian justice. Nevertheless, this is an important question. It should be noticed, however, that justice is normally considered an important value that, except for extreme cases, tends to outweigh other values. Rawls for instance famously asserted that:

> Justice is the first virtue of social institutions, as truth is of systems of thought. A theory however elegant and economical must be rejected or revised if it is untrue; likewise laws and institutions no matter how efficient and well-arranged must be reformed or abolished if they are unjust. Each person possesses an inviolability founded on justice that even the welfare of society as a whole cannot override. For this reason justice denies that the loss of freedom for some is made right by a greater good shared by others. It does not allow that the sacrifices imposed on a few are outweighed by the larger sum of advantages enjoyed by many. Therefore in a just society the liberties of equal citizenship are taken as settled; the rights secured by justice are not subject to political bargaining or to the calculus of social interests. (Rawls 1971: 3)

Others, e.g. Cohen, have tended to downplay the role of justice. Note, however, that luck egalitarianism does not capture all, if anything, of what Rawls has in mind in this quote. Suppose we can bring about equality by killing better-off persons. Presumably, Rawls, and many others, would say that doing so would clash with the inviolability of persons even if it would bring about perfect distributive justice. Accordingly, there are aspects of justice in the sense that Rawls has in mind here that are not captured by distributive justice.

This leads me to distinguish between three levels at which pluralism might be true. First, there might be different and conflicting values, justice being one of them, that together determine what we ought to do, all things considered, and what is best, all things considered.

Second, there might be different justice values, distributive justice being one of them, that determine what is just, all things considered. For instance, distributive justice is often contrasted with retributive justice. Suppose that everyone is equally well off, but one person has culpably made all of us worse off than we would otherwise have been. In this case, it may be that an unequal distribution is just, all things considered, even if there is no objection from the point of view of luck egalitarian justice to the present equal distribution.

Finally, it might be that there are different distributive justice values, luck egalitarian justice being one of them. For instance, if we give a non-desert-based account of luck, in principle one could hold that which distribution is just is determined by desert as well as the luck egalitarian principle. Similarly, it might be that what is distributively just depends not only on luck egalitarian justice, but also on the overall sum of weighted well-being (Temkin 1993).

Having mentioned these possibilities, I will assume that luck egalitarianism provides a complete account of distributive justice but that it might clash with other justice values, e.g. individual rights to freedom, or with other non-justice-related moral values. In the final section of this book – Section 8.6 – I will address some doubts about this pluralistic framework as well as the nature of justice in general. Sections 8.2 to 8.5 will explore some possibly conflicting values, to wit, freedom, agent-relative permissions, publicity and community.

8.2. Freedom

Probably, the most common objection to equality is that it conflicts with freedom. Robert Nozick put forward this objection in a particularly forceful form in *Anarchy, State, and Utopia* forty years ago. Strictly speaking, the target of this objection was those who reject his 'entitlement conception of justice in holdings' (Nozick 1974: 160), e.g. because they accept so-called patterned principles of distributive justice, which includes equality but also many other principles, e.g. sufficiency and prioritarianism. Nozick, however, chose equality for the purpose of illustration, claiming that equality forbids 'capitalist acts between consenting adults' (Nozick 1974: 163).

Nozick's objection is the following: he asks the defender of a patterned principle of distributive justice to select his or her favoured distributive pattern. Suppose the selected pattern is equality. Next thing that happens is that Wilt Chamberlain – a talented basketball player at the time Nozick wrote *Anarchy, State, and Utopia* – freely decides to play basketball games provided that all spectators put 25 cents in a box with his name on. Many spectators freely decide to do so thinking that the price is well worth the show. After a while, Chamberlain is better off than others, so the resulting distribution should be unjust according to egalitarianism. But how can this be the case, Nozick asks? After all, the initial equal distribution was just by the lights of egalitarianism and the steps that took us from the initial equal distribution to the later unequal one only involved free and autonomous acts between consenting adults, where presumably people only exercised their property rights over what was theirs, e.g. money and time. Nozick's challenge has exercised philosophers with egalitarian leanings quite a lot. Below I shall describe two ways in which luck egalitarians may respond to the Wilt Chamberlain challenge, or, in the case of the second response, a revised version thereof.

The first response is to point out that either the initial situation described by Nozick is not just, or it is, in which case luck egalitarians need not object to the resulting inequality. Luck egalitarians might affirm the former disjunct, because it seems obvious from Nozick's description of the example that Chamberlain has better opportunities than others. He has a basketball talent that gives him a greater earning capacity than others. Accordingly, on a relevant metric of equality the situation Nozick describes is not really one of equality. In response, Nozickeans might simply stipulate that all persons involved have identical talents and, accordingly, anyone could have done what Chamberlain did – it is just that they did not use their opportunities as well as they could. However – and that is where the second horn of the dilemma becomes relevant – they just chose not to do so, in which case luck egalitarians do not find the resulting inequality one that is a result of bad luck and, thus, not one that is unjust in any way. In neither case has Nozick succeeded in describing a challenge to luck egalitarianism.

One counter-reply to this might be that all it shows is that luck egalitarianism is not a patterned principle. That is, assuming certain initial conditions are fulfilled in principle any pattern of distribution could be just provided it results directly, and unmediated by luck, from people's choices. Since Nozick's objection was an objection to patterned principles it is no surprise that a principle that is not patterned survives the objection and, thus, that Nozick's challenge stands undefeated.

However, given the dialectical context of Nozick's Wilt Chamberlain argument, this counter-reply is not particularly convincing. For luck egalitarianism undoubtedly is a competitor to Nozick's libertarianism. Moreover, it would seem to be one of the competitors which Nozick would like to defeat by this argument. Accordingly, if luck egalitarianism is simply immune to the Wilt Chamberlain argument, its relevance is much reduced. Accordingly, it is better for libertarians to see if they can reformulate the challenge in such a way that it avoids the first luck egalitarian reply. So let us assume instead that Chamberlain is a very lovable person comparatively speaking due to bad brute luck of others and that due to his being so lovable everyone gives him 25 cents, not to see him play basketball, but simply because they want to give him a gift. As a result he is now much better off. Because the inequality in question results not from ordinary market transactions, but simply from people freely acting on the basis of their affections, it may seem counterintuitive that the resulting unequal distribution should be objectionable.

In response to the revised version of the Wilt Chamberlain objection, luck egalitarians might invoke a distinction between justice and legitimacy (cf. Cohen 2011). A distribution is just if and only if no one is worse off than others through bad luck. A distribution might be legitimate even if some are worse off than others through bad luck. If, for instance, everyone, including the worse-off, consents to bringing about a certain outcome, it might be legitimate in the sense that it would be unjust to prevent this distribution from being brought about even if it is an unjust distribution. Arguably, the distinction between justice and legitimacy is also at stake in relation to cases of gambling where two gamblers freely choose to gamble and one has good option luck and the other has bad option luck. The resulting inequality is unjust because it reflects differential luck, but it might nevertheless be unjust for others to undo it given that both gamblers freely and autonomously decided to engage in the gamble. Finally, the distinction is one that most recognize in relation to democracy. Within limits, it is possible to democratically choose a law which is unjust. The law might be legitimate in the sense that it would be unjust for anyone to undo the law by force despite its injustice.

In the section above I have sketched how luck egalitarians might defeat a certain argument to the effect that freedom and equality clash. Even if this sketch succeeds it is possible that they do clash, though for reasons other than those brought out by the Wilt Chamberlain argument. Accordingly, it would be desirable if luck egalitarianism could offer a positive argument for why they do not clash – desirable in the sense that, if the two values do not clash, we are not forced to sacrifice equality for the sake of freedom or vice versa. Ronald Dworkin offers such an argument.

In a discussion about what distinguishes liberals from conservatives Dworkin describes the common view that liberty and equality sometimes come into conflict with one another and that liberals and conservatives differ in that, unlike conservatives, liberals give greater weight to equality than to liberty (Dworkin 1986: 188). However, this view is flawed in Dworkin's view for a simple reason. Any person favours restrictions on liberty. For instance, even conservatives are:

content that their liberty to drive as they wish … may be invaded for the sake, not of some important competing political ideal, but only for marginal gains in convenience or orderly patterns. But since traffic regulation plainly involves some loss of liberty, the conservative cannot be said to value liberty as such unless he is able to show that, for some reason, less liberty is lost by traffic regulation

than its absence (Dworkin 1986: 189). To do so presupposes a 'concept of liberty that is quantifiable' and liberty is not, Dworkin claims, relevantly quantifiable. Accordingly, conservatives do not value liberty as such more than liberals do. Indeed, in the absence of a way of determining the overall sum of freedom, it is doubtful that it makes sense to value liberty as such.

There is something to Dworkin's argument. While some have proposed quantitative measures of freedom (Carter 1999), these are controversial and in any case it is not clear that these are somehow inherent in the concept of liberty. Still, there is something unpersuasive about Dworkin's argument. First, perhaps one can say something similar about equality. Often when we compare two situations with one another, it is difficult to say which one is worse in terms of inequality (Temkin 1993). Is this a reason for denying that it makes sense to care about equality as such?

Second, some states of affairs might dominate others in terms of freedom, i.e. it may be that in one situation everyone has all the freedoms they have in that other situation as well as some additional ones. Suppose that in the situation with fewer freedoms, there is perfect equality, while there is not in the situation with additional freedoms. Here it makes sense to say that liberals distinguish themselves from conservatives in thinking that, *ceteris paribus*, the former situation is better than the latter. In response Dworkin might remind us that, on his view, equality is to be construed as a duty the state has to treat its citizens as equals and that, perhaps, if the state brought about the latter situation it would still treat its citizens as equals as no one's interests would be sacrificed for the benefit of others. Whatever the merits of this reply, it seems to throw us back to the first problem. For, according to Dworkin, there are different interpretations of what it is to treat people as equals. On his view, conservatives subscribe to this requirement as well, albeit their interpretation is less good. But then why can one not similarly say that there are different interpretations of maximum overall freedom and that an interpretation according to which a situation with traffic regulations and freedom of speech is better, freedom-wise, than one without traffic regulations and no freedom of speech, is a worse interpretation?

Despite these misgivings, I think there is something to Dworkin's scepticism regarding the existence of a conflict between freedom as such and equality. Indeed, to think that there is seems to involve some sort of category mistake. Equality is a distributive principle. As such it can conflict with other distributive principles, e.g. sufficientarianism. Freedom, however, is not a distributive principle. Indeed, it is something to which one can apply distributive principles as when liberals insist on *equal* liberty. Accordingly, there can be no conflict between liberty as such and equality. Similarly there can be no conflict between welfare as such and equality. No doubt there can be a conflict between maximizing the sum of welfare and equalizing welfare, but the relevant conflict reflects a conflict between two different distributive principles, as does the conflict between maximizing the overall sum of freedom and equal freedom.

That being said, there can be conflicts between equality and particular freedoms, e.g. the freedom to earn money without having to pay income tax or, to use an example which will occupy us in the next section, the freedom to pursue one's personal projects. But this is surely different from saying that equality and freedom as such are at loggerheads – the important point being that freedom, as so many other things, can be distributed differently across persons.

8.3. Demandingness

There is a distinction between what one might call non-moral and moral freedom. A person who is forced at gunpoint to work for someone else does not have the non-moral freedom not to work for that person – another agent makes it the case that the option of not working is and/or is believed to be very bad and much worse than working – but she has the moral freedom not to do so in the sense that she is not morally required to work for the person enslaving her. On an intermediate and moralized notion of freedom, freedom is non-moral freedom to do what one is morally permitted to do. For present purposes we can set this notion of freedom aside. The previous section makes most sense on the assumption that by 'freedom', I mean non-moral freedom. However, in the present section I will focus on moral freedom.

One of the more common objections to act consequentialism is that it is 'too demanding'. There are various ways of fleshing out this objection. First, on some views the very requirement to give no greater weight to one's own interests than to those of others is too demanding. Second, on other views it is the fact that, under some circumstances, consequentialism implies that agents are required to sacrifice core interests or basic projects of their own to benefit others (Williams 1973b). Third, on the view, which we briefly encountered in Chapter 6, some find consequentialism too demanding because of the epistemic uncertainly it involves – it is always possible that we discover the facts are such that we have to make large sacrifices for the benefit of others (Tan 2014). Finally, consequentialism can be thought to be too demanding because it implies that, sometimes, a person is morally required to make large sacrifices to provide tiny benefits to a large number of other people.

In response to these criticisms Scheffler has proposed a form of quasi-consequentialism that incorporates an element of partiality into what is otherwise act consequentialism. On Scheffler's proposal, agents are morally permitted to bring about an outcome that is not the best outcome from an agent-neutral point of view, but which is more beneficial to their own interests than the agent-neutrally best outcome provided that the agent's extra gain is not dispropor-tionate relative to the gains others lose if the agent promotes her own interests. The resulting moral principle, obviously, is immune to the first version of the demandingness objection, since it gives significant room for partiality. The second and the third versions of the objection might still apply to Scheffler's view, but in versions where it is not clear that they defeat his view. For on most moral theories, under some circumstances we can be morally required to make large sacrifices – e.g. to avoid disastrously bad consequences – and we cannot know in advance that we will not end up in such unfortunate circumstances. The fourth version of the objection is one that Scheffler's agent-prerogative does not address. With this in mind, we can now turn to luck egalitarianism.

Like act consequentialism, luck egalitarianism has been criticized for being too demanding. Too see how, put yourself in the shoes of a gifted person living in an otherwise perfectly egalitarian community. You face the following choice:

(a) Working as a doctor at $300,000 being much better off than others.

(b) Working as a performance artist at $20,000 being just as well
     off as others.

(c) Working as a doctor at $20,000 being just as well off as
     others. (cf. Cohen 2008: 185)

You strongly prefer (a) to (b) – because money is not nothing – and
(b) to (c) – because, in terms of self-realization (b) is much better
than (c). All others prefer (c) to (a), and (a) to (b). What does luck
egalitarianism tell you to do? Some luck egalitarians – institutionalists
(cf. Section 6.5) – will say that the site of distributive justice is institutions and, accordingly, on their version of luck egalitarianism, luck
egalitarianism has nothing to say about what *you* should do, although
it may say that institutions, e.g. taxation regimes, should be such
that no one had so good opportunities and that individuals have a
duty to support just institutions (cf. Dworkin 2000; Tan 2014).

Other luck egalitarians – non-institutionalists or, as we might
call them in parallel to act consequentialists, act luck egalitarians –
concede that luck egalitarianism does have something to say about
the situation. Indeed, it seems that they have to say that while you
are morally permitted to choose between (b) and (c), you must not
choose (a), since in choosing (a) you will bring about that others are
worse off than you are through their having the bad luck of not being
gifted in the way you are. However, not choosing (a) is a big sacrifice
on your part, and it will not leave others much better off. So is act
luck egalitarianism not vulnerable to the demandingness objection in
the same way that act consequentialism is?

In response act luck egalitarians might have several things to
say. If they are pluralists, they might remind their critics of the
fact that egalitarian justice is just one moral concern among others
and that what agents are morally required to do depends on moral
factors other than the one theorized by luck egalitarianism. One
such factor could be a Schefflerian agent-relative prerogative.
Cohen writes: 'only an extreme moral rigorist could deny that
every person has a right to pursue self-interest to some reasonable
extent (even when that makes things worse than they need be for
badly off people)' (Cohen 2008, 61). Presumably, if Cohen did not
mean to imply here that a person who sacrifices the interests of
the worse-off to pursue her self-interest to a reasonable extent

does not do anything morally wrong, he would not have used the term 'moral rigorist' here.

Another reply could be that while you are morally required not to choose doctor at $300,000, you have a moral right to do so such that others are not morally permitted to force you not to choose it. Even so, if you exercise this right by choosing doctor at $300,000, you do what you are not morally permitted to do. This reply connects well with how act luck egalitarians might respond to differential option luck and while it may not go all the way in alleviating the concerns expressed by the demandingness objection, it might undermine most of its force.

Finally, luck egalitarians might respond more directly to the demandingness objection. For instance, act luck egalitarians might point out that, unlike Scheffler's prerogative, their view is not vulnerable to the fourth version of the demandingness objection, at least not in the version where it is most damaging. Absent considerations about differential responsibility, luck egalitarianism does not recommend that worse-off people make big sacrifices to provide small benefits for many better-off people. Still, as the levelling down objection shows, it does recommend it as desirable that better-off people make sacrifices bringing about equality even though that benefits no one, so perhaps it is vulnerable to the demandingness objection. Something similar can be said about the first objection. Strictly speaking, it is immune to it, because act luck egalitarianism does not require agents to treat the interests of other as being as important as their own interests. However, it requires them to treat an impersonal value as being more important than their own interests and this seems no less, if not more, demanding than being impartial between one's own interests and the interests of others. Finally, luck egalitarianism seems potentially vulnerable to the second and third versions of the demandingness objections.

The overall upshot of this is that, on its own, act luck egalitarianism might be vulnerable to some version of the demandingness objection that is no weaker than the similar objection to consequentialism. This, however, should not discourage pluralist luck egalitarians, who can incorporate an agent-relative prerogative into their account of what agents are morally required to do, all things considered. Luck egalitarianism can be part of an overall moral theory which is not too demanding and, thus, the demandingness objection does not defeat luck egalitarianism, even assuming that the objection is a sound one.

Still, one doubt might remain. For on a luck egalitarian account, it would be permissible for you to choose working as a performance artist at $20,000 rather than (a) on account of self-realization. However, you would, as would all others, prefer doctoring at $300,000 to being a performance artist making $20,000. So it seems that on the luck egalitarian account there is no way to reconcile Pareto, moral freedom in relation to freedom of occupation, and equality. However, as Cohen has pointed out, you could still choose doctor at $20,000 (cf. Cohen 2008: 87–115). In that case you would still enjoy freedom of occupation – no one interferes with your choice and you were free to choose otherwise. Equality obtains and neither doctoring at $300,000, nor being a performance artist making $20,000, is Pareto superior to doctoring at $20,000. The first option is not Pareto superior to the last, because while you would be better off doctoring at $300,000 than doctoring at $20,000 others would be worse off, since they would have to pay you more for the same doctoring services. Being a performance artist making $20,000 is not Pareto superior to doctoring at the same modest income level, because while you would be better off doing the former than you would doing the latter, others would be worse off, since while they just might get some enjoyment from your doing performance art, this far from compensates them for the loss of your doctoring services. Hence, there is a way out of the luck egalitarian trilemma.

At this point, however, one might ask why anyone should doctor at $20,000, when they could choose an alternative living that would involve the same earning but which would also allow them to realize themselves. At this point, we should turn to a discussion of the relation between equality and community.

8.4. Community

I return to the luck egalitarian trilemma shortly. However, first I want to remind the reader that we have already had some look at the notion of community. In Chapter 7 I introduced Cohen's interpersonal test, which he employs to criticize incentives-based justifications of inequality, and we encountered his notion of a justificatory community, i.e. one where members of the community are willing to justify their action to others whenever they affect them. So here some ideal of community played a role in justifying greater equality. However, in some of his last publications, Cohen also hinted at how he thought community was valuable independently of equality and, indeed, that sometimes one ought to do things in the interest of community that are not required – perhaps not even permitted – by luck egalitarian principles (Cohen 2009: 34; cf. Vrousalis 2010). Taking a broader historical perspective, we should also recall the motto of the French Revolution – 'Liberty, Equality, Fraternity' or, as it was initially more dramatically put, 'Liberty, Equality, Fraternity or Death'. Fraternity, despite its sexist twist, is a form of community, so also from the perspective of real-life egalitarians it is of considerable interest to clarify the relation between equality and community. While 'community' might mean many different things, here I want to focus on community in some senses that have been influential in recent luck egalitarian literature exploring possible conflicts between equality and community. Hence, I will disregard the literature on how luck egalitarian justice might support promoting minorities defined by a shared cultural structure (cf. Kymlicka 1991; Lippert-Rasmussen 2009).

Return to the egalitarian trilemma and the question of why someone would sacrifice self-realization when doing so would bring no compensating self-interested benefits. Cohen answers this question by appealing to the notion of an egalitarian ethos. An egalitarian ethos exists in a society when in that society there is a social norm to the effect that one should be guided by, in significant part at least, a concern for equality in the choices, e.g. in relation to choice of career or how one spends one's income one makes in one's daily life and, generally speaking, members of this community have internalized this norm and act in accordance with it. While Cohen does not think that it is impossible for a just distribution to be brought about without an egalitarian ethos, he also thinks that it is extremely unlikely that in a world like ours it will be so in its absence (Cohen 2008: 123–4). To put it simplistically: if luck egalitarian justice is to be realized, it does not just require that people vote for The Equality

Party and then seek to maximize their income in their daily lives. They should vote for The Equality Party but they should also, in the course of their daily lives, seek to promote equality.

A society that is permeated by an egalitarian ethos is characterized by a certain kind of justificatory community. In such a community any policy, or to extend the scope of Cohen's test, any norm or practice satisfies the interpersonal test (cf. Section 7.6). This test determines:

> how robust a policy argument is, by subjecting it to variation with respect to who is speaking and/or who is listening when the argument is presented. The test asks whether the argument could serve as a justification of a mooted policy when uttered by any member of society to any other member ... If, *because* of who is presenting it, and/or to whom it is presented, the argument cannot serve as a justification of the policy, then whether or not it passes as such under other dialogical conditions, it fails (tout court) to provide a comprehensive justification of the policy. (Cohen 2008: 42)

The justificatory communal relations that obtain when all policy arguments offered in a community pass the interpersonal test, so Cohen contends, preclude incentives-based inequalities. Any argument in favour of policies of providing inequality-producing incentives for talented people would fail the interpersonal test, because, when uttered by talented people, they would be the ones that make inequality necessary to improve the situation of the worse-off and such a stance is indefensible in the light of luck egalitarianism. So here is a case where luck egalitarian justice and (justificatory) community are not just compatible with one another, but, indeed, one where the non-satisfaction of the latter suggests non-satisfaction of the former (cf. Scheffler 2003a: 37 n.77). I will move on to two other aspects of community that are more in tension with luck egalitarian justice shortly, but before doing so let me just register one line of doubt about Cohen's optimistic view on the relation between justificatory community and egalitarian justice.

Suppose talented as well as untalented people influence not only the overall sum of benefits but also how it is distributed. Suppose, realistically, they all need to make an effort to secure the highest level of benefits. Suppose, finally, that untalented people make no efforts as a result of which worse-off people will be worse off than they would have been had untalented people made an effort comparable to the effort of talented people, whether or not talented people insist on inequality-inducing incentives. In such a case, which admittedly might be highly unusual, it may well be the case that talented people can offer an argument for inequality-inducing incentives that passes the interpersonal test, since talented people can deny that untalented people are in a position to complain about their (comparable) lack of efforts. If so, at least in some cases the existence of a justificatory communal relation does not require luck egalitarian justice (cf. Lippert-Rasmussen 2008b).

I will now move on to two further aspects of community which Cohen briefly explored in some of his last work and which, so he conceded, might clash with luck egalitarian justice – namely, community of life experience and communal motivation. On Cohen's view, for people to enjoy community of life experience the 'challenges' that they face in life have to be more or less the same in such a way that large inequalities rule out this valuable form of community: 'We cannot enjoy full community, you and I, if you make, and keep, say, ten times as much money as I do, because my life will then labor under challenges that you will never face, challenges that you could help me cope with, but do not, because you keep your money' (Cohen 2009: 35). By way of illustration of Cohen's thought here recall the utterance normally attributed to Queen Marie Antoinette shortly before the French Revolution – 'Let them eat cake' – in response to her being informed that her peasants had run out of bread.

In principle, however, such unfriendly inequalities in community of life experience can arise in a way that appears compatible with luck egalitarian justice, e.g. Joshua gets much richer than Jill because Jill is lazy and Joshua is not or because both gamble and one is lucky and the other one is not. In response, Cohen 'believe[s] that certain inequalities that cannot be forbidden in the name of socialist equality of opportunity should nevertheless be forbidden, in the name of community' (Cohen 2009: 37). Cohen declares himself agnostic on whether luck egalitarian justice and community, tragically, are 'potentially incompatible moral ideals' (Cohen 2009: 37) or whether the ideal of community 'define[s] the terms within which justice will operate' (Cohen 2009: 37). However, it is unclear what, by his own light, his grounds for his agnostic, as opposed to a tragic, stance rests upon. Given his earlier distinction between egalitarian objections and objections to equality that derive from other values, it seems clear that objections to luck egalitarian justice based on an ideal of community of life experience is an objection of the latter type.

In fact, it seems that the distance between luck egalitarian justice and community of life experience is greater than Cohen imagines. In principle at least, people can enjoy community of life experience even if great inequalities obtain and not enjoy community of life experience even if no overall inequality in life conditions obtain. The former seems possible if the people who are now rich were poor in the past (and have not forgotten what this was like) and people who are now poor (and were rich in the past and have not forgotten what that was like) and both parties recall that the differences between them are all compatible with luck egalitarian justice. The latter seems possible because the kind of challenges people face might be very different, even if, overall, they are equally challenging. A person who is charming and gets along with others very easily, but is dumb, faces challenges that are very different from people who are smart but not charming and are difficult to get along with. Both persons face challenges that might be equally difficult to face up to and yet they might not enjoy community of life experience precisely because the challenges they face are so different.

I now turn to the third aspect of community – communal relations. Luck egalitarianism – at least in its telic form – is concerned with the achievement of a certain distributive pattern. In principle such a pattern can be achieved by agents acting with many different kinds of motivation, provided the settings within which they act are suitably adjusted to the motivational structure. However, according to Cohen socialists care about motivations independently of how they contribute to the achievement of egalitarian justice. This comes out clearly in his story of a camping trip. Imagine you and some friends are on a camping trip. Presumably, almost everyone would agree that it would be horrible if you and the others cooperated because each of you sought to achieve benefits for yourself and believed that the only way to do so would be to cooperate with the other people on the camping trip. This kind of motivation is typical of market reciprocity. Rather, we would want such a community to be characterized by a spirit of, what Cohen labels, socialist reciprocity:

> I serve you in the expectation that (if you are able to) you will also serve me. My commitment to socialist community does not require me to be a sucker who serves you regardless of whether (if you are able to do so) you serve me, but I nevertheless find value in both parts of the conjunction – I serve you and you serve me – and in the conjunction itself: I do not regard the part – I serve you – as simply a means to my real end, which is that you serve me. (Cohen 2009: 43)

Cohen seems to suggest that luck egalitarian justice can be realized independently of communal motivations, but that luck egalitarianism is not enough for 'human relationships to take a desirable form' – communal relations are needed too (Cohen 2009: 39). Of course, this does not answer the question of whether the ideal of socialist reciprocity could ever conflict with luck egalitarian justice and, if they can, whether one should sometimes allow luck egalitarian injustice in the interest of realizing socialist motivations. On this score such a conflict seems possible and to the extent that it materializes, it would seem odd, given Cohen's view regarding the nature of desirable human relations as expressed by his story of the camping trip, to claim that some loss in terms of luck egalitarian justice might not be outweighed, in terms of overall desirability, by a gain in communal motivation. For instance, it seems not psychologically extraordinary for people's sense of obligation towards others to be reduced when they can count on institutions to take care of these obligations. Indeed, this is one of several common complaints about the welfare state. Suppose that some such psychological tendency obtains and suppose that institutions are actually better at implementing luck egalitarian justice, e.g. because the information needed to implement it is hard to survey by individuals. This is something I will take up in the next section. For present purposes, however, my point is that assuming that individuals are only slightly less good at implementing luck egalitarian justice, it might be that, tragically, there is a trade-off between implementing luck egalitarian justice and promoting communal motivations. More generally, it seems that luck egalitarian justice is only quite loosely connected with community in the three senses that I have explored here and, indeed, that it is possible, if not in some cases quite realistic, that they will come into conflict.

8.5. Publicity and stability

The conclusion of the previous section was that distributive justice, at least in the form of luck egalitarian justice, might come into conflict with community. However, some might take a more optimistic view here on the ground that they take a more critical view on the relevance of how people's actions in their daily lives, as informed by communal *ethē*, bear on justice. Some have a certain liberal meta-constraint on the nature of justice: that principle of justice be public. There are various ways publicity could be cashed out. Andrew Williams has argued that justice must be public in the sense that 'individuals are able to attain common knowledge of the rules' (i) general applicability, (ii) their particular requirements, and (iii) the extent to which individuals conform to those requirements' (1998: 233; cf. Cohen 2008: 346). So, assuming that it is impossible to publicly establish that everyone has the same amount of welfare and, thus, impossible to have common knowledge of what the particular requirements are that follow from equality of welfare (ad. ii) and to have common knowledge of who conforms to those requirements and who does not (ad. iii), justice cannot require equality of welfare. Similarly, if it is impossible to publicly establish whether everyone has complied with an egalitarian *ethos*, then the demands of justice cannot require that people act in accordance with it (Cohen 2008: 345).

Another meta-constraint, which is well known from Rawls, is that principles of justice must be stable. Again the stability requirement can be cashed out in different ways, but one way of doing so is to say that principles of justice, once 'instituted, have a propensity to last' (Cohen 2008: 327). Assuming that human beings are naturally selfish, it may be that a regime where incentives are not implemented does not lastingly promote equality, or at least not equality at the highest feasible level, as a result of human selfishness.

There are at least four questions that need to be addressed here and I shall only say something about the last one. First, the publicity and stability constraints can be fleshed out differently and which way of doing so is the most plausible one is an important issue. For instance, in relation to Williams' publicity requirement's third condition there is an issue about whether it is most plausibly construed as a requirement that we can identify particular conformers and non-conformers, or whether it requires that we know the general distribution of individuals across conformers and non-conformers even though we are unable to tell who is who, or both. Also, Williams' publicity condition seems different, and in some ways more demanding, than Rawls' publicity condition, which is first and foremost a matter of 'shared knowledge and belief about acceptance and justification of principles' (Cohen 2008: 358). Similarly, stability is a matter of degree, so a stability requirement can be more or less demanding depending on how stable principles must be in order for them to qualify as principles of justice.

Second, once the two constraints have been suitably specified, we must determine if it is really the case that egalitarian justice satisfies neither of them. For instance, perhaps the publicity constraint, suitably construed, can be met if people volunteer relevant information about their happiness level. Similarly, perhaps human selfishness is a result of market society and might weaken or even disappear in an egalitarian society such that it can conform to egalitarian principles *and* be stable.

Third, there is the question of whether standard non-ethos-requiring principles of justice meet the relevant publicity criterion. If they do not, it seems that rather than rejecting the idea of an egalitarian ethos, one should reject the publicity requirement, at least under the relevant interpretation, as being implausibly demanding. So, for instance, if governments are unable to tell whether the basic structure conforms to the difference principle, then defenders of the standard Rawlsian construal of the difference principle as something that applies to the basic structure only, and has no implications for how people should conduct themselves vis-à-vis incentive-seeking, cannot object to an egalitarian ethos on grounds of lack of publicity (Cohen 2008: 362; Lippert-Rasmussen 2008a).

Fourth, there is the question of whether it is plausible to say that publicity and stability should be seen as meta-constraints on theories of justice. If not, this would seem to strengthen luck egalitarianism given the doubts some have over its ability to satisfy the two constraints. In the rest of this section I will sketch Cohen's rejection of these meta-constraints. His argument raises some questions about the nature of justice, which I will then address in the book's last section.

Crucial to Cohen's rejection of the publicity and stability constraints is his distinction between fundamental principles of justice and rules of regulation. The former do not reflect any facts about which states of affairs we can bring about or can bring about without sacrificing values other than justice. The latter guide us towards realization of fundamental ideals, including the ideal of justice, as effectively as possible – or, as Cohen puts it: 'if rules for social living [i.e. rules of regulation] are soundly based, they will reflect both values other than justice and practical constraints that restrict the extent to which justice can be applied. That being so, justice itself could not be what is specified by such rules' (Cohen 2008: 3). Applying this distinction to the publicity constraint it might be argued that while publicity is a constraint that rules of regulation pertaining to distributive justice should meet, or at least a desideratum that they should satisfy, fundamental principles of distributive justice have to do neither. Just as truth may sometimes elude us, so might justice. Rules of regulation are supposed to guide us, so for that reason it has to be roughly clear when one complies with them and when one does not and to enforce them it is also fine if we can distinguish compliers from non-compliers. Similarly, principles of regulation should accommodate reasonably foreseeable non-compliance in a way that fundamental principles of justice should not. As Cohen puts it: 'justice is not the only virtue that should influence the content of principles of regulation. They need to serve other virtues, such as stability, a healthy respect for Pareto, and certain forms of publicity' (Cohen 2008: 286). Finally, rules of regulation must take into account the cost of collecting information and, thereby, the amount of resources that cannot be used on realizing other values, if spent on collecting information necessary for applying rules of regulation.

These concerns mean that Cohen has an explanation of why publicity is a desirable feature of rules of regulation which is compatible with publicity not being a constraint on fundamental principles of justice. Moreover, assuming that we have not been clear about the distinction between fundamental principles of justice and rules of regulation, any plausibility that we ascribe to publicity might simply reflect this lack of clarity. Similar reasoning applies to the stability constraint. It is desirable that a rule of regulation is stable, but the fact that it is not might simply reflect the fact that human beings often are disposed to injustice, and while rules of regulation must reflect this fact, fundamental principles of justice, by definition, do not.

Cohen offers additional reasons to think that neither publicity nor stability is required at the level of fundamental principles of justice. During the Second World War Britain was informed by an ethos that everyone had to make sacrifices for the sake of the war effort. Obviously, the requirement – 'Do your bit' – was very vague and yet it was understood and applied as a requirement of justice (Cohen 2008: 353). Moreover, take racist discrimination. Plausibly, it is a fundamental principle of justice that one does not discriminate on racial grounds. Yet, much racial discrimination takes place subliminally – that is, racial discriminators are unaware, perhaps even non-culpably unaware, of the fact that they engage in racial discrimination. So, at least in one sense, a principle to the effect that one should not racially discriminate is non-public in that it is not possible for people to tell if the rule is being complied with or, indeed, whether they themselves comply with the rule. Hence, in the light of this fact we do not retract the claim that racial discrimination is unjust, we must reject the publicity constraint as a constraint on justice (Cohen 2008: 356).

Similarly, suppose that non-racist regimes are unstable in that we are hardwired to engage in racist discrimination. Surely, should that be so, we would conclude not that racism is not unjust, but that, regrettably, we are disposed to be unjust. If so, stability is not a requirement of justice. Also, if stability were a requirement of justice, we could not, Cohen claims, 'say such intelligible things as

"This society is at the moment just, but it is likely to lose that feature very soon; justice is such a fragile achievement"; or "We don't want our society to be just only for the time being; we want its justice to last"' (Cohen 2008: 327–8). Since such claims make perfect sense, stability is not a requirement of justice. The confused belief that it is might derive from the reasonable wish that justice is not permanently at risk. But the very coherence of that *fear* shows that stability is not a feature of justice itself (Cohen 2008: 328).

These points seem well taken. Some might respond that while they might show that stability is not a part of the concept of justice, they do not show that it is not a substantive truth about justice that a necessary condition for something to be unjust is that it violates principles that are stable. They might say that similarly the fact that, as Moore's open question argument shows or at least supports, welfare maximization is not part of our concept of morally right actions does not show that it is not a substantive truth about morally right action that they maximize welfare.

However, Cohen's observations are easily reformulated in such a way that they have bite against this claim also. For presumably the fact that, say, we can coherently fear that justice does not last also manifests that we do not believe that it is a substantive truth about justice that a necessary condition for something to be unjust is that it violates principles that are stable. And, to the extent that our considered moral beliefs are reliable, this shows that the stability condition is not a substantive truth about justice. Similar reasoning applies to the publicity constraint. Hence, if the Cohenian line that I have endorsed in this section is correct, publicity and stability should not be construed as values that constrain or conflict with justice. Rather, they are values that bear on what rules of regulation should be and not values that clash with the fundamental value of justice. Still, the present discussion, along with the arguments addressed in the previous sections, raises a couple of more general questions about the nature of justice to which I shall now turn.

8.6. Reflections

Many of the discussions in this chapter and in the previous ones have been informed by certain assumptions about how two meta-questions should be answered and it is fitting to bring these two questions out in the open in this final section of the book. First, in my discussion of the proper egalitarian *equalisandum* in Chapter 4 and in my discussion of how egalitarian justice relates to other values I have more or less assumed a pluralist view of values. That is, I have assumed that different values, and their contours, can be determined independently of one another and that they can conflict with one another such that, tragically, we have to trade off values against one another, e.g. egalitarian justice vs. community. Pluralism about values is not an uncommon view, but not everyone accepts it. A few people are monists, because they think that there is only one value, e.g. welfare. More theorists are holists about value. Unlike monists, they think that there is more than one value, but, unlike pluralists, they deny these values are independent of one another. More specifically, they think that the value of justice is such that it is compatible with realizing other values, or at least that it is such that the probability of it coming into conflict with other values is minimized. I shall not say anything about monism, but I will reflect on the views of a prominent holist – Dworkin.

Second, throughout this book I have assumed that injustice can obtain even if everyone has done everything they could reasonably be expected to do in order to comply with the demands of equality. Indeed, I have assumed – e.g. in my discussion of inequalities across generations in Chapter 6 – that injustice might obtain even if everyone has successfully complied with the demands of justice. This implies the possibility of pure natural injustice, i.e. injustices that it is beyond human agency to prevent. As we saw in Chapter 5, many deontic egalitarians reject this possibility and social relations egalitarians, whose views we encountered in Chapter 7, similarly reject this possibility. While people who hold this view are normally taken to disagree with telic egalitarians, there is also the possibility that they simply have different things in mind when they use the term 'justice'. Some people might have in mind outcomes not characterized by unfairness, where nature and human agents alike can be unfair. Other people might have in mind, say, a set of rules that pertain to the basic structure of society and which can be realized compatibly with respecting the stability and publicity constraints. If that is the case, it is a real possibility that people who apparently disagree about whether distributive injustice can exist even if no one can eliminate it or could have avoided it, are simply addressing different questions and, thus, are talking past each other.

I shall start with the pluralism versus holism issue. In his Isaac Marks Memorial Lecture Dworkin asks the question whether political values such as equality and freedom, democracy and individual rights, freedom and true community conflict with one another such that sometimes whatever we do, we will do something that is 'bad or wrong' (Dworkin 2001: 252). That such tragic conflicts occur is the conventional wisdom, but Dworkin rejects it. More specifically, he argues that the postulated conflict between freedom and equality is illusory and indeed, that we should 'hope for a plausible theory of all central political values ... that shows each of these as growing out of and reflected in all the others, an account that conceives equality ... not only as compatible with liberty but as a value that someone who prized liberty would therefore also prize' (Dworkin 2000: 4).

To show that the conflict between equality and freedom is illusory, Dworkin distinguishes between two conceptions of equality and freedom of which he favours the latter: flat and dynamic conceptions. A dynamic, unlike a flat, conception operates under the following constraint: it 'must aim to show what is good about the virtue in question. It must aim to show why, if the virtue is compromised, something bad has happened, something of value has been lost, people have not been treated as they have a right to be treated' (Dworkin 2001: 255). This scope for the constraint is wide, because Dworkin argues that political concepts – such as freedom and equality – have no fixed descriptive meaning in ordinary language, but are subject to interpretation under the quoted constraint. Dworkin then moves on to argue that equality and freedom interpreted in the light of this constraint are indeed compatible. While he does not explicitly assert that there are no political values, dynamically construed, that conflict, he seems optimistic about this not being the case.

In response to Dworkin's position, I want to point out that his desirability constraint is too strong and, in any case, ambiguous in a way that renders it unable to support holism about values, i.e. the view that values are determined in part by their compossibility with other values. On the first point, compare Dworkin's desirability constraint with a weaker one to the effect that a conception of a political value like equality is more plausible to the extent that it can be shown that equality is often desirable, but not necessarily always so. Take for instance levelling down. Suppose you think that not levelling down involves nothing bad whatsoever. Given Dworkin's desirability constraint you would have to infer that the best conception of equality does not imply that levelling down promotes equality. But hang on. Levelling down involves moving from inequality to equality. How can an ideal of equality not deem the latter situation better than the former? It seems perfectly reasonably to say that the levelling down objection shows that even if inequality in many, if not most, situations involves a loss – to wit, a loss of welfare to those who would have been better off in the absence of levelling down – equality implies that not levelling down involves a loss and, in view of the fact that it does not, prioritarianism, not equality, is the relevant political value that distributions should realize. As should be obvious from my discussion of the levelling down objection in Chapter 5, I do not think that this is the right conclusion to draw. However, this is immaterial to the point I make here – namely, that such an inference is ruled out by Dworkin's desirability constraint which, at least when understood as a constraint and not just as a desideratum, rules out that political values on his favoured list turn out not to be values at all.

Second, even if the desirability constraint were defensible it would not support holism in the way Dworkin seems to assume. For the formulation 'something *bad* has happened', etc., hides an important ambiguity. To see this, suppose we apply Dworkin's desirability constraint in relation to the interpretation of equality in levelling down situations. By 'something bad' does Dworkin mean 'something bad *with regard to equality*' or 'something bad *all things considered*'? If he means the former, then the desirability constraint does no work in showing that different values are compossible. In the case at hand, an interpretation of equality might, compatibly with the first reading of the desirability constraint, imply that levelling down is in one respect good. But in the situation equality conflicts with welfare. If he means the latter, then the desirability constraint would do some work in showing that different values are compossible. For in that case, how we should understand, say, equality in relation to the levelling down situation is partly determined by how levelling down will be assessed in relation to other values, e.g. welfare, and if levelling down is bad in relation to these other values, then on the all-things-considered reading of the desirability constraint, that is a reason for construing equality in such a way that it does not imply that there is anything good about levelling down and in that way securing harmony between equality and welfare.

As a matter of fact it seems that Dworkin himself applies the all-things-considered reading of the desirability constraint. So, for instance, in relation to equality he thinks that a dynamic conception of equality will not object to pure differential option luck even though such inequality, he concedes, 'is not sensibly attributable to any difference in the choices that we have made' (Dworkin 2001: 258). The reason that the dynamic conception of equality will not object to pure differential option luck is that 'erasing this kind of difference between us would eliminate gambles ... from our lives, and make us all worse off' (Dworkin 2001: 258). One can certainly agree that a concern for welfare speaks in favour of letting differential option luck stand. But unless Dworkin uses the desirability constraint in the all-things-considered sense, it is difficult to see why a concern for a loss – possibly an equal loss from a situation of equality – of welfare for all of us should motivate a certain conception of equality.

However, using the desirability constraint in the all-things-considered sense is illegitimate in the dialectical context in which Dworkin wants to employ it – that is, an argument against pluralism. Pluralists think that values such as freedom, equality and welfare are distinct values. It seems to follow directly from their view that when determining how equality should be construed we should not assume that promoting equality will never reduce overall welfare. Hence, the desirability constraint in its all-things-considered reading, unlike in its with-regard-to-one-particular-value reading, begs the question against pluralists. Since, as Dworkin acknowledges, pluralism is the received view and since that would appear to place the burden of argument on people such as Dworkin, the failure of his argument allows pluralism about political values to stand unscathed by his criticisms.

Let me now move on to the second question that I want to address in this section, i.e. whether the existence of apparently conflicting views about luck egalitarian justice simply reflects that people have different things in mind when they use the term 'justice'. In a very helpful piece, Peter Vallentyne distinguishes between five different senses of justice. First, "[j]ustice" is sometimes understood to mean (something like) *moral permissibility of social institutions* (e.g. legal systems)' (Vallentyne 2014: 40). In this sense of the term, strictly speaking distributions can be neither just nor unjust, although they might be so in a loose sense, e.g. a distribution can be unjust in the sense that it results from impermissible social institutions. While the term is sometimes used in this way, I submit that, with the possible exception of the disagreement between pluralist Cohenians, on the one hand, and holist Dworkinians, on the other hand, none of the disputes that have been covered in this book are illusory in the sense that one party to the disagreement uses 'justice' to refer to moral permissibility of social institutions while the other party does not. The possible exception reflects that on Dworkin's interpretative account of political values, it might be a constraint on, or at least a desideratum in relation to, how we understand equality that it does not conflict with other values.

Second, 'justice' might refer to 'interpersonal morality understood as *the duties that we morally owe each other*' (Vallentyne 2014: 41). On this view, pure natural inequalities cannot be unjust, just as pure natural equalities cannot be just, since they do not reflect that anyone has failed to fulfil the duties that they morally owe others. It is at least possible, though not likely in the light of Section 7.5, that part of the disagreement between Elizabeth Anderson and luck egalitarians simply reflects such terminological difference, i.e. that by 'justice' she means 'interpersonal morality justice' whereas luck egalitarians mean something else. This is not to suggest that there is no substantive disagreement between them. First, luck egalitarians think that natural inequalities affect which duties we owe one another, whereas Anderson rejects this view. Second, presumably both Anderson and luck egalitarians will want to claim that justice in their sense is what people have in mind when they complain about or regret injustice. Or, to the extent that they concede that 'justice' is used in different senses in ordinary language, their sense of justice captures a, or the most important, sense of the term, when people make assessments of justice.

Third, on some uses '"justice" is concerned with *enforceable duties* – with those moral duties we have that others are morally permitted to force us to fulfil' (Vallentyne 2014: 41). The term is no doubt sometimes used in this sense. Indeed, it is possible that Anderson uses the term in a way that combines the second and third sense such that 'justice' refers to interpersonal morality understood as *the duties that we morally owe each other* and that others are morally permitted to force us to fulfil. However, I suspect that what Vallentyne is after here is a related but slightly different sense of justice, i.e. as those moral duties that others have a moral right to force us to fulfil. To see the difference between this sense and Vallentyne's third sense, consider a case where someone attempts to steal something from me, which he has a duty not to take. I could prevent him from doing so, but if I did so, a powerful friend of his would blow up an entire city. Here I might have a moral right to enforce his duty not to steal from me, even if it would be morally impermissible for me to enforce it. Hence, stealing from me would not be unjust in Vallentyne's third sense, but it would be so in my related sense. Since most people who use the term in an enforcement-related sense would consider this unjust, this suggests that my related sense captures better what Vallentyne has in mind than his own third sense.

Fourth, on some usages justice is that everyone gets what he or she deserves. 'Justice' in this sense is narrow in that it is tied to desert and many theorists want to flesh out what justice requires independently of desert. This includes many luck egalitarians as well as critics of luck egalitarianism. For instance, desert plays no role in Cohen's and Dworkin's luck egalitarianism and Anderson explicitly rejects its significance, so it is unlikely that their disagreement simply reflects that some of them use 'justice' in the present desert-based sense whereas others do not. Not only is this notion of justice perhaps not so relevant in the present contexts, I also doubt that anyone really uses the term in this way. For suppose I believe that justice obtains when everyone has equal well-being whether or not they are equally deserving. Here it seems more plausible to say that while I disagree with someone who thinks that justice obtains when everyone gets what he or she deserves about when justice obtains, I mean the same by 'justice' as my opponent does. Similarly, two people might share the same view about what a humiliating act is, but disagree about which acts are humiliating.

Fifth and finally, Vallentyne notes that sometimes 'justice' is understood as '*fairness*, where this is understood as a *purely comparative* concern for ensuring that each individual gets *what she is due* to the same extent as others' (Vallentyne 2014: 42). He also notes that Anderson claims that 'luck egalitarianism's focus on the fairness of distributions (justice in the fifth sense) makes it a non-contender for a theory of justice as the duties we owe each other' (Vallentyne 2014: 42). So, perhaps, what appears to be a substantive disagreement between Anderson and luck egalitarians is at least in part a matter of the two parties using 'justice' in the present fairness-focused sense and Anderson's using the term in a different sense.

Again I want to resist this suggestion. First, as already noted, I assume that 'justice' has a reasonably clear meaning in ordinary language and that the disagreements noted are disagreements about what people complain about when they complain about justice. *Pace* Dworkin, I think that 'justice' has a rough lexicographical meaning. Second, as Vallentyne argues, the fairness sense of justice bears on justice as something that concerns duties that we owe one another. For one might think that because inequalities due to luck are unfair and thus unjust in his fifth sense, we have a duty of justice in his second and/or third sense to reduce inequalities that are unjust in the fifth sense as much as we can. Social relations egalitarians reject any such duty, whereas luck egalitarians accept it. Hence, they do have substantive disagreements, which cannot be shown to reflect mere terminological differences.

One final worry might linger on even if the reader accepts the claim that luck egalitarians do not simply use 'justice' differently from others, e.g. social relations egalitarians: the important question is which distribution we ought to seek to bring about. Once we have settled that, it is irrelevant whether we think that the reasons why we ought to bring them about are reasons of justice in one sense or reasons of justice in another, or, for that matter, non-justice reasons.

If the aim of political philosophy simply were to say what we ought to do, all things considered, this worry would be warranted. However, it has at least three additional aims and that, in the light of these aims, we also want to know for what reasons we ought to bring about a certain outcome. First, if we know what distribution we ought to aim for, but do not know the reasons why we ought to aim for that distribution, we cannot extrapolate from our commitments regarding the present situation what we ought to do in a different situation. However, political philosophy also aims to say something about what we ought to do in circumstances different from the actual ones and doing so is difficult if we cannot say anything about the different factors that together determine what we ought to do in the actual situation. Indeed, acquiring such information is useful for understanding what we ought to do in the actual situation and this is the second aim I have in mind: political philosophy also aims to explain *why* we ought to do what we ought to do in the actual situation. Doing so requires that we understand the nature of different moral factors at work.

Finally, political philosophy aims to say something about not just what we ought to do in certain circumstances, but also something about what is desirable, e.g. from a point of justice. Suppose that some kind of simplistic historical materialism is true and that the technological level of the development of the means of production constrains the mode of production such that, say, in the ancient world people could not have eliminated slavery. On the assumption that 'ought' implies 'can' and perhaps an additional one about the impossibility of controlling the technological level of development of the means of production, it follows that it is not the case that ancient Greeks and Romans ought to have eliminated slavery. Political philosophy should not rest content with this claim. Rather, we want political philosophy to explain why, even given the present assumptions, slavery was an undesirable feature of ancient Greece and Rome. Similarly, even if some inequalities cannot be eliminated, we still want to know what is undesirable about them. Luck egalitarianism offers a good account thereof.

8.7. Summary

This completes this book. While it aims to offer a balanced overview of the main issues of contention among luck egalitarians as well as some of the main issues that separate luck egalitarians from friends of other distributive principles, I have made no secret of the fact that I am favourably inclined towards luck egalitarianism of a particular kind. More specifically, I have defended a fairness-based account of the presumption of equality (Chapter 2); briefly suggested a desert-based account of luck (Chapter 3); argued, in a way that coheres with my defence of the presumption in favour of equality, that the metric of egalitarian justice is the satisfaction of (a subset of) people's non-instrumental concerns (Chapter 4); denied that the distinction between deontic and telic egalitarianism is as significant as it is commonly thought to be and that the levelling down objection defeats neither form of egalitarianism (Chapter 5); defended a broad-scoped version of cosmopolitan and time-neutral luck egalitarianism whose primary scope ranges over persons' whole lives (Chapter 6); argued that social relations egalitarianism neither defeats, nor can replace, luck egalitarianism as an account of egalitarian justice (Chapter 7); and finally that the value of egalitarian justice does not clash with freedom, demandingness, publicity or stability, though it might do so with certain forms of community (Chapter 8). Obviously, it is up to the reader to form his or her own opinion about the attractiveness of this position and the strength of my arguments for it. While I aspire to convince readers that I am right, one should be realistic. Hence, I am content if many find luck egalitarianism in general and my favoured version of it in particular sufficiently plausible and well defended to be worth thinking about and perhaps even worth criticizing. But being content, of course, while not nothing, is not being happy.

Bibliography

Abizadeh, A. (2007), 'Cooperation, Pervasive Impact, and Coercion: On the Scope (not Site) of Distributive Justice', *Philosophy* and *Public Affairs*, 35 (4): 318–58.

Adler, M. (2000), 'Expressive Theories of Law: A Skeptical Overview', *University of Pennsylvania Law Review*, 148: 1363–1502.

Albertsen, A. and Midtgaard, S. F. (2014), 'Unjust Equalities', *Ethical Theory and Moral Practice*, 17 (2): 335–46.

Albertsen, A. and Knight, C. (2015), 'A Framework for Luck Egalitarianism in Health and Healthcare', *Journal of Medical Ethics*, 41 (2): 165–9.

Andersen, M. M. (2014) 'What Does Society Owe Me if I Am Responsible for Being Worse Off?', *Journal of Applied Philosophy*, 31 (3): 271–86.

Andersen, M. M. and Nielsen, M. E. J. (forthcoming), 'Luck Egalitarianism, Universal Health Care, and Non-Responsibility-Based-Reasons for Responsibilization', *Res Publica*.

Anderson, E. (1999a), 'What Is the Point of Equality?' *Ethics*, 109 (2): 287–337.

Anderson, E. (1999b), 'Reply', *Bears Symposium* on Anderson. Available online: http://www.brown.edu/Departments/Philosophy/bears/9912ande.html/

Anderson, E. (2010a), 'The Fundamental Disagreement between Luck Egalitarians and Relational Egalitarians', *Canadian Journal of Philosophy*, suppl. vol. 36: 1–23.

Anderson, E. (2010b), *The Imperative of Integration*, Princeton, NJ: Princeton University Press.

Arneson, R. J. (1989), 'Equality and Equal Opportunity for Welfare', *Philosophical Studies*, 56: 77–93.

Arneson, R. J. (1990), 'Liberalism, Distributive Subjectivism, and Equal Opportunity for Welfare', *Philosophy* and *Public Affairs*, 19: 158–94.

Arneson, R. J. (1999a), 'Egalitarianism and Responsibility', *Journal of Ethics*, 3: 225–47.

Arneson, R. J. (1999b), 'Comment', *Bears Symposium* on Anderson. Available online: http://www.brown.edu/Departments/Philosophy/bears/9904arne.html/

Arneson, R. J. (1999c), 'What, if Anything, Renders All Human Beings Morally Equal?', in D. Jamieson (ed.), *Singer and His Critics*, Oxford: Blackwell.

Arneson, R. J. (2000a), 'Luck Egalitarianism and Prioritarianism', *Ethics*, 110: 339–49.

Arneson, R. J. (2000b), 'Welfare Should Be the Currency of Justice', *Canadian Journal of Philosophy*, 30: 497–524.

Arneson, R. J. (2001), 'Luck and Equality', *Proceedings of Aristotelian Society*, suppl. vol. 75: 73–90.

Arneson, R. J. (2008), 'Equality of Opportunity', in E. Zalta (ed.), *The Stanford Encyclopedia of Philosophy*. Available online: http://plato. stanford.edu/archives/fall2008/entries/equal-opportunity/

Axelsen, D. and Nielsen, L. (2014) 'Sufficiency as Freedom from Duress', *Journal of Political Philosophy*, 23 (1). Available online: DOI: 10.1111/jopp.12048.

Ayer, A. J. (1982), 'Freedom and Necessity', in G. Watson (ed.), *Free Will*, Oxford University Press, 15–23.

Barry, B. (1989), *Theories of Justice*, vol. 1, Berkeley: University of California Press.

Barry, B. (2005), *Why Social Justice Matters*, Cambridge: Polity Press.

Barry, N. (2006), 'Defending Luck Egalitarianism', *Journal of Applied Philosophy*, 23 (1): 89–107.

Barry, N. (2008), 'Reassessing Luck Egalitarianism', *Journal of Politics*, 70: 136–50.

Beitz, C. (1975), 'Justice and International Relations', *Philosophy* and *Public Affairs* 4 (4): 360–89.

Benbaji, Y. (2005), 'The Doctrine of Sufficiency: A Defence', *Utilitas*, 17: 310–32.

Bidadanure, J. (forthcoming), 'Making Sense of Age Group Justice: A Time for Relational Equality?'.

Blake, M. (2001), 'Distributive Justice, State Coercion, and Autonomy', *Philosophy* and *Public Affairs*, 30 (3): 257–96.

Broome, J. (1991), *Weighing Goods*, Oxford: Blackwell.

Brown, A. (2005), 'Luck Egalitarianism and Democratic Equality', *Ethical Perspectives*, 12 (3): 293–339.

Caney, S. (2005), *Justice Beyond Borders: A Global Political Theory*, Oxford: Oxford University Press.

Caney, S. (2008), 'Global Distributive Justice and the State', *Political Theory*, 56: 487–518.

Caney, S. (2011), 'Humanity, Associations, and Global Justice: In Defence of Humanity-Centred Cosmopolitan Egalitarianism', *The Monist*, 94 (4): 506–34.

Carter, I. (1999), *A Measure of Freedom*, Oxford: Oxford University Press.

Carter, I. (2011), 'Respect and the Basis of Equality', *Ethics*, 121: 538–71.

Casal, P. (2007), 'Why Sufficiency is not Enough', *Ethics*, 117 (2): 296–326.

Christiano, T. (1999), 'Comment', *Bears Symposium* on Anderson. Available online: http://www.brown.edu/Departments/Philosophy/bears/9904chri.html/

Christiano, T. (2006), 'A Foundation for Egalitarianism', in N. Holtug and K. Lippert-Rasmussen (eds), *Egalitarianism: New Essays on the Nature and Value of Equality*, Oxford: Oxford University Press, 41–82.

Cohen, G. A. (1995), *Self-Ownership, Freedom and Equality*, Cambridge: Cambridge University Press.

Cohen, G. A. (2008), *Rescuing Justice and Equality*, Cambridge, MA: Harvard University Press.

Cohen, G. A. (2009), *Why Not Socialism?* Princeton, NJ: Princeton University Press.

Cohen, G. A. (2011), *On the Currency of Egalitarian Justice: And Other Essays in Political Philosophy*, Princeton, NJ: Princeton University Press.

Cohen, G. A. (2013), *Finding Oneself in the Other*, Princeton, NJ: Princeton University Press.

Cohen, M. C. (2004), 'Talent, Slavery, and Envy', in J. Burley (ed.), *Dworkin and His Critics*, Oxford: Blackwell, 30–44.

Darwall, S. (2006), *The Second-Person Standpoint: Morality, Respect, and Accountability*, Cambridge, MA: Harvard University Press.

Dworkin, R. (1986), *A Matter of Principle*, Cambridge, MA: Harvard University Press.

Dworkin, R. (2001), 'Do Values Conflict? A Hedgehog's Approach', *Arizona Law Review*, 43 (2): 251–9.

Dworkin, R. (2000), *Sovereign Virtue*, Cambridge, MA: Harvard University Press.

Dworkin, R. (2002), *Sovereign Virtue* Revisited, *Ethics*, 113: 106–43.

Dworkin, R. (2003), 'Equality, Luck and Hierarchy', *Philosophy* and *Public Affairs*, 31 (2): 190–98.

Dworkin, R. (2004), 'Replies', in J. Burley (ed), *Dworkin and His Critics*, Oxford: Blackwell, 339–95.

Elford, G. (2012), 'Men Who Would Be Kings: Choice, Inequality, and Counterfactual Responsibility', *Social Theory and Practice*, 38 (2): 193–212.

Elford, G. (2013), 'Equality of Opportunity and Other-Affecting Choice: Why Luck Egalitarianism Does Not Require Brute Luck Equality', *Ethical Theory and Moral Practice*, 16: 39–49.

Eyal, N. (2007), 'Egalitarian Justice and Innocent Choice', *Journal of Ethics and Social Philosophy*, 2 (1): 1–19.

Fabre, C. (2006), 'Global Distributive Justice: An Egalitarian Perspective', *Canadian Journal of Philosophy*, suppl. vol. 31: 139–64.

Fabre, C. (2012), *Cosmopolitan War*, Oxford: Oxford University Press.

Feldman, F. (1997), *Utilitarianism, Hedonism, and Desert*, Cambridge: Cambridge University Press.

Firth, J. (2013), 'What's So Shameful about Shameful Revelations', *Law, Ethics, and Philosophy*, 1: 31–51.

Fischer, J. M. (1994), *The Metaphysics of Free Will*, Oxford: Blackwell.

Fischer, J. M. (2006), *My Way: Essays on Moral Responsibility*, Oxford: Oxford University Press.

Fischer, J. M. and Ravizza, M. (1998), *Responsibility and Control*, Cambridge: Cambridge University Press.

Fleurbaey, M. (1995), 'Equal Opportunity or Equal Social Outcome', *Economics and Philosophy*, 11 (1): 25–55.

Fleurbaey, M. (2001), 'Egalitarian Opportunities', *Law and Philosophy*, 20: 499–530.

Fleurbaey, M. (2008), *Fairness, Responsibility, and Welfare*, Oxford: Oxford University Press.

Fourie, C. (2012), 'What is Social Equality? An Analysis of Status Equality as a Strongly Egalitarian Ideal', *Res Publica* 18: 107–26.

Frankfurt, H. (1987), 'Equality as a Moral Ideal', *Ethics*, 98: 21–43.

Frankfurt, H. (1988), *The Importance of What We Care About*, Cambridge: Cambridge University Press.

Freeman, S. (2007), 'Rawls and Luck Egalitarianism', in S. Freeman (ed.), *Justice and the Social Contract*, New York: Oxford University Press, 111–42.

Glover, J. (2006), *Choosing Children*, Oxford: Oxford University Press.

Goodin, R. E. (2007), 'Enfranchising All Affected Interests, and Its Alternatives', *Philosophy and Public Affairs*, 35 (1): 40–68.

Gosseries, A. and Meyer, L. (2009), *Intergenerational Justice*, Oxford: Oxford University Press.

Griffin, J. (1986), *Well-Being*, Oxford: Clarendon Press.

Hirose, I. (2014) *Egalitarianism*, New York: Routledge.

Holtug, N. (2003), 'Good for Whom?' *Theoria*, 69: 65–85.

Holtug, N. (2010), *Persons, Interests, and Justice*, Oxford: Oxford University Press.

Holtug, N. and Lippert-Rasmussen, K. (eds) (2006), *Egalitarianism: New Essays on the Nature and Value of Equality*, Oxford: Oxford University Press.

Hurley, S. (1993), 'Justice without Constitutive Luck', in A. P. Griffith (ed), *Ethics, Royal Institute of Philosophy Supplement*, 35, Cambridge: Cambridge University Press, 179–212.

Hurley, S. L. (2003), *Justice, Luck, and Knowledge*, Cambridge, MA: Harvard University Press.

Hurley, S. L. (2006), 'Replies', *Philosophy and Phenomenological Research*, 72: 447–65.

Huseby, R. (2010), 'Sufficiency: Restated and Defended', *Journal of Political Philosophy*, 18 (2): 178–97.

Kagan, S. (1992), 'The Limits of Well-Being', *Social Philosophy and Policy*, 9 (2): 169–89.

Kagan, S. (2012) *The Geometry of Desert*, Oxford: Oxford University Press.

Kamm, F. M. (2013), *Bioethical Prescriptions*, Oxford: Oxford University Press.

Kant, I. ([1785] 2002), *Groundwork for the Metaphysics of Morals*, New Haven, CT: Yale University Press.

Kaufman, A. (2004), 'Choice, Responsibility, and Equality', *Political Studies*, 52: 819–36.

Knight, C. (2009), *Luck Egalitarianism: Equality, Responsibility, and Justice*, Edinburgh: Edinburgh University Press.

Knight, C. (2013) 'Egalitarian Justice and Expected Value', *Ethical Theory and Moral Practice*, 16: 1061–73.

Knight, C. and Stemplowska, Z. (2011a), 'Responsibility and Distributive Justice: An Introduction', in C. Knight and Z. Stemplowska, *Responsibility and Distributive Justice*, Oxford: Oxford University Press, 1–23.

Knight, C. and Stemplowska, Z. (eds) (2011b), *Responsibility and Distributive Justice*, Oxford: Oxford University Press.

Kymlicka, W. (1990), *Contemporary Political Philosophy: An Introduction*, Oxford: Oxford University Press.

Kymlicka, W. (1991), *Liberalism, Community, and Culture*, Oxford: Clarendon Press.

Kymlicka, W. (2002), *Contemporary Political Philosophy: An Introduction*, 2nd edn, Oxford: Oxford University Press.

Lang, G. (2006), 'Luck Egalitarianism and the Sew-Saw Objection', *American Philosophical Quarterly*, 43 (1): 43–56.

Lazenby, H. (2010), 'One Kiss Too Many? Giving, Luck Egalitarianism and Other-Affecting Choice', *Journal of Political Philosophy*, 18 (3): 271–86.

Lazenby, H. (2014), 'Luck, Risk, and the Market', *Ethical Theory and Moral Practice*, 17: 667–80.

Lippert-Rasmussen, K. (1999), 'Arneson on Equality of Opportunity for Welfare', *The Journal of Political Philosophy*, 7 (4): 478–87.

Lippert-Rasmussen, K. (2001), 'Equality, Option Luck, and Responsibility', *Ethics*, 111: 548–79.

Lippert-Rasmussen, K. (2005), 'Hurley on Egalitarianism and the Luck-neutralizing Aim', *Politics, Philosophy, and Economics*, 4 (2): 249–65.

Lippert-Rasmussen, K. (2006), 'Telic versus Deontic Egalitarianism', in N. Holtug and K. Lippert-Rasmussen (eds), *Egalitarianism: New Essays on the Nature and Value of Equality*, Oxford: Oxford University Press, 101–24.

Lippert-Rasmussen, K. (2008a), 'Publicity and Egalitarian Justice',
    Journal of Moral Philosophy, 5 (1): 7–25.
Lippert-Rasmussen, K. (2008b), 'Inequality, Incentives, and the
    Interpersonal Test', *Ratio*, 21 (4): 421–39.
Lippert-Rasmussen, K. (2009), 'The Luck-Egalitarian Argument for
    Group Rights', in S. Lægaard, N. Holtug and K. Lippert-Rasmussen
    (eds), *Nationalism and Multiculturalism in a World of Immigration*,
    London: Palgrave Macmillan, 53–80.
Lippert-Rasmussen, K. (2011a), 'Luck Egalitarianism: Faults and
    Collective Choice', *Economics and Philosophy*, 27 (2): 208–15.
Lippert-Rasmussen, K. (2011b), 'Luck Egalitarianism and Group
    Responsibility', in C. Knight and Z. Stemplowska (eds),
    Responsibility and Distributive Justice, Oxford: Oxford University
    Press, 98–114.
Lippert-Rasmussen, K. (2012a), 'Immigrants, Multiculturalism, and
    Expensive Cultural Tastes: Quong on Luck-Egalitarianism and
    Cultural Minority Rights', *Athelier d'Ethique*, 6 (2): 176–92.
Lippert-Rasmussen, K. (2012b), 'Luck Egalitarianism vs. Social Relations
    Egalitarianism: What is at Stake?' *Philosophical Topics*, 40 (1):
    117–34.
Lippert-Rasmussen, K. (2013a), 'When Group Measures of Health
    Should Matter', in E. Nir, S. Hurst, O. Norheim and D. Wikler (eds),
    Justice and Health, Oxford: Oxford University Press: 52–65.
Lippert-Rasmussen, K. (2013b), *Born Free and Equal: A Philosophical
    Inquiry into the Nature of Discrimination*, Oxford University Press.
Lippert-Rasmussen, K. (2014a), 'Offensive Preferences, Snobbish
    Tastes, and Egalitarian Justice', *Journal of Social Philosophy*, 44 (4):
    439–58.
Lippert-Rasmussen, K. (2014b), 'A Just Distribution of Climate Burdens
    and Benefits: A Luck-Egalitarian View', in J. Moss (ed.), *Climate
    Justice*, Oxford: Oxford University Press.
Lippert-Rasmussen, K. (forthcoming), 'Luck Egalitarians vs. Relational
    Egalitarians: On the Prospects of a Pluralist Account of Egalitarian
    Justice', *Canadian Journal of Philosophy*.
Lægaard, S., Holtug, N. and Lippert-Rasmussen, K. (eds) (2009),
    Nationalism and Multiculturalism in A World of Immigration, London:
    Palgrave Macmillan.
McKerlie, D. (1996), 'Equality', *Ethics*, 106: 274–96.
McKerlie, D. (2001), 'Justice between the Young and the Old',
    Philosophy and *Public Affairs*, 30 (2): 342–79.
McMahan, J. (2002), *The Ethics of Killing: Problem at the Margins of
    Life*, Oxford: Oxford University Press.
McMahan, J. (2010), 'The Just Distribution of Harm between
    Combatants and Noncombatants', *Philosophy* and *Public Affairs*, 38
    (4): 342–79.

Mandle, J. (2009), *Rawls' A Theory of Justice: An Introduction*, Cambridge: Cambridge University Press.

Mason, A. (2001), 'Egalitarianism and the Levelling Down Objection', *Analysis*, 61 (3): 246–54.

Mason, A. (2006), *Levelling the Playing Field: The Ideal of Equal Opportunity and its Place in Egalitarian Thought*, Oxford: Oxford University Press.

Matravers, M. (2007), *Responsibility and Justice*, Cambridge: Polity Press.

Miller, D. (1995), *On Nationality*, Oxford: Oxford University Press.

Miller, D. (1998), 'Equality and Justice', in A. Mason (ed.), *Ideals of Equality*, Oxford: Blackwell, 21–36.

Miller, D. (2008), *National Responsibility and Global Justice*, Oxford: Oxford University Press.

Moore, G. E. ([1912] 1955), *Ethics*, Oxford: Oxford University Press.

Nagel, T. (1979), *Mortal Questions*, Cambridge: Cambridge University Press.

Nagel, T. (1991), *Equality and Partiality*, Oxford: Oxford University Press.

Nagel, T. (1997), 'Justice and Nature', *Oxford Journal of Legal Studies*, 17: 303–21.

Navin, M. (2011), 'Luck and oppression', *Ethical Theory and Moral Practice*, 14: 533–47.

Norheim, O. and Cappellen, A. (2005), 'Responsibility in Health Care: A Liberal Egalitarian Approach', *Journal of Medical Ethics*, 31: 476–80.

Nozick, R. (1974), *Anarchy, State, and Utopia*, Oxford: Basil Blackwell.

Nussbaum, M. (2000), *Women and Human Development: The Capabilities Approach*, Cambridge: Cambridge University Press.

Olsaretti, S. (2009), 'The Consequences of Choice', *Proceedings of the Aristotelian Society*, 109: 165–88.

Olsaretti, S. (2013), 'Rescuing Justice and Equality from Libertarianism', *Economics and Philosophy*, 29 (1): 43–63.

Olson, K. M. (2010), 'The Endowment Tax Puzzle', *Philosophy and Public Affairs*, 38 (3): 240–71.

O'Neill, M. (2008), 'What Should Egalitarians Believe?', *Philosophy and Public Affairs*, 36 (2): 119–56.

Otsuka, M. (2002), 'Luck, Insurance, and Equality', *Ethics*, 113: 40–54.

Otsuka, M. (2004), 'Equality, Insurance and Ambition', *Proceedings of Aristotelian Society*, 78: 151–66.

Otsuka, M. and Voorhoeve, A. (2009), 'Why It Matters that Some Are Worse Off than Others: An Argument against the Priority View', *Philosophy and Public Affairs*, 37: 171–99.

Parfit, D. (1984), *Reasons and Persons*, Oxford: Oxford University Press.

Parfit, D. (1995), 'Equality or Priority?' University of Kansas: The Lindley Lecture.

Parfit, D. (1998), 'Equality and Priority', in A. Mason (ed.), *Ideals of Equality*, Oxford: Blackwell, 1–20.

Parfit, D. (2002), 'Equality or Priority?' in M. Clayton and A. Williams (eds), *The Ideal of Equality*. Houndmills: Palgrave Macmillan, 81–125.

Pereboom, D. (2001), *Living Without Free Will*, Cambridge: Cambridge University Press.

Persson, I. (2006), 'A Defence of Extreme Egalitarianism', in N. Holtug and K. Lippert-Rasmussen (eds), *Egalitarianism: New Essays on the Nature and Value of Equality*, Oxford: Oxford University Press, 83–96.

Persson, I. (2008), 'Why Levelling Down Could be Worse for Prioritarianism than for Egalitarianism', *Ethical Theory and Moral Practice*, 11 (3): 295–303.

Price, T. L. (1999), 'Egalitarian Justice, Luck, and the Costs of Chosen Ends', *American Philosophical, Quarterly*, 36: 267–78.

Pritchard, D. (2005), *Epistemic Luck*, Oxford: Clarendon Press.

Rakowski, E. (1991), *Equal Justice*, Oxford: Clarendon Press.

Rawls, J. (1971), *A Theory of Justice*, Oxford: Oxford University Press.

Rawls, J. (1999), *The Law of Peoples*, Cambridge, MA: Harvard University Press.

Rescher, N. (1993), 'Moral Luck', in D. Statman (ed.), *Moral Luck*, Albany, NY: State University of New York Press, 141–66.

Ripstein, A. (1994), 'Equality, Luck, and Responsibility', *Philosophy and Public Affairs*, 23: 1–23.

Roemer, J. E. (1993), 'A Pragmatic Theory of Responsibility for the Egalitarian Planner', *Philosophy & Public Affairs*, 22: 146–66.

Roemer, J. E. (1996), *Theories of Distributive Justice*, Cambridge, MA: Harvard University Press.

Roemer, J. E. (2000), *Equality of Opportunity*, Cambridge, MA: Harvard University Press.

Sandbu, P. (2004), 'On Dworkin's Brute-Luck-Option-Luck Distinction and the Consistency of Brute-Luck Egalitarianism', *Politics, Philosophy & Economics*, 3: 283–12.

Sangiovanni, A. (2007), 'Global Justice, Reciprocity, and the State', *Philosophy and Public Affairs*, 35 (1): 3–39.

Sangiovanni, A. (2011), 'Global Justice and the Moral Arbitrariness of Birth', *The Monist*, 94 (4): 571–58.

Scanlon, T. M. (1975), 'Preference and Urgency', *Journal of Philosophy*, 72: 655–69.

Scanlon, T. M. (1982), 'Contractualism and Utilitarianism', in A. Sen and B. Williams (eds), *Utilitarianism and Beyond*, Cambridge: Cambridge University Press, 103–28.

Scanlon, T. M. (2000), *The Difficulty of Tolerance*, Cambridge: Cambridge University Press.

Scheffler, S. (2003a), 'What is Egalitarianism?' *Philosophy and Public Affairs*, 31 (1): 5–39.

Scheffler, S. (2003b), 'Equality as the Virtue of Sovereigns: A Reply to Ronald Dworkin', *Philosophy and Public Affairs*, 31 (2): 199–206.

Scheffler, S. (2005), 'Choice, Circumstance, and the Value of Equality', *Politics, Philosophy, and Economics*, 4 (4): 5–28.

Scheffler, S. (2006), 'Is the Basic Structure Basic?' in C. Sypnowich (ed.), *The Egalitarian Conscience: Essays in Honour of G. A. Cohen*, Oxford: Oxford University Press, 102–29.

Schemmel, C. (forthcoming), 'Luck Egalitarianism as Democratic Reciprocity: A Response to Tan', *Journal of Philosophy*.

Segall, S. (2007), 'In Solidarity with the Imprudent: A Defence of Luck-Egalitarianism', *Social Theory & Practice*, 33: 177–98.

Segall, S. (2010), *Health, Luck and Justice*, Princeton, NJ: Princeton University Press.

Segall, S. (2012), 'Why Egalitarians Should Not Care About Equality', *Ethical Theory* and *Moral Practice*, 15 (4): 507–19.

Segall, S. (2013), *Equality and Opportunity*, Oxford: Oxford University Press.

Segall, S. (2014), 'In Defense of Priority and (Equality)', *Politics, Philosophy, and Economics*. Available online: DOI: 10.1177/1470594X14550966

Segall, S. (forthcoming), 'Incas and Aliens', *Economics and Philosophy*.

Seligman, M. (2007), 'Luck, Leverage, and Equality: A Bargaining Problem for Luck Egalitarians', *Philosophy & Public Affairs*, 35: 266–92.

Sen, A. (1980), 'Equality of What?' in S. McMurrin (ed.), *The Tanner Lectures on Human Values*, vol. 1, Cambridge: Cambridge University Press.

Sen, A. (1985), *Commodities and Capabilities*, Amsterdam: North-Holland.

Sen, A. (2005), 'Human Rights and Capabilities', *Journal of Human Development*, 6 (2): 151–66.

Sen, A. (2009), *The Idea of Justice*, Cambridge, MA: Harvard University Press.

Sher, G. (1987), *Desert*, Princeton, NJ: Princeton University Press.

Sher, G. (1997), *Approximate Justice: Studies in Non-Ideal Theory*, Lanham, Maryland: Rowman & Littlefield.

Silvers, A., Wasserman, D. and Mahowald, M. B. (1998), *Disability, Difference, and Discrimination*, New York: Rowman & Littlefield.

Singer, P. (1993) *Practical Ethics*, Cambridge: Cambridge University Press.

Sobel, D. (1999), 'Comment on Anderson', *Bears Symposium* on

Anderson. Available online: http://www.brown.edu/Departments/
    Philosophy/bears/9912ande.html/
Statman, D. (ed) (1993), *Moral Luck*, Albany, NY: State University of
    New York Press.
Steiner, H. (2002), 'How Equality Matters', *Social Philosophy and Policy*,
    19: 342–56.
Stemplowska, Z. (2008), 'Holding People Responsible for what
    They Do Not Control', *Politics, Philosophy & Economics*, 7:
    377–99.
Stemplowska, Z. (2009), 'Making Justice Sensitive to Responsibility',
    Political Studies, 57: 237–59.
Stemplowska, Z. (2013), 'Rescuing Luck Egalitarianism', *Journal of
    Social Philosophy*, 44 (4): 402–19.
Stone, P. (2007), 'Why Lotteries Are Just', *Journal of Political
    Philosophy*, 15: 276–95.
Strawson, G. (1994), 'The Impossibility of Moral Responsibility',
    Philosophical Studies, 75: 5–24.
Tamir, Y. (1993), *Liberal Nationalism*, Princeton, NJ: Princeton University
    Press.
Tan, K.-C. (2014), *Justice, Institutions and Luck: The Site, Ground, and
    Scope of Equality*, Oxford: Oxford University Press.
Temkin, L. (1987), 'Intransitivity and the Mere Addition Paradox',
    Philosophy and Public Affairs, 16: 138–87.
Temkin, L. (1993), *Inequality*, Oxford: Oxford University Press.
Temkin, L. (1995), 'Justice and Equality', in E. Paul, F. D. Miller, and
    J. Paul (eds), *The Just Society*, Cambridge: Cambridge University
    Press, 72–104.
Temkin, L. (2003a), 'Equality, Priority, or What?' *Economics and
    Philosophy*, 19: 61–87.
Temkin, L. (2003b), 'Personal versus Impersonal Principles:
    Reconsidering the Slogan', *Theoria*, 69: 21–31.
Temkin, L. (2008), 'Exploring the Roots of Egalitarian Concerns',
    Theoria, 69: 125–51.
Temkin, L. (2011), 'Justice, Equality, Fairness, Desert, Rights, Free Will,
    Responsibility, and Luck', in C. Knight and Z. Stemplowska (eds),
    Responsibility and Distributive Justice, Oxford: Oxford University
    Press, 51–76.
Tungodden, B. (2003), 'The Value of Equality', *Economics and
    Philosophy*, 19: 1–44.
Vallentyne, P. (2002), 'Brute Luck, Option Luck, and Equality of Initial
    Opportunities', *Ethics*, 112: 529–57.
Vallentyne, P. (2006a), 'Hurley on Justice and Responsibility', *Philosophy
    and Phenomenological Research*, 72: 433–8.
Vallentyne, P. (2006b), 'Of Mice and Men: Equality and Animals',
    in N. Holtug and K. Lippert-Rasmussen (eds), *Egalitarianism:*

New Essays on the Nature and Value of Equality, Oxford: Oxford University Press, 211–38.

Vallentyne, P. (2008), 'Brute Luck and Responsibility', *Politics, Philosophy & Economics*, 7: 57–80.

Vallentyne, P. (2014), 'Justice, Interpersonal Morality, and Luck Egalitarianism', in A. Kaufman (ed.), *Distributive Justice and Access to Advantage: G. A. Cohen's Egalitarianism*, Cambridge: Cambridge University Press, 40–9.

Veen, R. van der (2002), 'Equality of Talent Resources: Procedures or Outcomes', *Ethics*, 113: 55–81.

Parijs, P. van (1991), 'Why Surfers Should Be Fed: The Liberal Case for an Unconditional Basic Income', *Philosophy* and *Public Affairs*, 20: 101–31.

Parijs, P. van (1995), *Real Freedom for All: What (if anything) Can Justify Capitalism?* Oxford: Oxford University Press.

Voigt, K. (2007), 'The Harshness Objection: Is Luck Egalitarianism Too Harsh on the Victims of Options Luck?', *Ethical Theory and Moral Practice*, 10: 389–407.

Vrousalis, N. (2010), 'G. A. Cohen on Socialism', *Journal of Ethics*, 14: 185–216.

Watson, G. (1982), *Free Will*, Oxford: Oxford University Press.

Watson, G. (2006), 'The Problematic Role of Responsibility in Contexts of Distributive Justice', *Philosophy and Phenomenological Research*, 72: 425–32.

Williams, A. (1998), 'Incentives, Inequality and Publicity', *Philosophy* and *Public* Affairs, 27 (3): 225–47.

Williams, A. (2013) 'How Gifts and Gambles Preserve Justice', *Economics and Philosophy* 29 (1): 65–85.

Williams, B. (1973a), *Problems of the Self*, Cambridge: Cambridge University Press.

Williams, B. (1973b), 'A Critique of Utilitarianism', in B. Williams and J. J. C. Smart, *Utilitarianism: For and Against*, Cambridge: Cambridge University Press, 77–150.

Williams, B., 1981, *Moral Luck*, Cambridge: Cambridge University Press).

Wolff, J. (1998), 'Fairness, Respect, and the Egalitarian Ethos', *Philosophy* and *Public Affairs*, 27: 97–122.

Wolff, J. (2010), 'Fairness, Respect and the Egalitarian Ethos Revisited', *Journal of Ethics*, 14: 335–50.

Young, I. M. (1990), *Justice and the Politics of Difference*, Princeton, NJ: Princeton University Press.

Zaitchik, A. (1977), 'On deserving to deserve', *Philosophy and Public Affairs*, 6: 370–88.

Zimmerman, M. J. (1993), 'Luck and Moral Responsibility', in D. Statman (ed.), *Moral Luck*, Albany, NY: State University of New York Press, 217–34.

Index

advantage 70, 90
  access to 89, 90, 98
age inequality 156
agency 123, 126, 127, 128
  moral 40, 49
  rational 40, 41
agential capacities 45, 47
  variable 45
altruism 99
ambition 12, 13, 17, 18, 19, 23, 32, 33
Anarchy, State and Utopia 211–12
Anderson, Elizabeth 184–8
  democratic equality 184–8
animals 174, 175
antecedent circumstances 56
Apartheid 2, 180
appropriation, Locke's theory of 142
arbitrariness, moral 9
Arneson, Richard 1, 19–22, 24
auction test 102–3, 107

bad luck 75–6, 158
badness 118, 119, 120, 133, 144, 177
basic needs 10, 170, 183
belief 61
  moral 230
benefits 67, 141, 148, 186, 222, 224
brute luck 17–18, 67–72, 76, 164, 170, 176, 186, 193

capability theory 110–11
Carter, Ian 36, 43, 50
caste, ideologies of 187

children 180
children of God 41
choice 5, 60, 61, 68, 118, 220
  collective 172
  group 163
  individual 163
Christianity 41
class, ideologies of 188
Cohen, G. A. 1, 3, 22–5
collective choice 172
commitments, moral 133
communal motivation 223
communal relations 224
community 220–26
compensation 13, 18, 19, 20, 61, 71, 75, 85, 86, 96, 155, 156, 184, 186, 192
  reverse compensation 75
condescension 182
conditional egalitarianism 136–9, 158, 159
connectedness 155
consciousness 41–2
  reflective 42
consequentialism 27, 114, 146, 216–17, 218, 219
  quasi-consequentialism 217
conservatives 215
constitutive luck 66–7
consumption 172
continuity 155
control 5, 60, 61, 63
cooperation 224–5
cosmopolitan egalitarianism 165, 166, 168, 169, 170
cosmopolitanism 166, 168
criminal justice 148
currency 78

decision trees 20
demandingness 216–20
democratic egalitarianism 194
deontic egalitarianism 113–50
    levelling down objection
        140–47
deontology 114
desert 37, 55, 62, 63, 118, 200,
    236
    comparative 59
desert luck 58, 59, 61–2, 65
deservingness, moral 5, 199
desirability constraint 233–4
determinism 63, 64, 122
diachronic envy 145
difference principle 7, 30
disability 2
disability objection 84–7
disadvantage 92, 195
    involuntary 23
discrimination 74, 89, 90, 91,
    120–21, 124
    racial 229
distribution 31, 32, 33, 73, 75,
    91, 108, 122, 133, 155,
    159, 172, 186, 202, 212,
    213–14, 221, 222, 224, 237,
    238
    principles 216
distributive justice 132, 170
distributive theories 53
duty 44, 45, 47
    enforceable 236
    humanitarian 170
    justice duties 47
    moral 236
    opacity duty 45, 46, 47
Dworkin, Richard 1, 11–19, 20,
    22, 23, 24, 101–8
    Sovereign Virtue 11

egalitarianism 46, 47, 48, 49, 50,
    51
    conditional 158, 159

endowment 12, 16, 17, 18, 23,
    145
envy 14–15, 19, 102
    diachronic 145
equal standing 36
equal treatment 50, 52, 54
equalisanda 85, 88, 101, 108,
    183, 195, 196, 231
equality 12, 22, 26, 29, 35–6,
    39–40, 41, 43, 44, 45, 48,
    50, 69, 72–5, 82, 87, 91,
    94, 96, 116, 125, 126, 131,
    139, 145, 149, 153, 160,
    162, 165, 168, 183, 191,
    193, 212, 214, 215, 216,
    220, 221, 222, 227, 232,
    233, 235
    democratic 184–8, 190, 193,
        194, 195, 197, 206, 207
    formal 36–9
    functionings 196
    presumption of 39, 40
    resources 14, 102
    scope 122–9
equality of opportunity 8, 9, 20,
    31–2
equalization 45
equilibrium, reflective 53
essentialism
    origin 157
ethics
    virtue ethics 142
eugenics 187
exegesis 46
expensive tastes 13–14, 19, 20,
    23, 92, 93–8
exploitation 3, 188

fairness 52, 54, 151, 156, 159,
    166, 168, 207, 237
fetishism 99, 109
foetuses 173
food 110
fraternity 221

free will 49
freedom 211–16, 232, 234
    moral 216, 220
    non-moral 216
    of occupation 220
    quantitative measures 215
friends 44, 46
functionings 198, 199
    equality of 196

gains 67
gamblers 214
gambling 18, 70, 71, 72, 76, 173, 223
gender 39
generations 156–61
genes 69
geneses 118, 119, 122, 125, 126, 128, 146
global agency 122
global tracing 121, 123
globalization 197
good luck 75–6
goodness 43, 130, 147
    moral 3
    outcomes 140–41
goods 81, 94, 104, 186, 195, 196
    distribution 202–3
    primary 108, 110
groups 161–5
    choice 163
    inequality 162–3
guilt 61

handicaps 16, 19, 106
happiness 24
harshness 189–94, 197, 206, 207
hedonism 13, 79–80, 81
hierarchical relations 181, 190
holism 231, 232, 233
    value 172
humanitarian assistance 170
humanitarian duty 170

humble preferences 95–6
humiliation 189–94, 206, 207, 237

incentives 56
income 76
    inequality 24
incompatibilism 64
indeterminacy 189
individuals 162, 173–7
inequality 6, 9, 15, 17, 18, 29, 31, 33, 39, 40, 61, 63, 68, 69, 73, 74, 75, 76, 77, 89, 90, 115, 116, 117, 119, 120, 121, 124, 125, 126, 127, 128, 129, 130, 135, 137, 138, 143, 146, 147, 148, 154, 158, 159, 161, 162, 163, 166, 174, 175, 176, 177, 205, 223, 224, 231, 233, 235
    age 156
    disvalue 136–7
    global 170
    groups 162–3
    income 24
    internationalism 167
    intrinsic value 138
    justification 221
    permissibility 38
    racial 155
    social 139, 163
    socioeconomic 191
    unavoidable 203
infants, new-born 173
inferiority 192, 193
injustice 4, 6, 7, 13, 69, 70, 91, 117, 118, 120, 126, 127, 128, 133, 143, 154, 155, 167, 168, 190, 198, 202–3, 231, 236
    natural 128
institutionalism 171
intelligence 42, 45
interpersonal test 205, 222

investment 172
involuntary disadvantage 23

judgements, moral 53
justice 3, 4, 5, 6, 10, 12, 19, 23,
    24, 31, 35, 36, 38, 43, 51,
    58, 63, 69, 70, 71, 75, 77,
    79, 82, 83, 85, 87, 90, 91,
    100, 111, 113, 119, 146,
    152, 153, 154, 162, 163,
    164, 165, 166, 168, 170,
    172, 173, 174, 176, 177,
    179, 185, 192, 195, 196,
    210, 213, 214, 223, 225,
    226, 227, 228, 229, 230,
    231, 235, 236, 237
  contours of 201–2
  criminal 148
  distributive 1, 77, 104, 132,
    170, 210–11, 226
  duties 47
  egalitarian 77–8, 108
  market 105
  retributive 211
  social 171
  theories 11, 228
  values 201, 211
  welfare 13
justification 202, 203, 205, 221
  context-sensitive 203

Kant, Immanuel 41, 44
  exegesis 46

labour 107, 108
labour power 15
laissez-faire libertarianism 7, 9
legitimacy 213, 214
levelling down 129–48, 160, 161,
    219, 233, 234
liberals 215
libertarianism 49, 213
  Nozickean 11
liberty 216

life experience 223, 224
lifetime egalitarianism 154
loan markets 107–8
local agency 122
local tracing 122
Locke, John
  theory of appropriation 142
losses 67
lotteries 8, 9, 63, 66–7, 70, 130
lottery luck 62

market 14
  justice of 105
market reciprocity 225
market society 227
materialism 238
maximalist view 175, 176
mental states 80
minimalism 176, 177
money 78, 108, 218
monism 231
moral agency 40, 49
moral arbitrariness 9
moral beliefs 230
moral commitments 133
moral deservingness 5, 199
moral goodness 3
moral judgements 53
moral permissibility 3, 26
moral responsibility 65, 92
moral standing 38, 49, 50, 51,
    52, 53, 167
moral status 39, 47, 48, 180
moral value 29, 30, 38
motivation 9, 224, 225
  communal 223, 225
  socialist 225

nationalism 187
neutral tastes 96
neutralization 72–5
non-egalitarians 49
non-humans 174, 175
normality bias 86

Nozick, Robert 49, 51, 115, 133, 142, 187
  Anarchy, State and Utopia 211–13
  libertarianism 11, 34, 213

obligation 225
offensive preferences 82, 87–92, 116–17
offensive tastes 85, 96
opacity 45
opacity duty 45, 46, 47
opacity respect 44, 48
opaqueness 43–8
opportunity 19, 24, 212
  equality of 20, 31–2, 110
option luck 186, 189, 199, 67–72, 76
origin essentialism 157
outcomes 19, 52, 56, 64–5, 70, 71, 73, 88, 100, 115, 117, 118, 119, 122, 124, 125, 126, 127, 130, 134, 137, 146, 154, 190, 238
  badness 133
  goodness 130–31, 140–41
  injustice 128
  unequal 144

pain 79, 83, 106
partiality 217
permissibility, moral 3, 26
person-affecting principle 147, 149
personal relations 81
pleasure 79, 81
pluralism 172, 202, 206, 210, 211, 218, 219, 231, 232, 235
  value 170–71, 172
political institutions 166
political philosophers 2
political relations 188
preferences 21, 22, 80–81, 84, 89, 95, 109

humble 95–6
offensive 82, 87–92, 116–17
second-best 100
snobbish 88
prejudice, racial 117
primary goods 108, 110
prioritarianism 29–30, 31, 38, 39, 49, 132, 144, 149, 170, 174, 212
priority principle 38
privacy 88
privilege 182
productivity 37, 106
publicity 51, 226–30, 232
punishment 198

quasi-consequentialism 217

race 39
racial discrimination 229
racism 2, 3, 22, 117, 187, 229
range properties 42, 43
rational agency 40, 41
rationality 173
Rawls, John 42–3, 47
reason-responsiveness 63
reasons-sensitive mechanisms 57
reciprocity
  market 225
  socialist 225
redistribution 39, 166
reflective equilibrium 53
regulation
  rules 228–30
relations, communal 224
relativities 143, 145
representations 123, 124, 128
resources 14–15, 17, 25, 29, 38, 83, 85, 87, 94, 101–2, 103, 104, 107, 108, 109, 145, 196
  deficiency 86
  distribution 108

equality of 102
resourcism 104, 105, 106, 108,
    109, 110, 111
resourcist luck 105
respect 43–8
    opacity respect 44, 48
responsibility 35, 36, 52, 55, 57,
    59, 60, 62, 63, 158, 183,
    189, 192, 195, 197, 198,
    199, 200
    differential 219
    moral 65, 92
responsibility luck 58, 61, 64,
    65, 73
restricted scope 123, 125
resultant luck 58
reverse compensation 75
right-holders 47
right-libertarianism 34
rights 49, 116
risk 18, 67, 68
    aversion 70
rule-utilitarianism 142

Saudi Arabia 180
scalar properties 42, 43
scope 151–78
    restricted 123, 125
    unrestricted 123, 126
self-awareness 41, 173
self-consciousness 173
self-determination 172
    national 173
self-interest 218–19
selfishness 227
self-ownership 10
self-realization 218, 220, 221
Sen, Amartya
    capability metric 108–11, 196
sentience 175
sexism 22, 33, 74, 120
slavery 109
    slavery of the talented 103–4
Slogan 141, 143, 148

Deontic 141–2, 147
Telic 141–2, 147
snobbish tastes 82, 88, 93–8
snobs 97–8
social cooperation 166, 167–8
social divisions 181
social inequality 163
social justice 171
social lottery 56
social relations 179–207, 237
    egalitarianism 206
    hierarchical 190
social standing 181, 195
social status 182
social structure 163
social upbringing 9
socialist reciprocity 225
South Africa 2, 180
Sovereign Virtue 11
specification objection 82–4
stability 226–30, 232
states 165–73
statist egalitarianism 165, 167,
    168–9
sufficiency 28–9, 175, 212
sufficientarianism 27–9, 49, 55,
    77, 134, 170, 174, 175, 185
    hedonist 82
    non-relational 134
    relational 134
superiority 94, 182

talent 102–3, 106, 107, 120,
    204–5, 212, 222–3
tastes 17
telic egalitarianism 113–50
    levelling down objection
    135–40
temperament 86
thick luck 59–62, 64, 76
thin luck 57–9
tracing approach 139
trading 14
truth 228, 230

unfairness 159, 232
unrestricted scope 123, 126
utilitarianism 25–7, 30, 36, 50,
        53, 74

value
    extrinsic 135
    instrumental 135
    intrinsic 135, 136, 138
    non-instrumental 135, 138
value holism 172
value pluralism 170–71, 172
values 53, 231, 233, 234
    justice 201, 211
virtue ethics 142

weighting 144, 148
welfare 12, 13, 17, 19, 20, 21, 22,
        24, 26, 27, 30, 35, 36, 72,
78–82, 83, 84, 87, 89, 92,
        93, 98–9, 100, 101, 105,
        106, 130, 131, 137, 144,
        159–61, 176, 196, 216, 226,
        230, 233
    deficit 88, 94, 95, 96
    inequality 160
    theories 160
welfarism 87, 104, 108, 109, 111,
        112
well-being 25, 26, 29, 81, 100,
        127, 144, 149, 154
whole lives 152–6
    segments 153, 154
Williams, Bernard 40–42, 43, 51
wrong-doing 126